Challenging the Right, Augmenting the Left

Recasting Leftist Imagination

Edited by
Robert Latham
A.T. Kingsmith
Julian von Bargen
Niko Block

FERNWOOD PUBLISHING
HALIFAX & WINNIPEG

Copyright © 2020 authors

All rights reserved. No part of this book may be reproduced or transmitted in any form by any means without permission in writing from the publisher, except by a reviewer, who may quote brief passages in a review.

Editing: Jenn Harris
Cover design: Evan Marnoch
Printed and bound in Canada

Published by Fernwood Publishing
32 Oceanvista Lane, Black Point, Nova Scotia, B0J 1B0
and 748 Broadway Avenue, Winnipeg, Manitoba, R3G 0X3
www.fernwoodpublishing.ca

Fernwood Publishing Company Limited gratefully acknowledges the financial support of the Government of Canada, the Canada Council for the Arts, the Manitoba Department of Culture, Heritage and Tourism under the Manitoba Publishers Marketing Assistance Program and the Province of Manitoba, through the Book Publishing Tax Credit, for our publishing program. We are pleased to work in partnership with the Province of Nova Scotia to develop and promote our creative industries for the benefit of all Nova Scotians.

Library and Archives Canada Cataloguing in Publication

Title: Challenging the right, augmenting the left :
recasting leftist imagination / edited by
   Robert Latham, A.T. Kingsmith, Julian von Bargen and Niko Block.
Names: Latham, Robert, 1956- editor. | Kingsmith, A.
T., 1989- editor. | Bargen, Julian von, 1982-
   editor. | Block, Niko, 1988- editor.
Description: Includes bibliographical references and index.
Identifiers: Canadiana (print) 20200163582 | Canadiana
(ebook) 20200163612 | ISBN 9781773632292
   (softcover) | ISBN 9781773632308 (EPUB) | ISBN 9781773632315 (Kindle)
Subjects: LCSH: Right and left (Political science)
Classification: LCC JA83 .C37 2020 | DDC 320.5—dc23

Contents

Acknowledgements / vii
Contributors / viii

Introduction
    Augmenting the Left:
    Challenging the Right, Reimagining Transformation / 1
    Niko Block

Section 1 — Engaging the Working Class / 15

1. Organizing the Contending Masses:
   From a Struggle With to a Struggle Against Capitalism / 16
   Robert Latham

       The Search for Potential Anti-Capitalist Forces / 18
       A Radicalizing Detroit / 21
       Conclusions / 23

2. Augmentation and Organization / 28
   Jordan House

       Organizations, Sectarianism, and Leadership / 30
       Education / 32
       Provocation / 33
       Mobilization / 34
       Organizing / 36

3. Can Studying Workers' Class Consciousness Help to Raise It? / 38
   Bertell Ollman

       My Questions / 38
       The Theory that Underlies this Practice / 44
       Conclusion / 47

Section 2 — Organizing Class and Identity / 49

4. Psychological Wage and the Trump Phenomenon / 50
   Paul Kellogg

       Populist Reductionism / 51
       The Colour Line / 52
       Misogyny / 54
       Narrow Trade Unionism / 55
       Implications for Left Politics / 58

5. "Rising Powers" and Authoritarian Populism:
   Beyond Northern Left Perspectives / 62
   Sedef Arat-Koç and Aparna Sundar

   > The Cultural(ist) Logic of the Post–Cold War World / 65
   > "Rising Power" Populism in Turkey and India / 66
   > Conclusion / 72

6. Migration "Crises" and the Left: In Search of the Political / 74
   Özgün E. Topak

   > Governing Migrants through Criminalization / 75
   > Governing Migrants through Humanitarianism / 78
   > In Search of the Political / 80

7. Navigating Contemporary Struggles:
   Class Composition and Social Reproduction / 86
   Elise Thorburn and Gary Kinsman

   > Starting within Class and Social Struggles / 86
   > Class Composition and Cycles of Struggle / 89
   > Social Reproduction as a Site
   > of Struggle and Transformation / 90
   > A Recomposition of Struggle? / 92
   > Recomposing Class Struggles
   > with a Focus on Social Reproduction / 94

8. Class-Based Organizing in an Identity-Based World / 98
   Assya Moustaqim-Barrette

   > The Process of Politicization / 99
   > How Left Organizations Can Recruit Politicized Liberals / 101

Section 3 — Building Parties or Movements? / 107

9. Experiences on the Socialist Left: Winning, Losing, and Continuing / 108
   Herman Rosenfeld

   > Socialist Project, First Incarnation / 110
   > Greater Toronto Workers' Assembly / 112
   > Second Incarnation of the Socialist Project / 114
   > How I See Socialist Movement Building Today / 116

10. What's Left after the Breakup of the CPGB? / 117
    Bruce Curtis and Justin Paulson

11. Building Political Infrastructure for the Present / 128
    Lina Nasr El Hag Ali

    > The Current Context / 129
    > Toronto: Sites of Mutation / 130
    > Conclusions / 133

12. Class Struggle in the Marketplace of Ideas:
    Toward a Leftist Framework of Civil Liberties / 135
    Julian von Bargen

    > What Are Civil Liberties? / 136
    > Conceptions of Civil Liberties beyond the Marketplace of Ideas / 137
    > Contemporary Challenges to Civil Liberties / 141
    > Augmenting the Left / 143

Section 4 — Advancing Eco-socialism / 145

13. The Anthropocene and Us: Grounds for an Augmented Left? / 146
    David Ravensbergen

    > Untenable Futures: From Ecomodernism
    > to Green Social Democracy / 148
    > Embracing a Contingent Future / 153

14. Environmental Contradiction:
    The Need for an Eco-socialist Paradigm on the Brazilian Left / 158
    Sabrina Fernandes

    > The Brazilian Pink Tide's Ecological Record / 160
    > The Radical Left's Own Environmental Contradictions / 161
    > The Brazilian Left Needs a New Paradigm / 163
    > Grassroots Resistance and Eco-socialist Proposals / 165

15. Andean Intercultural Eco-socialism in Times of *Buen-Vivir*?
    A Red-Green-Culturalist Approach / 169
    Javier Cuestas-Caza, Rickard Lalander, and Magnus Lembke

    > A Hobsbawmian Approach to Particularism-Universalism / 170
    > Universalist and Particularist Perspectives of *Buen-Vivir* / 172
    > The Citizens' Revolution and Neo-extractivism / 174
    > Concluding Reflections: *Buen-Vivir*
    > as Andean Intercultural Eco-socialism / 176

Section 5 — Generating Cultural Interventions / 183

16. Movement, Image, History:
    Walter Benjamin and Operational Politics / 184
    AK Thompson

    > Walter Benjamin / 189
    > Operational Politics / 191
    > Conclusion / 194

17. Disintegration of the Neoliberal Order
    and the Challenges for the Radical Left / 196
    Terry Maley

    > The Complexities of State Capture / 197
    > Illiberal Democracy under Neoliberalism / 200
    > Structural and Moral Disintegration / 202
    > Conclusions / 204

18. Late-Stage Capitalism, Anxiety, and Tactical Art Terrorism / 208
    William S. Jaques

    > Art Terrorism and Affective Liberation / 209
    > Cognitive Bias: "Information" and (in)Action / 212
    > Regions of Consciousness: Visceral Fields of Affect and Action / 214

19. *Détourne* Down for What?
    Culture Jamming in the Age of General Anxiety / 219
    A.T. Kingsmith

    > *Détournement* as Active Force / 220
    > The Age of General Anxiety / 223
    > A Self-Jamming System / 225
    > Communalizing the Public Secret / 227

20. Thirteen Theses Toward a Materialist Theory of Revenge Capitalism / 231
    Max Haiven

    > I. Revenge Capital / 231
    > II. Vengeful Accumulation
    > III. Torture as Economic Policy / 233
    > IV. Collective Revenge Fantasies / 233
    > V. Revenge and Reaction / 234
    > VI. Witch Hunt / 234
    > VII. Avenged Ancestors / 235
    > VIII. Revanchist Cities / 236
    > IX. Prison: Revenge Factory / 237
    > X. Cultural Illogic / 238
    > XI. The Means and Ends of History / 238
    > XII. Profits of Forgiveness / 239
    > XIII. Dig Two Graves / 240
    > XIV. Conclusion / 241

Afterword
> Augmenting the Left or Rethinking Progressive Politics? / 243
> *Ronaldo Munck*

Index / 249

Acknowledgements

We wish to thank the various faculty and staff at the Ontario College of Art and Design University (OCADU) who helped facilitate and organize the workshop in Toronto, Augmenting the Left, that was the starting point for this volume. Special thanks go to b.h. Yael, who advanced the project at OCADU in its early stages and was an insightful participant at the workshop. We also recognize the insightful contributions of presenters at the workshop who do not appear in the volume, including Raju Das, Tim McCaskell, Nick Dyer-Witheford, Svitlana Matviyenko, Steve Maher, Karen Murray, Roni Gechtman, James Beirne, Tyler Chartrand, Scott Forsythe, Niloofar Golkar, and Karl Gardner.

Without the substantial support of the Faculty of Liberal Arts and Professional Studies at York, this project would not have been possible; we extend our gratitude to the staff and relevant committees that made that possible. We also received general support from the York Department of Politics and extend special thanks to its chair, David Mutimer, and administrative assistant, Margo Barreto. A number of other programs and departments at York also offered funding including: Social Science, Humanities, Social and Political Thought, Geography, and Sociology. The efforts of the staff and program directors from those units to extend such help is greatly appreciated.

At Fernwood Publishing, we thank Errol Sharpe, who early saw the worth of this project. It has been a great pleasure to get to know him and finally work directly with him.

Contributors

Sedef Arat-Koç is associate professor in the Department of Politics and Public Administration at Ryerson University.

Niko Block is a doctoral student in political science at York University. His writings have appeared in *The Guardian, Canadian Dimension, New Internationalist,* and *Jacobin*.

Javier Cuestas-Caza has a PhD in local development from the Polytechnic University of Valencia. He is an assistant professor in the Department of Organizational Studies and Human Development, Escuela Politécnica Nacional, Ecuador.

Bruce Curtis is professor emeritus in the Department of Sociology and Anthropology at Carleton University.

Sabrina Fernandes has a PhD in sociology from Carleton University and is currently a full collaborating researcher at the University of Brasília. She studies leftist organizing and revolutionary ecologies in Latin America. Her book on the fragmentation of the left has recently come out in Brazil.

Max Haiven is the Canada Research Chair in Culture, Media and Social Justice at Lakehead University in Thunder Bay where he co-directs the ReImagining Value Action Lab. His latest book, published in 2018, is *Art After Money, Money After Art: Creative Strategies Against Financialization*.

Jordan House is a PhD candidate in political science at York University and an instructor in the Department of Labour Studies at Brock University. His research interests include the political economy of prison and prison labour, non-union workers' organizations, and labour movement renewal and strategy.

William S. Jaques is a PhD candidate in the Department of Politics at York University and an adjunct professor in the School of Liberal Arts and Sciences at Humber College.

Paul Kellogg teaches in the Faculty of Humanities and Social Sciences at Athabasca University and is chair of the Centre for Interdisciplinary Studies.

A.T. Kingsmith is a PhD candidate in the Department of Politics at York University and a mental health researcher at the University of British Columbia Urban Studies Lab. He teaches at Ryerson University and has written widely on digital networks, anxiety capitalism, and the political economy of mental health.

Gary Kinsman is a long-time queer liberation, anti-poverty, and anti-capitalist activist in solidarity with Indigenous struggles. He is the author of *The Regulation of Desire: Homo and Hetero Sexualities* and co-author of *The Canadian War on Queers*. He is professor emeritus at Laurentian University.

Rickard Lalander is an associate professor in Latin American studies, Department of World Cultures, University of Helsinki. He also teaches in global development studies at Södertörn University, Stockholm.

Robert Latham is a member of faculty in the Department of Politics at York University.

Magnus Lembke has worked for two decades at the Institute of Latin American studies at Stockholm University.

Terry Maley teaches critical and radical democratic theory in the Department of Politics and the Social and Political Thought Graduate Program at York University. He has written on participatory budgeting, radical democratic social movements, and neoliberalism.

Assya Moustaqim-Barrette is a PhD candidate in political science at York University.

Ronaldo Munck is the head of civic engagement at Dublin City University. He has written widely on Latin America and the impact of globalization on labour. He was a lead author for the International Panel on Social Progress Report "Rethinking Society for the Twenty-First Century."

Lina Nasr El Hag Ali is a doctoral candidate in politics at York University.

Bertell Ollman is a professor of politics at New York University. He has written or edited seventeen books of Marxist studies and in 2002 won the first Distinguished Career Award from the New Political

Science Section of the American Political Science Association. He is the creator of the *Class Struggle* board game.

Justin Paulson is a political sociologist and social theorist teaching in the Department of Sociology and Anthropology and the Institute of Political Economy at Carleton University.

David Ravensbergen is a union activist and PhD student in social and political thought at York University. He has published work on Marxism, climate change, and the political economy of the environment.

Herman Rosenfeld is a Toronto-based socialist activist, educator, organizer, and writer. He is a retired national staffer with the Canadian Auto Workers (now Unifor) in their Education Department. Before that, he worked on the line and served as an elected union representative in an auto assembly plant.

Aparna Sundar is a political scientist affiliated with Azim Premji University, India. She works on issues of labour and livelihoods, as well as the politics of democracy, nationalism, and fascism, with a focus on South Asia.

AK Thompson got kicked out of high school for publishing an underground newspaper called *The Agitator* and has been an activist, writer, and social theorist ever since. He is the author and editor of several books, including, most recently, *Premonitions: Selected Essays on the Culture of Revolt* (2018).

Özgün E. Topak is an assistant professor in the Department of Social Science at York University. His research areas include surveillance studies, migration, border studies, and human rights.

Julian von Bargen is a writer, researcher, teacher, and doctoral candidate in the Department of Political Science at York University, Toronto.

Introduction

Augmenting the Left
Challenging the Right, Reimagining Transformation

Niko Block

Beginning in January 2011, democratic uprisings across the Arab world rapidly toppled four governments and destabilized many more. Across Europe and North America, it had by then become obvious that any reforms stemming from the global financial crisis would be purely technocratic, not redistributive. For a left weary of liberal subterfuge and apology, the spectacle of the Egyptian revolution in Cairo's Tahrir Square was especially inspiring. What if people everywhere were to occupy key urban spaces and refuse to leave until their demands were met? In September of that year, the Occupy movement spread across the globe with a force that most would never have imagined possible. For several weeks, rising economic inequality became the top story even in the mainstream media. A stunning number of politicians acknowledged the disturbing concentration of wealth and income within the top 1 percent of their societies, and the proponents of business-friendly politics, it seemed, transformed from voices of reason into sweaty, stammering grifters pleading before an angry jury.

It looked for a moment as though change was inevitable — yet the movement declined almost as fast as it rose. Ironically, the original poster for Occupy Wall Street read, "What is our one demand?" Whereas the demand for democracy resonated across the Arab Spring, Occupy never answered this simple question and its lack of clear objectives led to growing impatience from the mainstream press. The movement was from the start also debilitated by internal disagreements and a lack of organization stemming from competing partisan and anarchist tendencies, and throughout the last two months of the year the encampments were gradually stamped out by direct state repression.

Not only did these transnational revolutionary waves fail to achieve their initial promise; eight years on, the forces of reactionary bigotry are now more powerful than any of us had predicted. Even for leftists who, over the past three decades, have ridiculed the assumption that the age of global liberalism was nigh, the recent surge of nationalist authoritarianism across the Philippines, India, Europe, Brazil, and the US has been dizzying. The Arab uprisings, meanwhile, have been either repressed by reconstituted dictatorships or, in the cases of Syria, Libya, and Yemen, collapsed into civil wars that persist to this day.

In a nutshell, the events of the past decade have made it clear that the hand of history will not intervene to neutralize the crises of capitalism. On the contrary, capitalism's self-reinforcing tendencies are strong enough to ensure that its own innate crises, specifically financial and environmental crises, will never spontaneously ignite systemic change. Rather, the transformative crisis must be a political one, charged with active discussion, organizing, and solidarity. This in turn raises the issue of what kinds of opportunities for *ideological* transformation exist in the twenty-first century. Will elite interests succeed in perpetuating capitalist ideology or will their increasingly obvious hypocrisy foment resistance?

Many on the left now talk about Occupy with disdain, try to forget about it, or even pretend that they were never involved. But in light of the work that needs to be done, I believe its history is instructive for a number of reasons. First, it was the single most important moment of consciousness raising in recent memory. In its wake, the concept of class conflict re-emerged, the socialist left in North America became increasingly self-confident, and a few key public intellectuals amplified their criticism of growing wealth and income inequality (Chomsky 2013; Stiglitz 2013; Piketty 2014). Second, we learned that the tactic of occupying public spaces carries major risks but does in fact work to garner attention, and it could probably succeed in pressing specific demands if it were more coherently organized. Third, we learned that there are thousands of people who are still drawn to the *idea* of revolutionary politics, but they are only likely to hit the streets when their imaginations have been sparked — a moment when the battle suddenly seems *winnable*. And fourth, we learned that it is also unwise to launch a movement before concrete demands have been articulated.

These last two themes — of narratives and vision — deserve some elaboration. This introduction will draw from the book's contributions to argue that the current left's shortcomings in these fields have rendered it difficult to develop a narrative and vision that garner popular support. Amidst the tumult and opportunity that marked the beginning of the twenty-tens, this crisis of vision has since become especially pressing.

Indeed, the central argument of this book is that the crises of the twenty-first century call for a radical recasting of the leftist imagination. This process involves building bridges between the real and the imaginary, so that the path to achieving political goals is plain to see. Accordingly, the articulation of leftist goals must resonate with people in concrete ways, so that it becomes obvious how the achievement of those goals would improve their day-to-day lives. The left, in this sense, must appeal to people's existing identities and not condescend the general public as victims of "false consciousness." All this means building movements of continual improvement and refusing to ask already vulnerable people for short-term losses on the abstract promise of long-term gains. As we will see below, this project also demands that we understand precisely why right-wing ideology retains a popular appeal in so many spaces. These were among the central themes addressed at the Augmenting the Left symposium held in downtown Toronto in May 2017, four months after the inauguration of Donald Trump.

By augmenting the left, then, we mean adapting it to the crises of our time and even getting ahead of them. We mean abandoning some of the wishful thinking that has persisted in left-wing thought, reconciling certain counterproductive divisions within the left, and strategizing for the work that lies ahead in this century. Five specific subjects call for attention, which are addressed in each of this book's sections. First, the left needs new ways to engage working-class people who are already disillusioned with the system they inhabit but who are nonetheless estranged from anti-capitalist organizing. Second, the left must find ways to undermine reactionary currents of ethnonationalism while at the same time supporting anti-colonial movements *in conjunction* with movements against class stratification. Third, the left needs to think about how to strategically build power both inside and outside the state apparatus. Fourth, the environmental crises of the twenty-first century, especially climate change, demand new forms of resistance that will have to challenge our existing systems of production in unprecedented ways. And finally, the left must understand the cultural dimensions of popular ideology in order to effectively promote notions of solidarity and ecological responsibility.

~

The left has a general appeal that many of us take to be self-evident: we want to fix the crises of inequality and ecological destruction that have been wrought by capitalism. But as several of the book's contributions observe (albeit in different terms), the left's political marginality can in many ways be explained by weaknesses in its narrative and objectives. On the other side of the spectrum, the narratives offered by the right typically have a more intuitive, nationalist character and follow the familiar U-shaped trajectory so common in biblical and other myths (Frye 2004). The protagonists begin from an immaculate and sacred status, then experience a tragic fall often at the hand of outsiders but eventually regain their past glory. It is a trajectory that remains strikingly persistent in Hollywood blockbusters, in which villains disrupt an excessively rosy version of our own world, but the heroes then vanquish the bad guys and return us to the *status quo ante*. The nostalgic character of the right offers us the same: a return to a time of mythologized national greatness, a sense of *destiny*. (Although primarily associated in the Anglophone world with slogans about "making America great again," this kind of irredentist rhetoric — promising a return to past national greatness — is hardly unique to the US, as Sedef Arat-Koç and Aparna Sundar's analysis of Turkish and Indian authoritarianism demonstrates.) Despite their deviations from the historical record, these visions of the past nonetheless resonate in the aggrieved and often paranoid minds of twenty-first century capitalism.

There is a perverse rationality at work in this style of aggrieved nationalism. The structures of power today operate in such obscure and confusing ways that even the most unflinchingly curious political scientists struggle to explain state behaviour. In much the same way that commodities are ascribed magical qualities because the labour that produced them remains hidden from the buyer (Marx 1976), the obscurity of political power today virtually demands that the gaps in our knowledge be filled by conjecture and even conspiracy theory. Yet all too often the outcome is ethnic scapegoating. The implications follow inexorably: once we escape the control of the "globalists," or exorcise the infiltration of immigrants, then we can be great again. (As Paul Kellogg argues in Chapter 4, tendencies of racial resentment are at the heart of nationalist authoritarianism in the United States today.)

Indeed, while these myths render national greatness an abstract but nonetheless *imaginable* outcome, the more concrete objectives offered by conservative demagogues are strikingly attainable. In other words, despite the grandiosity of their narratives, conservatives tend to offer policies that are almost comically modest: punish the villains and lower the taxes. Yet this modesty is their strength. After half a century in which progressive ambitions for the public sphere are almost always stymied, we should hardly be surprised if most voters have lowered their expectations. On top of the perverse rationality of paranoia, then, we might say there is also a cynical rationality within the reactionary mindset of today.

What follows is a cycle of chaos and anxiety that becomes difficult to break. In Trump's United States, for instance, we have witnessed an escalation of the state's sadistic and criminally negligent treatment of undocumented migrants, whose numbers continue to swell in concentration camps along the southern border. In Chapter 20, Max Haiven elaborates the revanchist character of these conservative tendencies, suggesting that the language of revenge has, amidst the crisis and confusion of the twenty-first century, become a dominant logic in politics. As Terry Maley similarly suggests, a certain "mix of fear, alienation, and desperation" has set in amidst the sense of despondency generated by the entrenchment of capitalist interests. As political hopes become frustrated, people become inured to the suffering of others and at times even desire it.

Liberal centrists (such as the Democratic Party or the Canadian Liberal Party) may forcefully rebuke the politics of scapegoating and *schadenfreude*, but they have virtually nothing to offer the typical pro-business voter who simply wants lower taxes and higher demand for labour in their locales. In particular, liberal parties around the world seem to be incapable of speaking to lower-middle-class rural voters who gain little from government services, whose local economies are propelled by the private sector, and who do in fact carry an unfair tax burden. Urban workers have only slightly more incentive to endorse liberal parties, who generally favour the professional middle class. As Robert Latham, Jordan

House, and Bertell Ollman all suggest, there is a really existing conflict between the lower and upper classes. Yet centrist liberals hardly bat an eye as they blame the poor for their poverty or claim that progressive income redistribution is simply impossible.

And what, we might ask, are the narratives and the objectives on offer from centrist liberals? Perhaps some empty words about the greatness of the Enlightenment, or a few familiar bromides about the wonders of our globalized economy. It hardly inspires, at this point. At the very least, there is a growing awareness that the liberals offer little of value on questions of inequality and the environment. (As Assya Moustaqim-Barrette argues, liberal prescriptions centred on lifestyle activism are hardly up to the task.) Indeed, if there is an opportunity for the socialist left today, it is because fewer and fewer people are drinking the Kool-Aid of liberal capitalism.

But what, then, does the socialist left offer by way of narrative and vision? If there is any truth in the above, then political power is largely built upon narratives that are romantic yet ring true, and objectives that seem both desirable and attainable. Some strands of left-wing ideology do have these characteristics, but today's left is so diverse that it is difficult to say anything sweeping about it. Certainly our historical narratives are contested. The most mollifying might relate to stories of emancipation for Blacks, women, or queer people. But historical victories in this vein are so often claimed — perhaps fairly — by liberals, while those on the socialist left tend to stress that these struggles are far from over. (The contribution from Elise Thorburn and Gary Kinsman is a case in point.) At the same time, the traditional Marxian narrative of class conflict and revolutionary uprising still resonates with many, as Occupy demonstrated. But when have such uprisings succeeded? The question has no straightforward answer. Perhaps we owe almost everything to the class struggles of the past, or perhaps we owe more to liberal reformism than we would like to admit.

In short, the values of the left may be shared — and they are the reason the left will never go extinct — but the stories are not. The result is that it is difficult for the left to capture the popular imagination, even in moments of crisis. Whereas the nationalist right is virtually constituted by mythologization, the socialist left, on the other hand, is organized around tedious historians attempting to explain the rise of capitalism, the process of neoliberalization, or why the promise of the workers' republic has so often resulted in the tragedy of totalitarianism. Whereas the right's utopian visions of the past and future can be depicted as glibly as the Flintstones and the Jetsons, the left is populated with inveterate pessimists insisting that no modern society has ever been truly free of exploitation or oppression. Whereas the right stands to gain from the absence of information, the left, so long as it has the courage of its convictions, pursues historical truths in all their amoral complexity. As such, the left's approach to history is fundamentally different from the right's. We study it not for the sake of irredentist propaganda, but for a theory of history that might guide our future struggles. "In contrast to the far right's stubborn recollections of mythic past greatness," writes AK Thompson in this volume, "the left opted for citations that could illuminate those internal relations that give discrete events their overarching coherence. Significantly, these citations recalled the enduring and unfulfilled dimensions of the broader struggle."

These divergent approaches to the truth have in this century become especially evident on questions of climate science. As Naomi Klein (2013) has observed, environmental science itself is telling us with ever-growing urgency that revolution is the only rational course of action, while fossil-friendly capitalist states "have had to find ever more thuggish ways to silence and intimidate their nations' scientists."

But the left's opposition to nationalist mythologization and censorial thuggery has done little for its ability to present appealing narratives nor helped it to present objectives that are both graspable and exciting. Certain goals are attainable within the realm of liberal democracy that we inhabit — improved social service provision or more bike lanes, for instance — but the revolutionary promise of the left at times seems difficult to justify. Strategically, the party often looks like a promising vehicle for change, but competent socialist parties have also foundered for simply failing to build an adequate constituency, as the essay by Bruce Curtis and Justin Paulson observes. Social movements outside the state, meanwhile, have sometimes won important gains of their own — especially on a local level, as Lina Nasr El Hag Ali demonstrates. But the question of how to build local, ground-level movements into forces capable of producing system change remains a difficult one, particularly when the nature of that change remains unclear. At what point might we be able to upend the system of exploitation that pervades our workplaces and our pathetically unfair housing market? At what point might we become truly empowered to the point that banks or oil developers no longer possess privileged seats in government? What, in short, *is* the socialism that we are fighting for? And how would it solve the truly momentous problems we face?

Our most wish-fulfilling proposal has in recent years become encapsulated in the idea of "fully automated luxury communism" (Srnicek and Williams 2015; Bastiani 2019). Arguably, the notion that new technologies will liberate people from work is dismissible as little more than a left-wing version of the Jetsonian pipe dream; indeed, the intellectual basis for the "post-work" or "post-scarcity" economy remains spurious, as David Ravensbergen suggests. But although loosely articulated, the idea has galvanized the much-needed conversation about what kind of future we on the left want to *build*. Most importantly, it has helped the left to break away from the long, self-imposed inertia of viewing revolutionary demands as naive and reformist demands as futile (Srnicek and Williams 2015). In that regard, the joint ambitions of curbing carbon emissions, shortening the workweek, and developing a universal basic income is not a bad place for socialists to start.

This means doing the hard and often dreary work of studying the concrete dynamics of political economy. It means conceptualizing the principles of modern history without naturalizing the exploitation, ecological devastation, and geopolitical competition that have defined it. Finally, it means making demands that are ambitious but attainable, and building mass movements on the basis of improving people's everyday lives. If narrative is constitutive of ideology, then it is incumbent upon us to act as both brutally honest historians and deliriously optimistic economists. Only then, I think, will we start to build a mass movement that avoids the pitfalls of its predecessors.

~

This volume responds to the complex, troubling forces that have brought us to the present moment and surveys strategies for finding a way out. Its contributions are united by a shared understanding of the gravity of the problems we face and the urgency with which we need to solve them. As noted, the following sections focus on strategies for working-class mobilization; the relation between contemporary class and identity politics; the question of the left's political infrastructure; the pressing need for ecological transformation; and, finally, the need for leftist cultural interventions.

Readers will find that each section contains a lively discussion, as the writers actively engage each other on the issues at hand.

In Section 1, authors survey both recent and historic strategies of class mobilization to understand how it can be effectively undertaken amidst the changing terrain of the twenty-first century. Robert Latham describes the subtle ferment of the present moment as a sort of in-betweenness, verging on neither political rupture nor political stability. Getting widespread dissatisfaction to transform into active resistance means obviating the ways in which so many people are *contending* with capitalism — a strategy that has in the past facilitated solidaristic struggles encompassing Black and white workers in the US. Bertell Ollman suggests that activating class consciousness is sometimes simply a matter of talking to workers directly, and putting questions *to them* rather than lecturing them about abstract theory. Jordan House, in a similar vein, stresses that the left, if it is worth its salt, must demonstrate its value to lower-class people on an ongoing basis by speaking in terms of the everyday obstacles they face and winning campaigns that concretely improve their lives.

The theme of nationalism re-emerges in Section 2, where contributors examine the complex ways in which identity shapes class politics, and vice versa. For Paul Kellogg, the unexpected rise of Donald Trump needs to be understood not merely as a "populist" insurgency, but as a campaign that deliberately capitalized on the still-powerful currents of racism and misogyny in the United States — forms of bigotry that appear to be fuelled by anxieties about the collapse of white privilege. Within this context, a critical mass of dispossessed whites, in supporting Trump, attempted to defend what W.E.B. Du Bois called the "psychological wage" of whiteness. Sedef Arat-Koç and Aparna Sundar observe that similar motives — the desire for ethnic privilege as well as geopolitical strength — are motivating support for India's Hindu-nationalist government under Narendra Modi, as well as Turkey's Sunni-nationalist government led by Recep Tayyip Erdoğan.

Assya Moustaqim-Barrette argues that ultimately it is class struggle that should be prioritized because class is fundamentally at the root of racial and gender discrimination. Consequently, the lifestyle- and identity-based politics that prevail in liberal culture are completely inadequate for dealing with the crises of our time. Elise Thorburn and Gary Kinsman flip the question somewhat on its head by arguing that identity-based movements like Black Lives Matter and Idle No More are in fact "at the *cutting edge* of class struggle, in that they mediate relations between race, colonialism, gender, and class." The question of the relation between identity and class is also addressed by Özgün Topak, who argues that the dominant discourse in the Global North reductively characterizes migrants and refugees either as villains or victims. Contrary to both, a reclamation of their identity as *workers* presents an opportunity to foster solidaristic links with domestic political movements.

The contributions in Section 3 focus on how the left needs to strategically engage with the state and the public from here on out. Herman Rosenfeld's chapter offers a series of honest reflections on decades of organizing in the Toronto area, looking at both the merits and the pitfalls of past struggles. Among these, the left needs to build coherent political infrastructures that are capable of exerting real pressure on parties and policymakers. Further, he stresses, the left needs to find a way to coherently engage both anti-oppression *and* class struggles without succumbing to infighting or false accusations.

Bruce Curtis and Justin Paulson, meanwhile, turn our attention to the difficult question of political parties in their analysis of the rise and decline of the Communist Party of Great Britain. They capture the extent to which this history was shaped by forces that surrounded the party, and therefore caution against unsubstantiated allegations that the party compromised to centrists by too much or too little. If we recognize that anti-capitalist parties cannot merely presume a constituency in the working class but should actively build one, then we must also ask: how are leftist constituencies built *in general*? Lina Nasr El Hag Ali responds to this pressing question — the one we started with — by stressing that successful left movements do not occur entirely within the boundaries of the party apparatus but, rather, are led by ground-level movements that succeed in *pushing* parties and public discourse in a leftward direction.

Julian von Bargen, approaching the state from a different angle, looks at how the left should approach the law itself. He argues that while the left has largely abandoned the notion of civil liberties, the concept has now been taken up to alarming effect by the right — especially in the right's churlish defences of hate speech. The result is that North American politics are characterized by an army for individual rights attacking only a few defenders of *collective* rights.

As we turn to the essays addressing the need to revolutionize our systems of ecological management, we are confronted with analyses that are perhaps even more sobering. David Ravensbergen observes that the dominant position on the climate embraced by liberal-left parties has an ecomodernist character, one that relies on clever technological solutions and geoengineering. But these ideas reflect a Holocene mentality that fails to grasp the scale of crisis at work in the Anthropocene. Rather, he suggests, we need to take seriously the argument that the ecological crises unfolding today can only be coherently addressed by a politics of degrowth that inherently challenges the foundations of capitalist production.

Sabrina Fernandes, focusing on Brazilian politics, confronts the fact that the left has not merely been relatively weak in its defence of the environment, but that industrial unions have in certain cases been straightforwardly regressive actors by campaigning for the protection of carbon-intensive jobs. Finally, the contribution from Javier Cuestas-Caza, Rickard Lalander, and Magnus Lembke examines the use and abuse of the idea of *Buen-Vivir* in the Ecuadorian and Bolivian governments that rose in the aughts. *Buen-Vivir* in its most reductive form signified living better and not with more, and it became laden with promises of an ecosocialist agenda that prioritized the particular interests of Indigenous Peoples. But as these governments attempted to square the impossible circle of progressive capitalist development, the concept that formerly encapsulated the manifold demands of the left ultimately became co-opted and lost its political resonance.

In the final section, authors examine the relations between popular culture, affect, and ideology in the rise of the contemporary right and analyze opportunities for leftist intervention. AK Thompson draws on the work of Walter Benjamin to suggest that it is precisely *because* the left approaches history with a truth-seeking mentality (rather than a propagandizing one) that it is more difficult to elaborate a leftist "selection of citable images and artifacts" that appeal to unconscious wish-images. Rather, the basis of ideological appeal for Thompson must be moved into the field of conscious, dialectical images, where the active *production* of new social relations can occur.

Terry Maley suggests that neoliberalism is distinguished in part by a self-legitimating cultural structure that shields the system from leftist movements and results in a profusion of social vulnerability. While that vulnerability becomes normalized, it also produces feelings of anxiety and anger that are often misdirected. Max Haiven, in a similar vein, suggests that capitalism has long relied upon forms of discipline that are framed as just revenge. The misdirected anger that drives the contemporary right, in this sense, has evolved out of these long-standing systems of discipline.

Will Jaques, in turn, suggests that because so much of the battle occurs in the field of affect and representation, the left should take seriously the tactics of art terrorism and insurgent art in order to "produce subversive and robust aesthetic experiences that involve a felt confrontation with the anxiety-producing contradictions of late-stage capitalism." A.T. Kingsmith, on the other hand, is circumspect, observing that the tradition of *détournement*, or culture jamming, has been taken up by the right, which now deploys memes, pranks, and misinformation in ways that do more to provoke anxiety than improve political consciousness. Across these contributions, we find consistently innovative approaches to the question of why the right has remobilized so rapidly in the present moment — approaches that weave together theories of political economy, state power, affect, and the unconscious with the complexity that the question demands.

~

The decade we now inhabit is by no means the first time that the left has, in a moment of retreat, had to rethink many of its long-standing assumptions. The value of these moments, however, is that everything becomes subject to interrogation, and the essays in this volume share that spirit of reflection. Throughout, there is a refreshingly sober examination of the general bases of solidarity the left must build, and yet also a sensitivity to the nuances of particular struggles.

And this is precisely the attitude we require to avoid further catastrophes: unbending solidarity in a time of divisive propaganda. Observe, for instance, the way that progressive voters were divided in the runup to the 2016 election in the US, when liberal centrists in the Democratic Party cynically accused their socialist rivals of holding reactionary views on race and gender. In the wake of the disaster that ensued, the left is just as heterogenous as it ever was, but there is a growing understanding that both social and economic justice must be pursued in unison. Accordingly, the left is in a unique position today to take advantage of the great diversity of approaches and issues that have been the hallmark of its otherwise bemoaned fragmentation. More precisely, the worldwide trend of popular disaffection presents a major opportunity for the left, if it is willing to take fragmentation, intra-left conflict, and a history of refusals and defeats as a starting point for next steps in the struggle against capitalism and the far right, rather than as the basis for more conflict or defeatism.

References

Bastiani, Aaron. 2019. *Fully Automated Luxury Communism: A Manifesto.* New York: Verso.

Chomsky, Noam. 2013. *Occupy.* New York: Zuccotti Park Press.

Frye, Northrop. 2004. *Biblical and Classical Myths: The Mythological Framework of Western Culture,* ed. Jay Macpherson. Toronto: University of Toronto Press.

Klein, Naomi. 2013. "How Science Is Telling Us All to Revolt." *New Statesman*, October 29. <newstatesman.com/2013/10/science-says-revolt>.

Marx, Karl. 1976. *Capital: A Critique of Political Economy, Volume I.* New York: Penguin Books.

Piketty, Thomas. 2014. *Capital in the Twenty-First Century.* Boston: Harvard University Press.

Srnicek, Nick, and Alex Williams. 2015. *Inventing the Future: Postcapitalism and a World Without Work.* New York: Verso.

Stiglitz, Joseph. 2013. *The Price of Inequality.* New York: Penguin.

Section 1

Engaging the Working Class

1. Organizing the Contending Masses
From a Struggle With to a Struggle Against Capitalism

Robert Latham

Today, in the heart of capitalist power (the Global North), when it comes to the possibilities for the development of anti-capitalism, we are living in the world of the in-between. There is no rupturing, revolutionary moment in sight (described famously by Lenin), nor a mobilized proletariat demanding change. But this is also not an age of capitalist stability, associated often with the 1950s. In this in-between world there is conformity, if not complacency; but there is also frustration and possibilities of contestation — the latter not just optimistically imagined but manifested in actions like protests and strikes. This in-between is not the slow transformation between two hegemonic orders (made famous by Gramsci) but rather a period of neither rupture nor stability.[1]

But are actions like strikes and protests evidence enough for this in-between? Such activity can be present in any period, even an apparently settled one like the 1950s. A more reliable indicator is whether potential anti-capitalist attitudes are widespread if not also deep and sustainable. Such attitudes emerged and then were realized in the 1960s and into the early 1970s in Europe and North America. They receded into the 1980s (the Reagan and Thatcher years), but that does not mean the in-between period drifted into an era of settled stability. From the 1980s on, across all economic dislocations, left defeats, and patterns of political quiescence, this potential remained and periodically broke the surface, as we saw with the early 2000s anti-globalization movements.

But from where come these potential anti-capitalist attitudes and orientations? How close to the surface of political and social life are they at any given time? And what does such closeness to the surface really mean? I want to consider all three questions and, more broadly, their implications for radical education, consciousness raising, and Marxist organizing overall.

I recognize that the second two questions mean nothing without initially being clear about the first. In the absence of an organizing proletariat, there must be some aggregate of people who constitute the force that makes anti-capitalism proximate — a force that can potentially converge as a very large and diverse body that has enough in common, emergent or otherwise, in relation to anti-capitalism to warrant this identity.

I will argue that this force is the masses of people who have in common lives that are constitutively shaped by their contending with capitalism, with contending understood in two senses: 1) struggling or coping with; and 2) challenging and opposing. The first sense represents the most immediate reality for "contending masses." They contend with substandard or insecure living conditions, crushing debt, job loss or insecurity, unpleasant and exploitative work in factories and fields, violence and imprisonment, and environmental harms. These factors have been traditionally engaged in Marxist thought and linked to working-class lives (if not also the petty bourgeoisie struggling in small shops or clerical positions). The question is whether such contending constitutes a common thread linking classes and other social categories as an emergent force.

I use the term contending *masses* to avoid any possible confusion that this is a class — in contrast to Guy Standing (2014), who has argued that there is now an emergent class of precarious people, which he labels the precariat. Moreover, as "contending" entails both struggling with and struggling against, it is not anchored only in adversity (as is the label "precariat") but also in a political standpoint vis-à-vis capitalism.

Overall, in any given national setting there are those who are at a minimum comfortable and secure (i.e., not contending with debt, work, food, housing, and health care pressures) and those who are not. There are, naturally, debatable boundaries as to who is really contending and who is not (e.g., a middle-class family losing its home?), but most social distinctions suffer from such issues, including class.[2] While the contending masses are composed of a variety of classes, the proletariat is the most important component.³

I am using *masses* in an unexceptional, commonplace way. I do not see the contending masses as a stand-in, potentially organized, historical agent along the lines of the proletariat, with a given ontological status. As Raymond Williams (1958: 300) suggested, "there are in fact no masses; there are only ways of seeing people as masses." There is no weighty framing or special meanings in development here; my focus is on the contending and what it implies for understanding potential challenges to capitalism. Also, the term's equivocalness is consistent with in-betweenness.

The Search for Potential Anti-Capitalist Forces

Identifying the contending masses as an aggregate force is only a preliminary step in establishing the potential proximity of anti-capitalist attitudes to the surface of a social fabric that has more or less endured since the 1970s. A next step is determining the political possibilities inherent in the contending masses' struggle with capitalism. One might look to well-known conditions like increasing economic insecurity, stagnating incomes, and rising inequality. But that would not account for the differences across the decades of the in-between. As the 1960s was a relatively robust economic context for the US — and even, in ways, the UK — it is tempting to look only to the 1970s and onward, allowing an alignment with the sorts of crises and transformations associated with neoliberalism's ascendance. However, that would overlook the movements of the 1960s that were an obvious break from the 1950s.

Rather than focus on conditions per se for what establishes proximity, I think it more useful to consider the emergence of apprehension — an awareness or recognition — of struggles with capitalism; this can stem from socioeconomic conditions but is nonetheless distinct. Apprehension does not require an understanding that it is capitalism (via its commodification, concentration, and exploitative wage system) that is central to relevant conditions. It can simply be an awareness of the problematic and oppressive nature of aspects of one's life situation. This is a long way from the sort of proletarian class consciousness Marxists have historically sought.

The emerging New Left — with its clearly anti-capitalist message — was a part of this increasing awareness, as was the very different 1970s culture of complaint around inflation and recession. It is not that criticism did not happen in the 1950s, but it was not as widespread and ingrained in the general culture.[4] It is important to distinguish more general discontents and forms of resentment, which can manifest as racism, anti-immigration, and sexism, from the discontents associated with capitalism (see Max Haiven's chapter). That there could be a coincidence of both does not invalidate discontent within capitalism.

How do we know discontent and apprehension are extensive? The question is not answered by the frequent surveys of economic pessimism or optimism that populate the financial media. Not only can these be flawed;[5] they often do not even capture the struggle with capitalism among the contending masses. Far better are first-hand studies of contending lives as we saw in Barbara Ehrenreich's (2010) book about low-wage work, *Nickel and Dimed: On (Not) Getting by in America*. There are also analyses that rely on the art of discerning the overall tenor of a given historical period, such as the 1980s (e.g., Rossinow 2015). Discontent and apprehension can manifest in the resonance of political appeals (populism, socialism, and specific protest movements like poor people's campaigns) across the ideological spectrum that take up causes of distress associated with capitalism.

Even when the discontent and apprehension of the contending masses move close to the surface, or even become part of capitalist society (evident, say, in support for discourses of dissatisfaction offered by parties or the media, or even participation in struggles against capitalism), they still remain only a *potential* anti-capitalist force. That is because they are not necessarily organized as anti-capitalist and may just be about *reforming* capitalism. What is needed is an anti-capitalist orientation as well as support for, and participation in, anti-capitalist action.

This anti-capitalism holds promise as a potential force for breaking through the surface of capitalist society. Much leftist thought and strategy has been dedicated to the notion that vanguards, radical intellectuals, or activists more generally could help make the oppressed more aware of the reasons behind their discontents and help point the way toward their transformation into revolutionary subjects. The list of party newspapers, journals, and pamphlets put out across the twentieth century written for a range of education levels is quite long. One of the most well-known advocates for radical education is Gramsci (1971: 334), who argued for the cultivation of a "critical self-consciousness" first among intellectual leaders, who then can actively engage with workers to establish processes for the development of "theory-practice" and proletarian revolutionary organizing. Gramsci had the experience of helping develop in 1919 the magazine *Ordine Nuovo* in Turin, where he got to pursue ideas developed in some prior years about how "socialism is organization and not only political and economic organization, but also, especially, organization of knowledge and will, obtained through cultural activity."[6] He was emphasizing that we need to focus on organizing society — its culture, knowledge, and ways of relating to one another — not just economies, even if they are socialist-oriented.

Gramsci, of course, had a mobilized working class before him in Turin at that time. We do not. Further, the reception to anti-capitalist ideas among the broader contending masses today remains limited — even where there is meaningful support for communist parties in countries like Portugal. Potential pathways of conversion are, thus, obscured. Rather than lapse into a sense of defeat yet again, one might consider whether, in struggling and coping with capitalism, individuals and groups inadvertently take anti-capitalist action by participating in or supporting some initiative that circumvents some dimension of capitalism. A quite mundane example in the US is community banking, where you have a given town or region — whose fiscal status is harmed by the flow of their funds to Wall Street financial institutions — that chooses to keep its funds within the community through a public bank. Another relevant example is squatting. While much attention has been given to squatting movements that have been self-consciously anti-capitalist, there is a long history of what Hans Pruijt (2013) calls "deprivation-based squatting" where this activist movement logic is absent. One might also put in this same category the relatively widespread emergence of worker cooperatives in Argentina after the early 2000s economic crisis (Vieta 2012), or the various social experiments that more recently have emerged in Greece after its crisis began (Kavoulakos and Gritzas 2015).

Rather than dismiss these acts of contending with capitalism as wrongheaded utopianism, one might see them as expressions of struggle and, in their departure from capitalism, even if by only a few degrees, as anti-capitalist. But acknowledging this does not mean anti-capitalism should stop with such endeavours. They clearly are not enough to undergird what I elsewhere call an "arc of anti-capitalism" that might scale up into a broad anti-capitalist front (Latham 2018). Explicitly anti-capitalist masses are necessary for such a front. But rather than assume that front asks too much of an in-between context — a concept meant to emphasize degrees of possibility rather than actuality — I want to go back to the relationship between activists, intellectuals, and the contending masses to consider what may predispose the contending masses, in the in-between, to appeals by vanguards and activists (when they are not already self-consciously proletarian).

A Radicalizing Detroit

A particularly instructive example of this was documented by Georgakas and Surkin (1998). The authors show how Black auto workers, struggling intensely with the ravages of capitalism in late 1960s and early 1970s Detroit, became radicalized. Crucial were the activist organizations and media, from the newspaper called the *Inner City Voice* that emerged out of the massive Detroit rebellion of 1967 to the Dodge Revolutionary Union Movement and the League of Black Revolutionary Workers. What these clearly radical activists had to say about how badly Black workers were being exploited and abused both in the workplace — above and beyond white workers — and in Detroit communities resonated with Black auto workers. They took a range of actions, such as frequent wildcat strikes, across factory sites. The message of the organizers was clearly anti-capitalist and revolutionary, promoting not just workers' control but the expropriation of the factories and the remaking of Detroit (from housing and schooling to health care) along egalitarian lines (Georgakas and Surkin 1998).

The example evokes common sense: When oppressed groups are acutely aware of their struggles within capitalism, especially because they are intense and extensive, they are more receptive to anti-capitalist approaches. But how generalizable is this example? Certainly the milieu of the 1960s enhanced their receptivity, as did recent experience of the insurrection of 1967 (the "Great Rebellion") — along perhaps with the history of Communist Party activity in the UAW (United Auto Workers), outreach by the Socialist Workers Party, and the pamphlets of the Boggs.[7]

Even more problematic, some may feel that Blacks were not representative of US workers, given this history and overall white working-class conformism.

Georgakas and Surkin (1998) point out that while there was some initial sympathy and resonance among white workers (some of whom participated in the wildcat strikes), white workers were coming from a position where they were deeply invested in and targeted by the main business-oriented UAW union. Despite that, as one organizer put it:

> White workers came to support us. Some wanted to work with us. But we found out that management knew how to divide the whites. We decided that we could work best by organizing alone. We told whites to do the same thing. Once they did that, we could work with them on a coalition basis. (47)

And strike they did. Regarding one wildcat strike involving whites, Georgakas and Surkin (1998) claim:

> The most significant aspect of the strike was that Black radicals had maintained a working alliance with white, mainly Polish workers, something that had not occurred at Dodge Main in 1968, at Eldon in 1969–70, or at the Chrysler Sterling stamping plant where white workers had rebelled in a week-long wildcat in 1969 over working-condition grievances similar to those voiced by DRUM [Detroit Revolutionary Union Movement] and ELRUM [Eldon Avenue Revolutionary Union Movement]. (230)

Georgakas and Surkin (1998) show in the end that the apprehension of white workers and their receptivity to radical action could also deepen in that rebellious moment in Detroit, even if whites remained anchored in the economistic UAW.

The contrast between white and Black workers in Detroit raises the question of how much of a group or individual's existence is shaped by or drawn into the struggle with capitalism and how that matters to contention. Any group or community may be composed of individuals, families and localities that face a variety of struggles in their lives based on their class and circumstances (e.g., unemployment or housing difficulties). Black Detroiters have long faced a wide range and scope of struggle, from work to community. Seemingly middle-class white communities face far more limited struggles. Further complication arises from political differences, as when some workers support different types of union and political party relationships (Communist, Socialist, Social Democratic, Liberal). While these complications, intersections, or even tensions can be seen as fetters, I disagree. Recognizing that struggles with capitalism and apprehensions can be partial or diverse (in the face of differing scopes and ranges of struggle, as in Detroit) suggests that a range of possibilities and emergent pathways of anti-capitalism is possible.

Conclusions

Detroit never became an American Petrograd as some on the left had hoped (Georgakas and Surkin 1998). If anything, in time, management clawed back many gains, and the conditions for workers and residents, especially Blacks, never saw substantial improvement. The extensive organizational efforts, from worker action to street publications — along with the pursuit of worker education — came and went. The gains were initially achieved in a particular time and place but were not squarely tied to a deeper and more sustained development of anti-capitalist consciousness regarding struggle. Management was hence free to act once that time passed. Such is life in the in-between.

One might be discouraged by this and by the ways that various circumventions that have emerged — perhaps most powerfully symbolized by the Mondragon cooperative — remain limited in scope and highly vulnerable to being subsumed within the logics and circuits of capitalism. Thinking pessimistically, one might infer that the in-between is condemned to remain neither a decisive, ruptural moment nor a relatively stable one. Within it, crises, radicalizations, or upsurges are trapped in a political purgatory shaped by counterforces, complacency, and the recourse to reform (e.g., wages, working conditions, or counter-austerity). At best, it might be seen as an enduring transfer point between stability and systemic crisis or political-economic rupture. Vanguards and activists may have an effect but sustaining and building a real mass anti-capitalist movement seems elusive.

So, do we just try to prepare the ground for rupture or systemic crisis, or do we seek to create the conditions in the in-between so that it can contain a substantial constellation of anti-capitalist strategies? As is well known, both orientations have taken hold across the twentieth century, either in militant movements (parties and vanguards focused on aspirations for national and international revolution) or in the long history of efforts to capture and, more importantly, transform state power, alter capitalist practices, and build alternative networks of power along dualistic lines. However, a gap remains between these strategies: The reality is that the contending masses who have no choice but to struggle with capitalism often do not make the choice to struggle against it. We might need to start rethinking what sort of leadership is required to help foster that struggle against.

Some may find consolation in the fact that there has been a persistent attempt by vanguards and activists across the decades to draw the contending masses toward the struggle against capitalism and to place hope in those upsurges of protest and resistance that are inevitable in the in-between. This consolation, alas, should not let itself be further buoyed by the hope that crisis will usher in the conditions for the conversion of the contending masses from struggle with to struggle against. Rather, we may need to reassess the potential terms and nature of such conversion and what it encompasses. This implies caution regarding knowledge building and education — to ostensibly dispel "false consciousness" — since it rests on the assumption that the contending masses are receptive to such theory and information. And even if some become so and take up the conscious struggle against capitalism, history suggests there is little room for inconclusive, drawn-out struggle, which risks apathetic acceptance that anti-capitalism is fruitless.

But rather than keep hoping they can be drawn to us, we might see how we can be drawn to them — on different terms than in the past — and in so doing, reorient various left approaches. Consider the circumventions that might entail unintended deflections from capitalism, such as efforts to keep community funds within a town or region, seek more control over job security, or in rejecting racism anchored in capitalist housing practices in Detroit. As a starting point in the in-between, groups do not need to recognize and accept anti-capitalism or become conscious proletarians — they just need to do things that divert away from what capitalism does in whatever minor or seemingly un-revolutionary way. The task of radical intellectuals and activists is to make the connections between these bottom-up endeavours — to theorize along with the groups what such diversions might mean, why they are necessary, how to possibly scale up and ultimately represent forms of anti-capitalism. Such thinkers become intellectuals who are organic to these deflections, not just a particular class.

Engaging in this way does not mean the exclusion of all the other left pathways; all of them must be continually pursued and developed, even the most self-consciously militant Leninist ones. Choices will have to be made about when and on what terms these different paths should intersect. This is what an arc of anti-capitalism entails.

Perhaps one of the great drawbacks to what has come to be labelled post-Marxism was that it generated a fear that long-developed positions among Marxists might have to be relinquished (along with political fidelity), limiting openness to different paths just when that was most needed. However, once again we might look to Marx's recognition not only of the Paris Commune as an important development (even though it was a relatively small-scale uprising) but also his consideration of the potential benefits of the Russian peasant communes for the development of anti-capitalism. One might read Marx — even in the wake of his political theories regarding the potential for proletarian revolution — as looking for anti-capitalism, over the course of his lifetime, wherever it might emerge and in whatever form held promise.

This may require, as suggested previously, a transformation — and sometimes even a tactical or strategic foregoing — by the far left of its long-standing commitment to radical education and explicit, up-front cultivation of critical self-consciousness based on traditional notions of class struggle and proletariat agency. This does not mean abandoning this commitment, becoming passive, or submerging Marxist and socialist adherence, but rather developing new ways of applying these in relation to anti-capitalism. This means cultivating even inadvertent anti-capitalist actions and tendencies among the contending masses. This can entail showing how, when some areas of local life — from banking to housing and education — are organized on a non-capitalist basis, these are forms of anti-capitalism that open the way for people to liberate themselves from centralizing capitalist interests within the state or corporations. Alternately, it can entail the encouragement of anti-capitalist organizational inclinations, as we see in Ollman's chapter. Without these new methods, transformations, and innovations in how the left pursues what lies below the surface of the in-between, the impediments to a widely developing anti-capitalism are likely to remain in place for some time — or at least until the next existential crisis of capitalism ushers in a long-awaited ruptural moment.

Notes
1. A hegemonic order is a particular organization of economic, social, political, and cultural life. An example is the order that came into being after World War II in North America and Europe, organized around liberal democratic capitalism (including large industrial corporations, welfare states, and consumer societies with expanding middle classes).
2. Consider debates about the aristocracy of labour; see Hobsbawm (2012).
3. Thomas Piketty's (2014) data shows that across times and places, 50 percent of the population typically has no assets — the classic understanding of the proletariat.
4. On the culture of dissatisfaction — for instance, in the UK — see Alt (1979).
5. On the limits of such measures, see De Boef and Kellstedt (2004).
6. Gramsci wrote this in 1918; see Clark (1977: 53).
7. Such conditions of receptivity are stressed by Geschwender (1977). He emphasizes that racism and Black nationalism were important background resonances for the workers responding to the league.

References
Alt, James. 1979. *The Politics of Economic Decline: Economic Management and Political Behaviour in Britain Since 1964*. Cambridge University Press.

Clark, Martin. 1977. *Antonio Gramsci and the Revolution that Failed*. New Haven: Yale University Press.

De Boef, Suzanna, and Paul M. Kellstedt. 2004. "The Political (and Economic) Origins of Consumer Confidence." *American Journal of Political Science*, 48, 4 (October).

Ehrenreich, Barbara. 2010. *Nickel and Dimed: On (Not) Getting by in America*. New York: Metropolitan Books.

Georgakas, Dan, and Marvin Surkin. 1998. *Detroit, I Do Mind Dying: A Study in Urban Revolution*. Cambridge: South End Press.

Geschwender, James. 1977. *Class, Race and Worker Insurgency: The League of Revolutionary Black Workers*. Cambridge University Press.

Gramsci, Antonio. 1971. *Selections from the Prison Notebooks of Antonio Gramsci*. London: Lawrence and Wishart.

Hobsbawm, Eric. 2012. "Lenin and the Aristocracy of Labor." *Monthly Review*, 64, 7 (December).

Kavoulakos, K.I., and G. Gritzas. 2015. "Movements and Alternative Spaces in an Era of Crisis: A New Civil Society." In N. Georgarakis and N.G. Demertzis (eds.), *The Political Portrait of Greece: Crisis and the Deconstruction of the Political*. Athens: Gutenberg/EKKE.

Latham, Robert. 2018. "Contemporary Capitalism, Uneven Development and the Arc of Anti-Capitalism." *Global Discourse*, 8, 2 (Spring).

Piketty, Thomas. 2014. *Capital in the Twenty-First Century.* Cambridge: Harvard University Press.
Pruijt, Hans. 2013. "The Logic of Urban Squatting." *International Journal of Urban and Regional Research,* 37, 1.
Rossinow, Doug. 2015. *The Reagan Era: A History of the 1980s.* New York: Columbia University Press.
Standing, Guy. 2014. "Understanding the Precariat Through Labour and Work." *Development and Change,* 45, 5.
Vieta, Marcelo Alejandro. 2012. "Taking Destiny into Their Own Hands: Autogestión and Cooperation in Argentina's Worker-Recuperated Enterprises." York University, PhD thesis.
Williams, Raymond. 1958. *Culture & Society: 1780–1950.* New York: Columbia University Press.

2. Augmentation and Organization

Jordan House

The transformation of society requires the collective efforts of large numbers of people. However, if one honestly assessed the activities of much of the left, it would be easy to conclude that building a movement premised upon mass participation isn't the goal. Instead, left groups settle for honing theoretical lines or conducting any number of other symbolic and inward-facing activities. If we want to "augment the left" — which aptly captures the desire for not just a larger movement, but also one that attempts to seriously overcome the limitations, bad ideas, and practices of previous movements — we need to do the difficult work of organizing. This means moving beyond a left made up largely of self-selected participants by engaging in deep organizing efforts and building campaigns capable of not only defending working people from ruling-class attacks but also winning meaningful reforms. We likewise need to build democratic working-class organizations that allow working-class people to learn, theorize, and develop collective resources and engage in struggle. Since much of what gets called "organizing" is in fact not, it is important to differentiate organizing from practices of education, provocation, and mobilization, which are divorced from deeper organizing efforts that attempt to win gains for working-class people and build class capacities.

To augment the left through organizing, we must clarify what we mean by "the left." Much has been written on this question but, at minimum, we need a left that confronts power beyond the realm of discourse. We need a left that is working class *rooted* and working class *focused*, and that seeks to transform society rather than reducing class to an identity and class power to an attitude (Panitch and Gindin 2016). In short, we need a socialist left committed to building working-class power and the revolutionary transformation of society.

Some might hesitate to use the term "working class" on the basis that it is insufficiently inclusive. Others might object on the basis that even if it existed in an earlier era, no working "class" meaningfully exists today. Both reservations are understandable, but they do not warrant the abandonment of class as the critical analytical category from which to rebuild a solid left-wing movement. The left must stop assuming the working class is synonymous with the industrial proletariat. The working class must be conceived broadly to include all those who rely on wages or state support to obtain the means to life as well as those engaged in both waged and unwaged social reproductive labour.

The second concern is also partially valid. Over the past century there has been a process of class decomposition that has seen the breakdown of working-class communities and organizations as well as intensified stratification and segmentation of working-class people. Neoliberalism, new technologies, and changes to labour processes have meant the increased ability to offshore and automate production, an increase in part-time, contract, and "gig" work, and increasingly complex and convoluted supply chains, among other things. These changes have created clear challenges for traditional working-class organizations such as trade unions; however, they have not meant the end of the working class. Instead, these shifts mean that the current task of the left is to recompose the class and develop class capacities. This will require organizing and organizations.

Organizing the working class, however, does not simply mean workplace organizing. In the words of Jane McAlevey, "the strategic front for the most successful movement effort is *still* the workplace, but not *only* the workplace" (McAlevey 2016). Given the economic transformations of the last forty years, individual workplaces may or may not be viable or important terrains of struggle. Critical areas of engagement for left organizations also include reproductive struggles, such as those around public services and housing, as well as fighting discrimination — for example, in connection with police violence and mass incarceration. The left should not reduce all concerns to "class issues," if these are meant merely as economic issues of distribution and inequality. Rather, the opposite is true: class power is the basis upon which ordinary people can best combat oppression and discrimination — seen, for example, in the role of the labour movement in winning universal maternity leave in Canada (Nichols 2012). Socialists have a long tradition of fighting for oppressed and marginalized people — and any number of movements, from feminist and queer to anti-racist, civil rights and anti-fascist struggles, have benefited from the organic participation and leadership of socialists and socialist organizations.

As our task is one of building the capacities of the working class to become a *class for itself*, it's critical that we differentiate this from the dead-end goal of "uniting" the left — which often amounts to organizing leftists into slightly larger but still marginal organizations or simply cobbling an organization together on a lowest-common-denominator basis. The worst manifestation of this strategy occurs in the activities of hypersectarian grouplets who spend most of their energies attacking their rivals in their newspapers and recruit primarily by attempting to poach already "developed" leftists instead of building bases in working-class communities and movements. Imitating the slogans, organizational models, and aesthetics of past movements is insufficient. Instead, we need to intervene in the everyday struggles of working-class people and do our best to convince them that the left has something to offer in terms of practical acts of solidarity and mutual aid, as well as plausible explanations of the forces shaping their lives. This means that organizations need analytical capacity — but they also need to concretely engage in politics and struggle.

Organizations, Sectarianism, and Leadership

In order to develop and empower what Latham (in this volume) calls the "contending masses" capable of transforming society — and in order to augment the left — we need to build organizations. In his chapter, Latham points to a variety of organizations that emerged in the 1960s and early 1970s in Detroit to help workers struggling against exploitation in the auto industry. Organizations included media outlets, a union movement, and a league of revolutionary workers who worked together to agitate on the shop floor and connect their labour struggles with broader concerns around housing, education, and health care. While this may be common sense to many, there are some on the left who would challenge the assertion that building organizations is the main task of leftists today. Anti-organizational anarchists, especially the insurrectionist and post-structuralist varieties, object to formal organization on the basis that organizations are inherently authoritarian and/or undemocratic. Or, taking a more moderate position, they hold that organizations, even democratic ones, tend toward bureaucratization and authoritarianism; as such, they should be avoided in favour of temporary organizations and/or small, closed affinity groups.

The first criticism misunderstands the basic nature of human social relations by assuming that there is such a thing as the individual outside of society. Far from being an impediment, relationships with others form the very basis of our capacities for freedom. To quote Mikhail Bakunin (1871), "I am truly free only when all human beings, men and women, are equally free. The freedom of other men, far from negating or limiting my freedom, is, on the contrary, its necessary premise and confirmation." As one cannot opt out of social relations, the real issue is the extent to which those relationships can and should be democratized — thus, the question of democracy and bureaucratization is significant, especially given the history and prominence of Leninist vanguard parties. Organizations can be more or less internally democratic, and we should strive to create the most democratic and participatory organizations possible — this is a basic prefigurative principal. If we want a free, democratic, and participatory society, we need to develop working-class people's democratic capacities for struggle in their organizations. Relatedly, in the current conjuncture, there is a particular need for organization in order to combat the atomistic and individualizing effects of neoliberalism and rebuild "cultures of solidarity" (Fantasia 1988). Organizations must be self-financed to avoid the "dependency and accommodation" that occur in state- and foundation-funded bodies (INCITE! 2017: 41). In particular, members' dues are fundamental for people, especially working people, to own their organizations (INCITE! 2017).

Critically, we must abandon the idea that small, dogmatic, and ideologically pure organizations are sufficient. We need broad swaths of working-class people to help build organizations, "raise expectations," and build solidarity and trust (McAlevey 2012). This can only occur by organizing concrete and collective action. Thus, initiatives to educate, provoke, or mobilize people outside of structured organizing campaigns are insufficient for the project of augmentation that is required in the face of rising inequality, an insurgent right, increased potential for global conflict, and intensifying ecological crisis. We therefore need organizations that are democratic and non-sectarian, outward facing, both accountable to and steered by the rank and file, and involved in theorization aimed at furthering real and concrete struggle.

Education

We cannot augment the left by education alone. The left's embeddedness in academia and the emphasis of certain tendencies on position-taking *as* political activity make a program based on left education tempting for many. However, if "day long lectures" and "well-crafted pamphlets" were the keys to left renewal, then the left would be a formidable force, our ivory towers fortresses instead of hideouts — the last places where "Marxism" means much to anyone (Workman 2011: 173–83). Likewise, if education in itself was the key to left renewal, the production and sale of esoteric newspapers would be the activity of large and growing organizations rather than tiny sects (for other responses to Workman, see Paulson and Schein 2012; Rosenfeld 2012; and Workman 2012).

Education will clearly be an important component of any successful augmentation of the left. But it cannot be divorced from struggle and the real-world issues facing working people. According to Thom Workman, in order for a "Promethean rebirth" of the left, "nation-wide gatherings every Saturday afternoon, safe places where we can talk and grumble and cry and commiserate and then talk some more, might just be the place to start. Our contribution to the conversation of humankind can grow from there." But we also need to stand Workman on his head. Political education must be directly linked to, and emerge from, the needs of people in regular, everyday struggle. This synthesis of theory and action — but with an emphasis on the necessity for struggle — is powerfully captured by the anarchist Rudolph Rocker (2004: 34), who writes that "only from the everyday conflicts between labour and capital could the doctrines of Socialism, which had arisen in the minds of individual thinkers, take on flesh and blood and acquire that peculiar character which make of them a mass movement, the embodiment of a new cultural idea for the future."

Ollman (in this volume) describes attempts he made to provoke class consciousness using focus groups drawn from New York City's working class. The discussions in the focus groups quickly led to participants realizing their shared predicament. In other words, Ollman's group members quickly found their way to the answer this chapter suggests they will: they wanted to build an organization capable of intervening in actual class struggles on behalf of the working class — in this case, in the form of a new party. This reaffirms the claims made in this chapter: education is not simply a matter of good arguments; people also need to have transformative experiences and learn by doing. Organizations can facilitate this, whereas education alone cannot.

Provocation

Provocation or agitation is a necessary part of organizing, seeking to connect emotional reactions and affective commitment to a political project. (For further discussion on this, see Kingsmith, Jaques, and Thompson in this volume.) However, it has become divorced from broader organizing efforts and substituted for organizing in different forms: propaganda of the deed, art provocations, "culture jamming," et cetera. Provocation-as-politics is elite-driven in the sense that self-selected individuals or groups attempt to expose a passive target population to a political line without any opportunity for those on the receiving end to participate in it. Moreover, provocations don't attempt to grapple with power, settling instead for "raised consciousness" (Bey 1985). Provocation as "propaganda of the deed" and left-wing terrorism has been disastrously counterproductive for movement building for the simple reason that "you can't blow up a social relationship."

Agitation in the form of "culture jamming" was a key strategy of the anti-globalization movement and a heavy emphasis on agitation in the form of Internet memes continues in our contemporary context. But even when provocations are actually provocative, there are problems of agitation in the absence of organizing. Agitation without education and organizing can be self-defeating. When a problem has been identified and feelings are stirred without a potential solution to the problem — without a way for agitated people to *do* anything — agitation is useless and disempowering. This issue is critical in relation to catastrophist environmental messaging. As Doug Henwood (2012) explains, "Catastrophe can be paralyzing, not mobilizing. Revolutionaries should be talking about possibilities of transformation, not spinning tales of great chaos and suffering. That's not to say that there isn't plenty of chaos and suffering in life. But looking to epochal quantities of both as the shocks that will awaken the masses out of their somnolence is not promising." If the world is over, why change anything at all?

Mobilization

Like agitation and education, mobilizing is a necessary part of political organizing. Mobilizing is important in that it attempts to move large groups of people into action, but it typically does so on the basis of a single campaign, like an election, or a single cause, like raising the minimum wage. It asks people to act, but it doesn't ask them to become responsible for strategizing, theorizing, or planning the campaign, and thus it doesn't build capacities. And it doesn't provide a means for people to remain involved in a struggle after a particular campaign has subsided. Transforming people's consciousness and building up new organizers may exist as goals but are not the main work of mobilizing campaigns. There are typically three kinds of mobilizing campaigns: 1) as part of a broader organizing campaign (for example, mobilizing for a rally to support a rent strike); 2) as grassroots protest activity, divorced from an organizing project; and 3) as the activity of a top-down campaign led by an organization, such as a union or non-profit. The latter two kinds of mobilizing, divorced from a commitment to organization and movement building, won't augment the left.

In term of grassroots activist mobilizing *as politics*, there is perhaps no better example than the "summit hopping" of the anti-globalization movement, where self-selecting activists travel from one trade summit protest to the next, with all the subcultural trappings of fans following a favourite band on tour. Critiques of "activistism" range from the tendency toward anti-intellectualism and faulty conceptions of politics and power to issues of basic strategy. For instance, activists may assume that marches and protests will build movements, when in fact effective protests are the *result* of organizing and movement building. Marches "only work when they demonstrate the power of an organized mass movement, proving that a mass base has unified around a particular demand. Put differently, organizing work must precede any successful march, and that work takes years, not months" (Kinnucan 2017). Much of mobilizing amounts to convincing oneself and others that *something has been done*, when in reality, there has not even been an attempt to significantly shift the balance of power.

In the top-down mobilizations typical of trade unions and NGOs, staff and organizational leaders possess agency, develop campaign demands and recruit activist "self-selectors" as participants and representatives of some larger constituency. As McAlevey (2012: 10) explains:

> Professional staff directs, manipulates and controls the mobilization; the staffers see themselves, not ordinary people, as the key agents of change. To them, it matters little who shows up, or, why, as long as a sufficient number of bodies appear — enough for a photo good enough to tweet and maybe generate earned media. The committed activists in the photo have had no part in developing a power analysis; they aren't informed about that or the resulting strategy, but they dutifully show up at protests that rarely matter to power.

In situations where these mobilizing campaigns make gains, leaders typically control negotiations and determine the compromises. Mobilizing campaigns of this type may win important victories from time to time, but they don't in themselves sustain an organizational capacity to win wholesale political, economic, and social transformation or to overcome the existence of strong, organized, resourced opposition.

Many mobilizing initiatives are implicitly premised on a notion of spontaneity — the idea that new movements will emerge of their own volition — and that the left should simply support, and perhaps seek leadership of, these movements as they develop. This position is flawed in two ways. First, it misunderstands the degree to which organization is necessary for "spontaneous" movements to emerge. Second, in practice, this strategy amounts to ambulance chasing — groups jumping from cause to cause as each becomes popular, but without meaningfully taking up any of the issues of the emergent movement or building any kind of base.

We need to abandon the idea that if we support the right hot-button issue at the right moment, a socialist movement will appear through some alchemy of historical materialism. It is hoped — and asserted — that single-issue campaigns will somehow converge and that a revolutionary socialist movement will appear. Instead, we need to do the organizing in and through already existing movements to build class power.

Organizing

We need to engage in mass political activity that not only creates left organizations but also develops groups of people with socialist capacities into movements capable of contending both *with* and *for* power. The first step is to adopt organizing methods that allow us to transcend the more-or-less passive recruitment of self-selectors. Most importantly, organizing "places the agency for success with a continually expanding base of ordinary people, a mass of people never previously involved, who don't consider themselves activists at all — that's the point of organizing" (McAlevey 2012: 10). Organizing, unlike the other models, identifies leaders of key constituencies and brings them (and their constituents) into the campaign or organization — which is what allows us to organize the class rather than just the left.

In order to do this, we need sustained contact with people, which is partially why organizing our co-workers and neighbours is strategic — we know them and have pre-existing relationships upon which to build. Following Rocker, we also have to appeal to people on the basis of their daily struggles in order to build class power — and so struggles against individual employers or landlords are the first necessary step to struggles against employers and landlords as a class. Likewise, campaigns against particular instances of police violence or tuition hikes are the first step to broader movements capable of larger political fights — but the key is to win fights and continue to build power.

Because of its mass — and class — character, an organizing model must, by its nature, be based on collective action and the exercise of working-class power. There is plenty of good organizing work to emulate. The Quebec student movement, with its ability to periodically call successful province-wide strikes like the one in 2012, serves as an impressive example of organizing. In the working-class neighbourhood of Parkdale in Toronto, tenants have successfully engaged in several rent strikes against landlords' increases and built on that organization to support union drives and strikes at the nearby Toronto Food Terminal, where many Parkdale residents work (Parkdale Organize n.d.). Now tenant organizing along the Parkdale model has spread to other working-class neighbourhoods in Toronto and to nearby Hamilton. These campaigns were built by organizations with clear, democratic, and transparent structures that continuously sought the participation of large numbers of people and aimed to build and exercise working-class power as students, workers, and tenants. It's only through *organizing* to build class power and infrastructures that we can truly augment the left.

References

Bakunin, Mikhail. 1871. "Man, Society, and Freedom." Marxists.org. <marxists.org/reference/archive/bakunin/works/1871/man-society.htm>.
Bey, Hakim. 1985. "The Temporary Autonomous Zone." <theanarchistlibrary.org/library/hakim-bey-t-a-z-the-temporary-autonomous-zone-ontological-anarchy-poetic-terrorism#toc45>.
Fantasia, Rick. 1988. *Cultures of Solidarity: Consciousness, Action, and Contemporary American Workers*. Berkeley: University of California Press.
Henwood, Doug. 2012. "Foreword: Dystopia Is for Losers." In Sasha Lilley, David McNally, Eddie Yuen and James Davis (eds.), *Catastrophism: The Apocalyptic Politics of Collapse and Rebirth*. Oakland: PM Press.
INCITE!. 2017. *The Revolution Will Not Be Funded: Beyond the Non-Profit Industrial Complex*. Durham: Duke University Press.
Kinnucan, Michael. 2017. "Don't March, Organize for Power." *Jacobin*. <jacobinmag.com/2017/07/march-single-payer-medicare-health-care-democratic-socialists-of-america-unions>.
McAlevey, Jane. 2012. *Raising Expectations (and Raising Hell): My Decade Fighting for the Labor Movement*. New York: Verso.
___. 2016. *No Shortcuts: Organizing for Power in the New Gilded Age*. New York: Oxford University Press.
Nichols, Leslie J. 2012. "Alliance Building to Create Change: The Women's Movement and the 1982 CUPW Strike." *Just Labour*, 19.
Panitch, Leo, and Sam Gindin. 2016. "Class, Party and the Challenge of State Transformation." *The Socialist Register 2017: Rethinking Revolution*. London: Merlin.
Parkdale Organize. n.d. <parkdaleorganize.ca/>.
Paulson, Justin, and Rebecca Schein. 2012. "Justin Paulson and Rebecca Schein's Response to 'The Left After Politics.'" *Studies in Political Economy*, 89.
Rocker, Rudolph. 2004. *Anarcho-Syndicalism: Theory and Practice*. London: AK Press.
Rosenfeld, Herman. 2012. "Herman Rosenfeld's Response to 'The Left After Politics.'" *Studies in Political Economy*, 89.
Workman, Thom. 2011. "The Left After Politics." *Studies in Political Economy*, 87.
___. 2012. "More on 'The Left After Politics.'" *Studies in Political Economy*, 90.

3. Can Studying Workers' Class Consciousness Help to Raise It?

Bertell Ollman

In 2008, I conducted two focus groups in New York with ten workers from different occupations in each one; my main task was to ask them questions, which were inspired by the questionnaire Marx prepared for the "Revue Socialiste" that was sent to several thousand French workers in 1880 but not published until much later. During the focus groups, only occasionally did I add a fact that helped them think about a question. None of the workers were radical. At first, each worker was asked the same question; after a short while, the questions were addressed to them in groups of two, five, and then ten. Each session went on for two hours.

Since the great majority of such studies are done by mainstream academics who try to remain neutral and take little or no account of the larger context in which workers find themselves, the results have usually been what the people who employ the workers like to see. Is there another approach to learning what workers think about the class to which they belong that openly takes their side and helps them to understand their situation as well as what can be done to improve it?

My Questions

I started the sessions with the following questions:

- What do you as a worker, but also other workers, deserve? This is not just about what would satisfy you, but what the whole society owes you, what you deserve because of the contribution the working class as a whole makes to the life of our society. This question can be broken up into several parts:

1) Do you and all other workers deserve a living wage, a real living wage, which is at least two or three times what the government calls the "minimum wage"?
2) Do you and other workers deserve job security?
3) Do you deserve a safe, pleasant, and ecologically sensitive work place — that is, one that doesn't poison you or your co-workers, or others in the neighbourhood, or those for whom you are providing products or services?
4) Do you and all other workers deserve shorter hours at the same pay, which would give you more free time to develop other interests and talents?
5) Do all workers deserve at least a month's paid vacation every year?
6) Do all workers deserve completely free medical coverage for themselves and their families?
7) Do workers deserve complete equality of opportunity and of treatment for everyone in their place of work, whatever their race, gender, religion, etc.?
8) Do all workers deserve pensions large enough to enable them to pay all their bills after they retire?
9) Do all workers deserve a chance to develop the skills and acquire the knowledge needed to advance to a better job, with the workplace picking up the entire tab?
10) Do workers deserve a chance to do a greater variety of things on their jobs to avoid boredom?
11) Do you and other workers deserve a chance to participate in some of the important decisions made in your workplace, like electing foremen and supervisors, for example? (Remember, I asked you to think about what you and other workers deserve, not about what is easy to get.)
12) Do you think all workers, those who already hold a job and those who are still looking for one, deserve to live in a society that has enough good jobs for everyone who wants one?

(My questions as well as your answers to them should help us understand what a good job is.)

13) And, finally, if our capitalist society is organized to maximize profits for owners and cannot deliver even most of the things you believe you deserve, doesn't it make sense to look for another economic system that could provide us with all of these things?

- Next, I want to ask whether you think many workers would disagree with the views you have just expressed about the kind of good jobs that all workers deserve?
- Would workers who can only find part-time or temporary jobs disagree with us? What about unemployed workers or retired workers? What about the families of workers? What about the workers who make more money, even a lot more money, than you do, but share with you most of the other problems that have come up in these questions?
- What about the workers who like to refer to themselves by some other label — like "associates," "assistants," "partners," "professionals," or even "middle class"? (There are many labels that muddy up the water as to who is a worker.)
- As regards professionals (doctors, engineers, teachers, lawyers, for example): if they have a boss who hired them and can fire them (and most do), who sets their wages and conditions of work and tells them what to do, wouldn't they benefit from the kind of good jobs we have been talking about? Doesn't that make them — despite their different specialties and no matter how much education they've had or how much money they make and even how they think of themselves — doesn't that make them members of the same broad working class as you ... and me?
- As for what's called the "middle class," insofar as the great majority of the middle-class work for someone else and receive a wage or a salary, doesn't the same thing I've said about professionals apply to them? No matter how they think of themselves and what kind of lifestyle they lead, aren't they also part of the broad working class and wouldn't they benefit from having the kind of good jobs we have been talking about?

- It would seem that there are a number of important changes in our work and lives that would benefit all workers, changes that Marx often refers to as "workers' class interests." But why do so many workers seem unaware of them? Are they really unaware, or are they pretending — or forced to pretend?

At this point I put my questions aside and asked one of the workers to pretend he is a boss and another one to play the part of a worker who has come to his boss's office to ask for a raise. After listening to their exchange for a couple of minutes, I picked another boss and asked two more workers to join the first one in asking for a raise. Then, after a few minutes, I added three more workers to the group and asked them to do the same. After changing the boss once again, I asked all the workers to approach the boss with the same request. With each increase in the number of workers, the exchange with the boss got louder and louder. Finally, I said it is my turn to play the boss. As soon as the workers entered "my" office, I asked, "Do you have an appointment with me?" When a couple of them said "no," I hollered, "Then get the hell out of here" — at which point they all dashed forward and threatened to throw me out the window.

After a brief discussion on what made these apparently similar encounters with the boss so different, we returned to my questions:

- Now, how about our bosses, all of our bosses taken together — would they be happy with the kind of changes needed to make good jobs for their workers? On such matters, is it even possible to make both the bosses and the workers happy? If not, which side do you choose? What side are you on? Why do so many workers seem to have chosen the other side?
- How have the bosses managed to keep things the way they want them to be? What percentage of the population in our country are owners of the means of production, distribution, or exchange (that's Karl Marx's definition of a capitalist)? I'm not talking about the tens of millions of people who have put some of their savings into the stock market. They don't own enough to quit their jobs. The capitalists, on the other hand, own much more than enough, so they don't have to look for a job and even hire others to manage their affairs, including their workers, for them.

- Are the capitalists 30 percent of the population in America or 10 percent? Or 5 percent? Or 1 percent? Does it surprise you that it's closer to 1 percent?
- What percentage of the population belongs to the working class, understood as those who don't own factories, banks, or stores, so they have to go to work for someone else who decides what they should do, how long and how fast they should do it, when they should start and finish their work, and, of course, what they will be paid?
- Is the working class — including all the different groups that should be included in the working class — 30 percent of the population, 50 percent, or 70 percent, or 90 percent? It's well over 90 percent, which is much more than it was fifty and especially one hundred years ago, when there was a large class of independent small farmers and most doctors, lawyers, and accountants worked for themselves. Now most of the people who do farming and doctoring and accounting work for a boss and are part of the extended working class.
- It is said that we live in a democracy, the best definition of which is "the rule of the people." But if the workers make up over 90 percent of the population and the bosses only 1 to 2 percent, how is it that they can get what they want, while it is so hard for workers to get what they deserve (like the good jobs we've described)? What is the basis of the owners' power in our society? If it isn't their charm or their intelligence, or — at least in capitalism — their aristocratic birth, what else can it be but their money?
- Money's first and greatest power is to make still more money, which very quickly gives capitalists enough power to buy ... what? Well, why do you think the government and the media and the universities try so hard to get the rest of us to accept this unfair division of power and wealth as normal and even necessary? Who owns them?
- In this situation, what does it mean to be "apolitical," refusing even take a stand on the major issues of the day? What do you think of workers who pretend to be "neutral" on these matters?
- With workers outnumbering capitalists about fifty to one, is it

really so hard to see that workers have much more potential power than the capitalists do? Have you ever thought of all that workers could do if we acted together as a class? Can you see any other way of getting all that we deserve and need as workers? If not, what can we do about it together, starting with helping more and more workers to share our understanding of what is terribly wrong with capitalism and how to right it or, if need be, to replace it?
- This leads, of course — if it hasn't already come to your mind — to the two most important questions of all those I have asked: What is to be done? And how should we organize those who have come this far in their thinking to do it? Well, what do you think needs to be done and how should we do it?

This was the last question, and by this time it seemed like everyone in both focus groups had evolved far enough that they had no difficulty treating this question as the obvious one with which to finish our session. After fifteen to twenty minutes of very lively discussion, the consensus, again in both focus groups, was that they needed to start a new workers' political party that would struggle for just these goals. Only one woman said she couldn't play an active role in such a party, because she was a single mother and between her job and her three young children she had no time, but she too fully supported what the others wanted to do.

What did I learn? The workers who participated in these sessions already knew the answers to most (if not all) of the questions I asked them. What was missing, for the most part, were the connections between their answers — or, at least, clarifying that part of the "bigger picture" on "what is to be done." This is, of course, a crucial element in what Marx called "dialectics." Does this mean that dialectics has a much bigger role in helping to raise workers' class consciousness than most people on the left have realized?

It was getting late and as I thanked all the participants for coming, adding that I hoped what we discussed would prove very useful to them, a few people in both focus groups got angry at me for not staying there to help them start the new political party. I don't recall exactly what I said, but it allowed us to part on friendly terms. The workers who had spoken out, however, were not satisfied. Nor, I must confess, after all these years, am I.

The Theory that Underlies this Practice

While discussions of "theory" usually precede any attempt to put it to use, I believe that the particular "practice" displayed in this chapter is simple enough to be understood and appreciated by a wider audience than would be attracted by what you're about to read here. If there is still a place for theory in this discussion, it has to do with contextualizing the connections you have already encountered above, recognizing the full range of possibilities in the conditions before us and never losing sight of the question, "What is to be done?"

It may be useful to begin this theoretical section by noting that if the most important category in Marx's analysis of capitalism is "value," the most important category with which to organize our efforts to replace capitalism is "class." There was never any doubt, for example, that Marx would begin *The Communist Manifesto*, his most famous work, with "the history of all hitherto existing society is the history of class struggles" and follow with an account of capitalism that draws heavily from this opening remark. But if "class" deserves all this attention — and it does — it is essential that we understand the layered meanings he ascribes to what most people, including most of his followers, take to be a relatively simple category.

For Marx, "class" is, first of all, a place in the social-economic system, together with the main functions that come from occupying this place. One such place is very large and full of people but empty of all they need to survive, so that their main function is to find a job that will pay them enough to live. A second, much smaller space within the same system contains relatively few people, but they own enough wealth to perform the function of hiring workers to make themselves even richer than they were before. "Class" stands out here as a simple relationship between a particular place in society and the function that attaches to that place. It is this relation between workers and their bosses, and not how much money they make — though the two are usually related — that determines who belongs to what class.

The situation of the people in these two classes carries in its wake a set of distinctive "class interests" having to do with what would benefit them as members of their class (even under capitalism). For the workers, the most important of these are a decent wage, job security, and safe working conditions, while the main "class interests" of capitalists lie in maximizing their profits. I can't imagine that there are many (or any) workers or capitalists who are not aware that they have at least these interests, though capitalists often try to convince their workers that their interests stop at having a job and receiving any salary at all, since doing anything more for them would interfere with the capitalist's ability to maximize profits.

Marx's use of the concept of "class" is stretched even further in the expression "class consciousness." To be sure, knowing that one has an interest in a decent wage and safe conditions of work is already to be conscious of them and to recognize that other workers have the same interests. But the range of meaning covered by "class consciousness" extends much further, starting with the recognition that only a workers' organization can obtain a serious improvement in workers' conditions and — in the case of a growing number of workers — leading eventually to the belief that a more egalitarian way of organizing the production and distribution of wealth in our society is both possible and necessary.

There are many factors that contribute to the development of the workers' class consciousness, of which the most effective are the range of pressures coming from their class interests — but just as many factors that hold it back, among which the widespread efforts by the capitalists and their hired propagandists (misnamed as journalists, professors, priests, publicists, and politicians) play the major role. With so many crisscrossing influences at play at any one time, class consciousness is a very volatile substance. Unlike class interests, which can remain the same over a long period, class consciousness is subject to relatively quick changes, even major ones both forward and backward, depending to a large degree on what one has just learned or experienced. And that cannot help but have a major influence on how one participates in the "class struggle."

"Class struggle" is the fourth and most developed sense in which Marx uses "class." And just as "class interests" can be viewed as an aspect of "class," and "class consciousness" as an aspect of both "class" and "class interests," "class struggle" is an aspect of all of these, which is to say it is already present in the others to one degree or another, as they are in it. It is simply not brought into focus very much when dealing with the less-developed forms of class, but the interaction between the majority of people who do most of the work in society and the few who benefit from that work has always included some elements of class struggle. It is only by making the internal relations between "class," "class interests," "class consciousness," and "class struggle" explicit, however, that we are in a position to study how "class struggle" acquired its current form. Treating "class" as a relation capable of highlighting all of its extended aspects also makes it the ideal vantage point from which to study the workings of the complex and rapidly evolving society that is capitalism and to develop the kind of politics needed to win the version of the class struggle in which we find ourselves.

This rough sketch of the relations between the different senses in which Marx uses "class" leaves a lot to be desired, but I hope it is enough to provide a useful framework for what I consider the most provocative conclusion to come out of the section on focus groups with which I began this chapter. I noted above that the workers who participated in these sessions already knew the answers to most (if not all) the questions I asked them. What was missing, for the most part, were the connections between their answers, or at least that much of the "bigger picture" needed to give them a clearer grasp of "what is to be done."

In short, trying to understand anything of importance — especially if it seems to call for some kind of action — while knowing only some of what is involved is never enough. But we live in a society where most of what we know is relegated to different disciplines and sub-disciplines — the social sciences being the worst offenders, in which the "bigger picture" for any significant problem never emerges. What we are left with are the bits and pieces of a problem, which may contain enough to appear relevant, without providing us with most of what we need to resolve it.

It is here that Marx's version of dialectics offers another approach, one that begins with the acceptance of a world in which everything is internally related to everything else directly or indirectly, often very indirectly, and therefore interacting and affecting each other a little or a lot, one way or another and at one speed or another. It is this that allowed me to treat the four aspects of class discussed earlier as internally related parts of the same broad relation, which has evolved from whatever gave rise to it to wherever its main thrust is likely to take it.

Dialectics consists of a lot more than what I've been able to describe here, but in treating everything as relations and processes that are internally related to one another — which I consider its most important characteristic — little of what we observe can be gleaned from first appearances. Instead, we are constantly being pressed to "connect the dots" again and again. It is not a matter of needing to know everything about a subject before being ready to act on it, but of most people knowing far too little about the interrelated conditions that affect their lives even when the information is readily available. In reconstructing a fuller — albeit still partial — "bigger picture" from their own disconnected understanding of their situation, all of the workers in my two focus groups seemed ready to adopt a practice that was much more in sync with their class interests. This connection has proven so difficult for most workers to make because the elements involved are usually viewed, and therefore also treated, as externally related and separate from one another. But it is only when the most important of these connections are fully grasped and a wave of "class consciousness" spills over into the rest of workers' lives that a truly radical transformation of capitalism becomes possible.

Conclusion

Finally, I must admit that one of my main aims in this chapter, as well as in my two focus groups, was to see how much one can do politically by substituting a shorter, common sense version of "big picture" dialectics for a fuller account of it. To be sure, the rest of dialectics is very important, but I have found that its complicated features often dissuade many of the people I want to reach from using any part of it. Emphasizing the "bigger picture," on the other hand, is usually enough to bring most workers around to making the connections needed to jump-start their class consciousness along with the kind of politics that generally goes with it. Let me suggest that any reader who still has doubts about this take another look at the reaction of the workers who attended my focus groups.

This doesn't mean that people should forego a more detailed study of dialectics when the time permits, for there is a major difference between knowing what dialectics "is," so one can recognize it when it appears, and being able to "think" dialectically, so that one can use it wherever it applies, which is almost everywhere. At its core, "thinking" dialectically is being able to focus, as a matter of course, on the main relations and processes that make up any problem, and having the flexibility to change one's focus as the problem evolves, as all problems do. It is the difference between taking a photo of an event and tracking it over time and space. Being able to actually think dialectically against all the hurdles thrown up by capitalism's growing number of partial and one-sided ideologies represents a major achievement for anyone. It is in this context that introducing the notion of the "bigger picture" becomes an extremely helpful first step for workers — but also for students — in coming to grips with the unusual combination of unity and difference that constitutes the core of Marx's dialectical method. The next step is to uncover all that Marx does with it.

My own attempts to provide a fuller account of Marx's use of dialectics can be found in the references below.

References
Ollman, Bertell. 1975. *Alienation: Marx's Conception of Man in Capitalist Society.* Cambridge University Press.

___. 1993. *Dialectical Investigations.* London: Routledge.

___. 2003. *Dance of the Dialectic.* Champagne: University of Illinois Press.

Section 2

Organizing Class and Identity

4. Psychological Wage and the Trump Phenomenon

Paul Kellogg

In the days following the election of US president Donald Trump in 2016, parents and teachers comforted the sobs of their fearful children and students. Thousands rallied and marched in dozens of cities under the banner "not my president."[1] January 21, 2017, the day after Trump's inauguration, one in every one hundred people in the United States took to the streets in the "Women's March" — the largest one-day protest in US history. On January 28, 2017, tens of thousands surged into airports across the country to protest Trump's attempt to ban immigration from a series of "Muslim" countries. In an earlier era, Antonio Gramsci wrote, "The crisis consists precisely in the fact that the old is dying and the new cannot be born; in this interregnum, a great variety of morbid symptoms appear" (Gramsci 1930: 276).

As the new society is trying to be born, the millions who have marched and voted against Trump recognize his elevation to the presidency as a morbid symptom of the crises in our own era. The left cannot play a meaningful role in this opposition unless it shares this affect — and that will require a careful and sober re-examination of widely held understandings of the Trump phenomenon. This chapter will suggest that reducing the Trump election to a "populist revolt" against elites has the effect of minimizing or obliterating the importance of the "colour line" in US politics. This minimizing of the colour line underpins the limits of narrow trade unionist responses that actually welcomed aspects of the Trump agenda. I will suggest the importance of deploying the category of the "psychological wage," introduced by W.E.B. Du Bois, and conclude with some comments on what this means for the left. Trump has carved out a political movement of the far right that combines racism, misogyny, and corporate power. The challenge is to put forward a solidaristic politics of the left — embracing the connections between race, class, and gender.

Populist Reductionism

It is not uncommon to see working-class populist anger portrayed as the key to the 2016 election campaign, fuelling both Bernie Sanders's insurgent challenge to Hillary Clinton and Donald Trump's takeover of the Republican Party. Gerald Seib, writing in the *Wall Street Journal,* called both Sanders and Trump "populist voices" and labelled Trump a "billionaire populist … who has somehow tapped into a deep vein of working-class anger." Also writing in the *Wall Street Journal,* Charles Murray said that "the central truth of Trumpism as a phenomenon is that the entire American working class has legitimate reasons to be angry at the ruling class." In dialogue with Murray, Clive Crook said, "Supporting Trump is an act of class protest." Timothy Carney, writing in Washington's *Examiner,* argued that a "huge swath of the electorate is angry because they agree that the country "is a mess" and the game is rigged. All of these pundits think it's self-evident, as Trump says, that "the American Dream is dead."

This "populist reductionism" approach to the Trump phenomenon is completely misleading. One of the most basic indicators that might provide a basis for a populist rebellion against elites would be a prolonged period of income stagnation and an increase in poverty. There is no question that such circumstances characterize the US economy in the twenty-first century. Between 2002 and 2014, overall poverty rates in the United States drifted upwards from 12.1 percent to 14.8 percent. It should not be surprising to anyone that this increase in poverty was deeply racialized. For the Latinx[2] population, poverty rates are almost double the national average — going from 21.8 percent in 2002 to 23.6 percent in 2014. For African-Americans, poverty rates are even higher — going from 24.1 percent in 2002 to 26.2 percent in 2014. Contrast these poverty rates with those experienced by the non-racialized (white) section of the population — also increasing, but only barely touching double digits, going from 8.0 percent to 10.1 percent — far lower than poverty rates for the country's racialized poor (US Census 2014). But, as we will see in this chapter, the racialized poor — with far more reason to be part of a rebellion against the elites than the non-racialized poor — voted in overwhelming numbers for Clinton. The non-racialized poor — with far less reason to "rebel against the elites" — were the ones who voted in overwhelming numbers for Trump. The "class" argument used by some to explain the Trump phenomenon only makes sense when it is seen as a *racialized* class argument.

The Colour Line

The "populist reductionism" visible in many of the analyses of Donald Trump universally ignores or minimizes the colour line in US politics. Not seeing the significance of this colour line makes it impossible to understand the dynamics of party politics or voting behaviour. Noam Chomsky was articulating a widely held commonsensical judgment when, in 2010, he said, "In the US, there is basically one party — the business party. It has two factions, called Democrats and Republicans" (McDonald 2010). This is a two-dimensional analysis that obliterates the impact of race and racism. At every Democratic Party convention this century, more than 20 percent of the delegates have been African-American — almost twice their share of the general population. The contrast with the overwhelmingly white Republican National Conventions is striking. In 2016, the Democratic Texas delegation alone, with seventy-one delegates and alternates, was four times larger than the entire African-American delegation to the overwhelmingly white Republican convention. The modern Republican Party has coalesced as a party that incubates not just neoliberalism, but also open concessions to a deeply racist politics.

Voting patterns clearly highlight this colour line. This century, in every presidential election, the Democratic candidate has won overwhelming majorities within racialized communities, outpolling Republicans by twelve million in 2004 and twenty million in the next three elections. By contrast, Republican presidential candidates completely dominate within the non-racialized electorate, outpolling Democrats by sixteen million and twelve million in 2004 and 2008, and then by twenty million in the next two elections. It is not just business and economic class that shape the party system in the United States. Race and racism are at least as important (Goldfield 1997).

Trump's entry into politics was not through business but through racism. In April 2011, he jumped to the front ranks of Republican presidential hopefuls by becoming a loud advocate for the "birther" movement — questioning whether President Obama had been born in the United States. In making this his issue, Trump was swimming in what Columbia University professor Marc Lamont Hill described as "the most racist smear campaign in American political history." He was also tapping into a mass racist sentiment. In 2010, more than 40 percent of those polled indicated they didn't believe President Obama was born in the US or didn't know. A 2011 poll showed that 25 percent of adults nationwide believed Obama was not born in the United States. For Republicans, the figure was 45 percent. This racism has found fertile ground in Trump's discourse on migration and his seeming acceptance of violence by his far-right supporters.

At first, Trump's candidacy in 2015 was seen by some as a reality TV joke. But none of this is funny. To rhetorically play with violence in front of an audience of millions legitimizes the recourse to violence by the extremist fringe of his supporters. A campaign against elites, on a racist basis, with an appeal to violence echoes all the key themes of the fascist movements of the early and mid-twentieth century. These are the "morbid symptoms" that millions felt in the days and weeks following Trump's elevation to the presidency.

The response from people of colour was very clear. Trump received only eight million votes from racialized voters, swamped by the twenty-nine million who supported Democratic presidential candidate Hillary Clinton. Among Latinx voters, Clinton outpolled Trump by 4.8 million (7.7 million to 2.9 million) and among African-American voters by thirteen million (14.5 million to 1.3 million).

The response from white people was also, tragically, clear. Clinton received the support of thirty-six million white voters. Trump crushed her in this category, winning fifty-six million votes — twenty million more than put an "X" beside Clinton's name. With her overwhelming support among voters of colour, Clinton was still able to win the popular vote. But Trump's crushing landslide among white voters was enough to allow him to narrowly win Michigan, Wisconsin, Pennsylvania, Florida, and North Carolina, and, through the Electoral College, take over the White House. Millions of racialized voters saw the clear threat that Trump's racism and violence represented and in overwhelming majorities chose Clinton. But the white electorate — exposed to the same racism and the same appeals to violence — chose Trump over Clinton in what can only be called a landslide. Nothing could more clearly indicate the fact that the 2016 election was completely about the colour line in US politics.

Misogyny

Trump played on themes other than race. In an extraordinary exposé just before the election, he was caught on tape virtually advocating sexual assault. Misogyny, in fact, is a core component of his politics and those of his allies. The Alabama special election of 2017 was a case in point. The Republican candidate was Roy Moore, endorsed by Trump with an infamous December 4 tweet saying, "Go get 'em Roy." Moore is an extremely reactionary figure. His campaign from the beginning was weighed down by controversy over allegations of attempted sexual assault on two fourteen-year-old girls. During the campaign, four more women came forward with accusations of sexual assault.

In addition to being an alleged predator, Moore was also a bigot. In the course of two appearances on a radio show in 2011, he advocated getting rid of all constitutional amendments after the tenth, saying this would "eliminate many problems." He was, in other words, advocating the elimination of the post-slavery thirteenth, fourteenth, and fifteenth amendments, which determined that "neither slavery nor involuntary servitude ... shall exist within the United States," giving the right to citizenship of "all persons born or naturalized in the United States" regardless of race, and asserting that the right "to vote shall not be denied ... on account of race, color, or previous condition of servitude." Moore furthermore would abolish the nineteenth amendment, which gave women the vote, and the civil rights–era twenty-fourth amendment that eliminated poll tax requirements for voting eligibility.

The important fact is not that, in the end, Roy Moore lost, but that he almost won, trailing Democrat Doug Jones by just twenty-one thousand votes. Had the election allowed only non-racialized (white) people to vote, Moore would have won in a landslide, 605,306 to 267,047. Jones only squeaked out a victory because he received an astonishing 96 percent of the votes cast by African-Americans, crushing Moore in that category,

375,484 to 15,645 (Alabama Votes 2017; The Sentencing Project 2017; *Washington Post* 2017).

This is only part of the story. The largest single bloc of votes supporting Jones and opposing Moore came from 220,000 African-American women. Just 9,000 of them supported Moore. The second largest bloc came from African-American men — 142,000 supporting Jones, just 6,000 supporting Moore.

One more fact must be brought into focus. The state of Alabama, like many others in the United States, has "felony disenfranchisement laws" that remove the right to vote for thousands because of criminal convictions. These laws disproportionately impact men and people of colour. (Fully 92 percent of Alabama's prison population is male and the custody rate for African-Americans is 355 per 100,000 population — more than three times the 110 per 100,000 custody rate for non-racialized (white) people in Alabama.) As a result, more than 130,000 African-American men were prevented from voting in the December special election because of felony disenfranchisement.

So, a candidate exposed as a pedophile, openly calling for the repeal of those amendments to the constitution that enfranchise and empower African-Americans and women, wins overwhelming support in the white electorate and is only defeated because of an unprecedented surge to the polls by African-American women, a surge strong enough to overcome the disenfranchisement of tens of thousands of African-American men. The deep problem of racism and the enormous significance of the colour line, again, are clear.

Narrow Trade Unionism

The left pays a price when it separates this politics of racism and misogyny from its understanding of dynamics inside the working class. Slavoj Žižek said that, had he been eligible, he would have voted for Trump (Žižek 2016). John Pilger argued that "Hillary Clinton is more dangerous than Donald Trump" (Pilger 2016). In the small arena of the left, the flippant positions of Pilger and Žižek can be seen as morbid symptoms of a politics that risks making itself irrelevant to the anti-Trump sentiment that has been embraced by millions. However, this minimizing of the threat of Trump — only possible if we close our eyes to the racist, misogynist, and violent foundations on which his politics are built — is unfortunately not simply the property of these two individuals.

On election night, Trump broke through the so-called Democratic "blue wall" in heavily unionized Michigan, Wisconsin, and Pennsylvania. Following a logic parallel to the "populist reductionism" outlined earlier, some argued that Trump was able to break this blue wall and win the support of ordinary working-class trade union voters because of his opposition to the trade deals that have devastated blue-collar employment in the United States. Rick Salutin, for instance, said that Trump "won because he carried four states in the rust belt, where factories once guaranteed people decent lives and which Democrats had always taken for granted.... In those states, the issue was hatred of free trade, largely in the form of NAFTA." Branko Milanovic, author of *Global Inequality: A New Approach for the Age of Globalization* (Milanovic 2016) — interviewed during the 2016 election campaign — argued that there is an "absence of growth, stagnation of incomes in the US middle class, not only from loss of jobs, but also from loss of dreams of upward mobility for many people." He added, "Direct competition with Asia or other emerging markets ... was clearly one strong element which explains Trump."

Key leaders in the workers' movement took a similar position. Dennis Williams, president of the United Auto Workers, gave "kudos" to Trump for his opposition to NAFTA. Williams's view was echoed in Canada by Jerry Dias, president of Unifor, who said the union "welcomes the renegotiation of the North American Free Trade Agreement," as well as by progressive journalists such as Thomas Walkom, who wrote, "If Trump kills NAFTA, Canada could benefit" (Bomey 2016; CNW 2017; Phillips 2016; Salutin 2017; Walkom 2016).

The left has to completely reject this approach. It is based on a profound misunderstanding of the real dynamics of the election campaign and an unwillingness to confront the issue of racism inside the working class. First, it was at his rallies that Trump made NAFTA and protectionism a big issue. While these rallies were massive, they were only attended by a small portion of the electorate. In the media coverage of his campaign, and in his campaign announcements, the issues that were by far the most prominent had to do with racism — building a wall bordering Mexico and banning immigration from Muslim countries. The tape exposing his misogyny and virtual advocacy of sexual assault went viral. For the vast majority who get their news not from mass meetings but from the media — social or otherwise — it was the wall, immigration, and the infamous tape that dominated all coverage of Trump.

Second, which blue-collar trade unionists are we talking about? We do not have direct figures for the votes of trade unionists as such, but we do have a useful proxy: the votes of people in union households, 24.6 million members of which voted in 2016, a small increase from 2012. Union households as a whole, by a small majority (55 percent to 45 percent) voted for the pro-NAFTA candidate, Clinton, and not the anti-NAFTA candidate, Trump. The fact that more trade union households voted for Clinton than for Trump undermines the NAFTA-centred analysis of the Trump phenomenon.

However, when the numbers are parsed into racialized categories, something really significant does appear. Racialized trade union households voted overwhelmingly for the pro-NAFTA Clinton compared to the anti-NAFTA Trump — Latinx households 2.1 million to 1.1 million; Asian households 800,000 to 500,000; African-American trade union households by an overwhelming margin — 3.5 million to 350,000. There was, however, one group of trade union household voters who chose Trump over Clinton: non-racialized (white) trade union households gave 8.3 million votes to Trump and just 6.1 million votes to Clinton.

These 8.3 million non-racialized trade union household voters were able to look past Trump's extraordinarily racist campaign and put an "X" by his name. Only two million racialized members of union households could make that move, swamped by the 6.5 million who voted for Clinton. Were these 6.5 million racialized voters in union households voting "for" free trade? Of course not. They were voting against Trump. His racially charged campaign was the issue, not his stance on NAFTA and other trade deals. If there was an "anti–free trade" trade unionist vote for Trump, it was exclusively reserved for white trade unionists.

In the 1980s and 1990s, corporate-backed politicians articulated a pro–free trade policy in an economically driven campaign to maximize corporate power and profits. Free trade was opposed by the left as a clearly neoliberal attempt to undermine social programs and workers' rights. But Trump's anti–free trade policies are not driven by economics. They are, in fact, economically irrational, threatening the world economy with escalating trade wars that, if taken to their logical conclusion, would lead to economic crises everywhere. Trump's anti-NAFTA policies are a blatant attempt to stoke anti-Mexican racism. Trump's trade war with China and his abandonment of the Trans-Pacific Partnership are parallel attempts to stoke anti-Asian racism. This politics of "othering" has to be seen as such and condemned, not welcomed.

Implications for Left Politics

Trump's opposition to trade deals are part of his white nationalist, "America First" racism, which has nothing in common with any progressive trade union agenda. Understanding this white nationalist politics takes us on a road different from either populist reductionism or narrow trade unionism. The best map for finding this road remains the "psychological wage" framework developed by W.E.B. Du Bois. Written to deal with nineteenth-century social psychology, it is still profoundly relevant in the twenty-first century.

> It must be remembered that the white group of laborers, while they received a low wage, were compensated in part by a sort of public and psychological wage. They were given public deference and titles of courtesy because they were white. They were admitted freely with all classes of white people to public functions, public parks, and the best schools. The police were drawn from their ranks, and the courts, dependent upon their votes, treated them with such leniency as to encourage lawlessness. (Du Bois 1935: 700)

Toni Morrison and Jamelle Bouie can help us translate this concept of a "psychological wage" into contemporary language. Morrison's compelling post-election article "Mourning for Whiteness" suggests that there is a fear in white US society "of a collapse of white privilege" to the extent that millions "flocked to a political platform that supports and translates violence against the defenseless as strength" (Morrison 2016). Bouie (2016), chief political correspondent for *Slate*, argued that a key factor in the 2016 election was a backlash in sections of the white electorate against the very fact of having had an African-American president for eight years.

In the primaries, the flagrantly rich billionaire Trump swept counties in Appalachia, home to some of the country's poorest people. Du

Bois's notion of the psychological wage is the key to explaining his otherwise counterintuitive ability to attract the votes of masses of poor and working-class white voters. There is a section of the white electorate that experienced eight years of an African-American in the White House — just as some of their forebears had experienced the civil rights movement — as a cut in their psychological wage. Trump's campaign crystallized a racism with deep roots in US political discourse. The left has to take up the challenge of looking beyond the economic wage and seriously engage with the psychological wage, which was the core reason that millions of workers voted against their material interests and supported a reactionary billionaire in the 2016 election.

To be clear, this is not simply saying that the left should tack on a "race matters" aspect to our pre-existing class analysis. Rather, no class analysis is even *possible* when questions of racism are minimized or ignored. The so-called class analyses of the Trump phenomenon that have fixated on populism and downplayed the deep racist vein mined by the Trump campaign — reflected in the shocking indifference to Trump's election from people like Žižek and Pilger — are inaccurate and misleading.

The polarization created by the Trump presidency is, if anything, intensifying, pushing millions toward politics on both the right and the left. In the 2018 elections for the House of Representatives, the Republican vote increased from 2014, going from thirty-nine million to fifty-one million — an increase of 27.7 percent. But the Democrats were able to win control of the House of Representatives because their vote increased even more dramatically, going from thirty-five million to sixty-one million, an increase of 72 percent (House of Representatives 2018). We must heed the African-American women of Alabama and all the other millions of racialized voters in the United States; if we carefully listen to them and observe the issues propelling mass movements at the polls, it will force a re-evaluation of key elements of left politics. We will have to re-examine the commonplace — and narrow — understanding of Trump as a "populist" and his elevation to the presidency as a "protest against elites." If we do this, we will have taken a step to combatting the politics of racism, misogyny, and violence with which Trump has polluted political discourse, confronting these instead with a solidaristic politics that refuses to see class, race, and gender as separate issues, but instead as inextricably linked both in political ideology and in political strategy.

Notes

1. For detailed footnotes providing sources for this chapter, see "Not My President" (Kellogg 2017). Throughout the chapter, statistics on the 2016 election are taken from this source.
2. Used throughout as a gender-neutral or non-binary alternative to Latino or Latina.

References

Alabama Votes. 2017. "Special Election Official Results." <sos.alabama.gov/alabama-votes/voter/election-night-official-results>.

Bomey, Nathan. 2016. "UAW Wants to Join Trump in Effort to Crush NAFTA." *USA Today*, November 10.

Bouie, Jamelle. 2016. "How Trump Happened." *Slate*, March 13.

CNW. 2017. "Unifor Welcomes Start of NAFTA Renegotiation." *Canada NewsWire*, August 16.

Du Bois, W.E.B. 1935. *Black Reconstruction: An Essay Toward a History of the Part Which Black Folk Played in the Attempt to Reconstruct Democracy in America, 1860–1880*. New York: Harcourt, Brace and Company.

Goldfield, Michael. 1997. *The Color of Politics: Race and the Mainsprings of American Politics*. New York: New Press.

Gramsci, Antonio. 1930. "Wave of Materialism" and "Crisis of Authority." In Q. Hoare and G. Nowell-Smith (eds.), *Selections from the Prison Notebooks of Antonio Gramsci*. New York: International Publishers.

House of Representatives. 2018. "Election Statistics, 1920 to Present." <history.house.gov/Institution/Election-Statistics/>.

Kellogg, Paul. 2017. "Not My President." US Election Notebook, January 18. <web.archive.org/web/20170121105536/http:/news.athabascau.ca:80/news/not-my-president>.

McDonald, Alyssa. 2010. "The NS Interview: Noam Chomsky." *New Statesman*, September 13. <newstatesman.com/international-politics/2010/09/war-crimes-interview-obama>.

Milanovic, Branko. 2016. *Global Inequality: A New Approach for the Age of Globalization*. Cambridge, MA: Harvard University Press.

Morrison, Toni. 2016. "Mourning for Whiteness." *New Yorker*, November 21.

Phillips, Matt. 2016. "The Hidden Economics behind the Rise of Donald Trump" [Interview with Branko Milanovic]. *Quartz*, March 1. <qz.com/626076/the-hidden-economics-behind-the-rise-of-donald-trump/>.

Pilger, John. 2016. "Why Hillary Clinton Is More Dangerous Than Donald Trump." *New Matilda*, March 23. <newmatilda.com/2016/03/23/john-pilger-why-hillary-clinton-is-more-dangerous-than-donald-trump/>.

Salutin, Rick. 2017. "Will Justin Trudeau Be the Last Neo-Liberal Standing?" Opinion, *Toronto Star*, January 6.

The Sentencing Project. 2017. "State-by-State Data." <sentencingproject.org/the-facts/#map?dataset-option=SIR>.

United States Census. 2014. "Income and Poverty in the United States." <census.gov/

library/publications/2015/demo/p60-252.html>.
Walkom, Thomas. 2016. "If Trump Kills NAFTA, Canada Could Benefit." *Toronto Star*, November 11.
Washington Post. 2017. "Exit Poll Results: How Different Groups Voted in Alabama." December 13. <washingtonpost.com/graphics/2017/politics/alabama-exit-polls/>.
Žižek, Slavoj. 2016. "Slavoj Žižek Would Vote for Trump." *Žižek.Uk*, November 3. <zizek.uk/slavoj-zizek-would-vote-for-trump/>.

5. "Rising Powers" and Authoritarian Populism
Beyond Northern Left Perspectives

Sedef Arat-Koç and Aparna Sundar

This chapter aims to augment the left's understanding of contemporary right-wing populisms by situating them in the geopolitical economy (Desai 2015) of the post–Cold War world. We focus on two non-European cases — Turkey and India — to make the case that, despite the contemporaneous rise of right-wing authoritarian populisms and, in some cases, even fascisms across the world, an adequate left response requires that we pay attention to differences arising from their specific historical and geopolitical-economic locations. Indeed, the need to understand these ascendant movements in their specificities is all the more pressing because fascism in its contemporary incarnation is likely to coexist with, and operate through, (il)liberal democratic forms (Giroux 2018; Finchelstein 2017).

As prominent instances of authoritarian populism (Hall 1979) outside the North, the cases of Turkey under Recep Tayyip Erdoğan and India under Narendra Modi illustrate some of these differences. Historically, these cases are characterized by the rise of civilizational discourses and what we call *culturalism*, which is a mode of both explaining and doing politics on the global scale. Within the contemporary context of the neoliberal capitalist world order, they represent the "rising power" populisms of the Global South, emerging from a complex mixture of grievances and aspirations, and simultaneously asserting both aggrieved anti-imperialism and great-nation ambition.

Left analyses understand right-wing populism in the North as a form of neoliberal crisis management or as a result of the social reaction to neoliberalism. Theorists have noted that the rise of contemporary right-wing populism in post–Cold War Europe has corresponded with a state of "post-democracy" (Mouffe 2005) or "unpolitical democracy" (Urbinati 2014) that offers no democratic alternatives to the neoliberal consensus. It is a consequence of a political environment where distinctions between the right and the left have blurred, where mainstream "democratic politics" is reduced to smoothing the functions of the market, as noted early on by Rancière (1998: 113): "The absolute identification of politics with the management of capital is no longer the shameful secret hidden behind the 'forms' of democracy; it is the openly declared truth by which our governments acquire legitimacy." Ian Bruff (2014: 124–5) argues that contemporary right-wing governments represent an "authoritarian fix" to the post-2007 crisis of capitalism, with "authoritarian neoliberalism" emerging as "a response both to the wider crisis of capitalism *and* [to] more specific legitimation crises of capitalist states." Wendy Brown (2017) concurs that authoritarian populism represents a simultaneous weakening and strengthening of the state, arising from the "hostility to politics, to social justice and even to democracy in favour of market justice and rationales combined with heavy statism." But Brown is also interested in the sociological basis of the phenomenon, including "the socio-economic frustrations, the instabilities, the precarities, the loss of national horizons, and the social disintegration that have fomented nationalism, racism, xenophobia and desire for authoritarian rule." Trump's social base is made up substantially of "*dethroned whites,*" whose loss of economic power and cultural pride of place is a result of neoliberal practices that have undermined living standards, exported jobs overseas, redistributed wealth upward, and weakened access to higher education. Yet they ascribe these shifts to "a *perceived* liberal political trajectory understood … to have demoted them and promoted historically excluded groups — women, racial and sexual minorities, the disabled, new immigrants and, above all, African Americans" (Brown 2017).

Neoliberal dislocations and chauvinistic backlash are without doubt also at the base of our two cases. But authoritarian populism in these states differs in significant ways from the Northern cases referenced above. In seeking to understand these differences, we draw insights from a geopolitical economy approach that recognizes "the materiality of nation-states" in processes of uneven and combined development (Desai 2015). Such an analysis argues for "the need to unite the normally separated economic and political logics of capitalism in an overall historical understanding" whereby combined development, often under the aegis of a developmental state, has been one of the principal ways of spreading productive power around the world. By insisting that "nations are material products of capitalist development just as much as classes are," geopolitical economy puts "the international struggle between dominant and contender powers and class struggles within them in a single frame" (Desai 2015: 450–52).

Neoliberal globalization has created further space for the rise of new economies on the world stage while also reproducing and reconfiguring uneven development at national and international levels (Desai 2015). The nationalism of "rising powers" such as Turkey and India as they seek to position themselves within this shifting geopolitical economy expresses not only the frustrations associated with the negative effects of neoliberal globalization, but also the aspirations and perceived opportunities of the new global order. These nationalisms take the form of populist platforms that combine cultural chauvinism with economic development to appeal to various social classes. Economic expansion has whetted the appetites of the big bourgeoisie and delivered a consumption economy to the rising middle classes. For other classes, for whom the gains from globalization are not as evident, the growing ethnicization and sectarianization of the polity has created a "gradation in citizenship" (Bannerji 2011: 58) based on ethnic, religious, or caste identity, providing some privileges for parts of the working class and peasantry in the form of psychological "wages" associated with Hinduness in India or conservative Sunni-Muslimness in Turkey. Our argument here thus shares the emphasis of Topak (in this volume) when he underlines the continued potency of appeals to nationalism in separating a global working class into categories such as the "European host" and "Muslim refugee." Likewise, we note that popular support for the ethnic/sectarian authoritarianisms in Turkey and India is based in different versions of the "psychological wage" identified by Kellogg (in this volume) to explain the higher levels of support for Trump among white men than among any other social group.

In the next section, we discuss the rise of culturalism as a frame through which right populisms in both the North and the South are constituted and mutually reinforced. Following that, we locate the new populisms of the Global South in the context of new openings created by the shifts in global capital, even as global inequality continues to increase and Northern/Western military and economic power seeks to re-entrench itself. We show how the attempted economic and cultural strategies of redistribution by "rising powers" may also interpolate upwardly mobile classes and social groups that see themselves as their beneficiaries. Thus, while authoritarian populisms proliferate across both the North and the South, we can gain a full understanding of their differences only through a historically and spatially contextualized geopolitical-economic account. Such an account also promises a better understanding of the complexity and contradictions of post–Cold War geopolitical economy and the interconnected dangers of culturalism for democracy and peace.

The Cultural(ist) Logic of the Post–Cold War World

Contemporary right-wing populisms in the Global North and the South are located in the economics of neoliberalism, on the one hand, and a politics of culturalism, on the other. In *Good Muslim, Bad Muslim*, Mahmood Mamdani (2004: 17) argues that the period after the Cold War, typically characterized as the era of globalization, is "marked by the ascendancy and rapid politicizing of a single term: 'culture.'" Culturalism is both a product and symptom of the (anti)politics of the post–Cold War era. In a period that has marked the end of "actually existing socialism" as well as the "assassination" of the "Third World Project" (Prashad 2007), when capitalism has appeared as having "no alternatives" and the global hegemony of capitalism has been celebrated as the "end of history," a specific conception of "culture" has captured a central place in the political imaginary. Very different from material and lived notions of culture, "culture talk" refers to assumed, essentialized, and absolute differences between civilizations that come in "large geo-packages" (Mamdani 2004: 17; Samuel Huntington's *Clash of Civilizations* [1996] is a case in point). This notion of civilization attributes specific political dispositions to human collectivities. It assumes that they "operate according to a sort of spiritualized genetic code called culture, so that their joint history is seen as a kind of natural history of congenital predispositions and incapacities" (Al-Azmeh 2012: 507). The notion of civilization as political disposition not only simplifies and distorts the characteristics assumed of the "self" and the "other," but it also occludes historical and political discussion by instead promoting the "displacement of the world's problems onto the realm of culture" (Dirlik 2002: 34).

Arif Dirlik's work helps locate the characteristics and contradictions of the culturalist logic of contemporary right-wing populisms. He focuses on the coexistence of two seemingly contradictory developments of recent decades: "economic and political globalization that is taken generally to point to unprecedented global integration, and the resurgence of religions or, more broadly, traditionalisms, that create new political and cultural fractures, or reopen old ones" (Dirlik 2003: 147). Despite the seeming contradiction, he argues, the "wedding of neoliberal capitalism and assertions of cultural autonomy has become a defining feature of contemporary global politics" (Dirlik 2015: 12). Contrary to the emphasis in some non-Western countries on their cultural differences from "the West" and their "alternative modernities," Dirlik (2003) insists that we all live now in a singular modernity — a "capitalist modernity" that is immersed in the policies and values of neoliberalism.

At both national and international levels, culturalism shapes a necessarily antagonistic, exclusionary, and authoritarian "post-politics," whereby politics plays out in the moral register, as the difference between good and evil, and political opponents are constructed not as "adversaries" but as "enemies" (Mouffe 2005: 75).

"Rising Power" Populism in Turkey and India

The end of the Cold War signalled the emergence of a single "capitalist modernity" around the world. While neoliberal globalization has created new spaces for the rise of new economies on the world stage, it has also reproduced and reconfigured uneven development at national and international levels (Desai 2015). On the one hand, the growing numbers of billionaires and of consumerist middle classes in India and China, along with increasing precarity in the North, suggests that there is a "flattening" of the world. At the same time, inequality between the world historical regions of North and South has continued to grow. Observing Global South countries' distinct structural locations within the global system, along with their complex mixtures of grievances and aspirations, provides a better understanding of their specific brands of authoritarian populism. In contrast to their Northern counterparts, contemporary Indian and

Turkish populisms express not only the frustrations associated with the negative effects of neoliberal globalization, but also the aspirations and perceived opportunities of the new global order. In both countries, the populist platforms that combined cultural chauvinism with economic development have appealed to various social classes: economic expansion has whetted the appetites of the big bourgeoisie and likewise delivered a consumption economy to the rising middle classes. Yet in the context of the growing ethnicization and sectarianization of the polity, there has been a "gradation in citizenship by establishing religious/ethnic terms for claims on the resources of the nation" (Bannerji 2011: 58). In this context, there have even been some privileges for parts of the working class and peasantry in the form of material and, as importantly, psychological "wages" associated with Hinduness in India or conservative Sunni-Muslimness in Turkey. Though decisively of the South, the basis of popular support for these ethnic authoritarianisms is similar to the "wages of whiteness" identified in David Roediger's (1991) analysis of working-class racism in the United States.

In the case of both the Bharatiya Janata Party (BJP) in India and the Justice and Development Party (AKP) in Turkey, we have seen the rise of religio-cultural definitions of nationhood. Using "univocal monopolistic interpretations of religion, culture, tradition and community," ethnic nationalists "rewrite or invent histories, substituting history and actual social relations with 'traditions' and scriptural injunctions" (Bannerji 2011: 44). In this political climate, we see what can be described as an (over)politicization of "culture" and a depoliticization of politics as "projects of social justice [become] unutterable and discredited, while putting in place collectivities of animosities and exclusion based primarily on religion" (Bannerji 2011: 45).

Vijay Prashad argues that with the demise of the "Third World Project," "dominant classes in these states adopted two postures, and sometimes both: an eagerness to be untethered from their societies and/or linked to their population through ascribed identities of faith and race" (Prashad 2007: 217). Turkey's AKP, in power since 2002, has simultaneously pursued both positions. Its rule has involved a wild, "vagabond capitalism": an aggressive hyper-developmentalism voraciously transforming space, people, and relationships with hardly any consideration for the social or ecological fabric; and political and ideological attempts to resolve the tensions associated with this strategy through authoritarian, nativist politics and neo-Ottoman aspirations for regional leadership. Like other cases of right-populism internationally, the rise of the AKP corresponded to a historical context, when the left was crushed through the 1980 military coup and mainstream parties experienced a crisis through the 1990s and the early 2000s. This milieu offered no political representation for the working class (including those in the sizable informal sector) or for small peasants. The largest opposition party, the Republican People's Party (CHP), which had adopted social democracy in the 1970s, shed this platform and instead placed a rather identitarian notion of secularism at the centre of its political agenda.

Since it was founded in 2001, the AKP has successfully constructed and popularized an image of its leadership as organically connected to "the real people" of the country, leading an epic struggle against an arrogant, Westernizing elite who are depicted as alienated from the "national self." This ideology posits conservative Sunni Muslims as the real, authentic national subjects, and characterizes their identity — including that of the Muslim bourgeoisie — as oppressed and marginalized by the Turkish cultural mainstream. Starting in its first term in office with "soft" (and reasonable) populist appeals for the democratic inclusion of devout Muslims in Turkish modernity, the AKP's populist project has moved in an increasingly exclusionary, sectarian, and totalitarian direction. This became apparent especially after the Gezi movement in 2013, which posed serious challenges not only to the AKP's development project, but also to its claims to represent "the people." Even as the AKP has undone any separation of powers, as it has fully captured all institutions of the state and started to act *as the state*, it continues to use culturalist arguments to invert relations of domination by representing those now holding power as the eternal underdogs of Turkish society.

What gives AKP populism its "rising power" quality is partly related to its neo-Ottoman aspirations, which have inspired a new political imaginary and changes in foreign policy. Even though Turkey does not have the size or resource base of other "rising powers" such as India or China, its strategic location in the Middle East and its historical relationship with NATO and some Muslim majority countries seemed to create possibilities — especially after 9/11 and during the Arab uprisings of 2011 — for Turkey to play the role of a regional power. Representing aspirations for a national reawakening, neo-Ottomanism involves grandiose visions that a "resurgent Turkey ... following the example of its Ottoman forebears, [would] lead Muslims from around the world to global recognition if not hegemony" (Dirlik 2015: 4).

Neo-Ottoman discourses not only advocate for ambitious changes in foreign policy through stronger ties and influence throughout the former Ottoman territories; they also have significant implications for national politics, in that they attempt to radically transform the national identity of modern Turkey. Posing an Islamist challenge to secular nationalism, neo-Ottomanism treats the last century and more of Turkey's history as one of subordination and humiliation in relation to the Western world. Representing this period as an anomalous diversion from Turkey's "authentic" historical legacy, neo-Ottomanism proposes to close the "hundred-year parentheses" and "return" Turkey to its teleological position of national greatness. The de-secularization of the Turkish polity and the more interventionist role Turkey has assumed in foreign policy have increased ethnic and sectarian divisions in Turkey, including those between conservative Muslims and secular people.

Neo-Ottoman discourses present neoliberal development projects as an integral part of national reinvigoration, contributing to the psychological "wage" for the working class in its feeling part of a great nation (Tokdoğan 2018). In practice, this means that any political or environmental opposition to these projects is delegitimized and dismissed as an attempt by internal enemies to stall Turkey's progress.

Neo-Ottomanism also serves to express grievances and resentment in regional and international relations (Tokdoğan 2018). As Turkey's Middle Eastern policy has faltered in recent years — most notably because of its continued insistence on regime change in Syria — and Turkish leadership has lost popularity among Middle Eastern neighbours as well as Western allies, this rapid fall has fuelled ultra-nationalist sentiments. Recent foreign policy discourses articulate culturalist, civilizational thinking with a politics of resentment and a paranoid nationalism, specifically the idea that Turkey's rise as a regional leader and global power is being attacked from all sides. This kind of thinking fuels authoritarianism at the national level, delegitimizing any critiques of national or foreign policy as treasonous.

In India, cultural nationalism and rising-power positioning play out in ways that are both similar to and different from those in Turkey. Hindutva or Hindu nationalism is a project dating to the anti-colonial movement of the early twentieth century, shaped by the globally circulating fascist ideologies of racial purity and violence of that period, and repudiated in the founding of the secular postcolonial state (Jaffrelot 2009). Its resurgence under the BJP is almost exactly contemporaneous with the opening up of the Indian economy to international capital in the early 1990s (Sud 2012). Although the BJP is not the party that moved the country to neoliberalism, it is the party that has grown the most under it — suggesting, if not a clear causal link between neoliberalism and Hindu nationalism, certainly an elective affinity.

Hindutva ideology casts India as an ancient Hindu civilization coming into its own again after a millennium of oppression under a series of Muslim invaders and then under the British. The task of the BJP and its affiliate organizations is to strengthen this revived nation by consolidating Hindu identity culturally and electorally. The project of creating a Hindu nation involves undermining India's constitutional commitment to secularism, the demonization of religious minorities (Muslims in particular), and the consolidation of a majority Hindu community out of a bewildering variety of regionally differentiated castes and ethnicities. Toward these ends, culture has become a key terrain, with cultural practices associated with religious "others" and lower castes — such as the sale and consumption of beef, inter-religious and inter-caste marriages, and literary or artistic creations that "hurt community sentiments" — becoming targets of violence by non-state actors granted impunity by the state. Critics of the rewriting of history and the remaking of community are branded "traitors to the nation." The particular targets of these insults are left and liberal intellectuals, artists, activists, and members of civil society organizations; they are portrayed as members of an established anglicized, "pseudo-secularist" elite, against which the BJP portrays itself, as did the AKP, as both the representative of the authentic nation and a perpetual underdog. Rural and Indigenous communities fighting dispossession of their land to make way for mines, factories, or infrastructure projects are also declared "anti-national" for opposing the nation's development and rise as an economic power. The BJP has strong support from sections of the rising middle classes and "provincial propertied classes" (Balagopal 2011 [1987]), especially those who have prospered from the opening of the market and overcome their own perceived lack of cultural capital. The

BJP represents the confidence and aspirations, but also the resentments, of this sizable new social formation.

The Hindutva project is riddled with contradictions, of course. The capture of the public sphere by the politics of culture means that other issues — of agrarian distress, faltering job creation, environmental crisis — have been made invisible. Especially thorny is the contradiction between Hindutva as simultaneously a project of revanchist Brahminical patriarchy *and* a project of Hindu consolidation. On the one hand, lower castes and especially Dalits (traditionally deemed to fall "outside" the Indian caste hierarchy) are seen as having become too assertive and needing to be put in their place. On the other, they are numerically essential to the construction of a Hindu "majority" and must be courted electorally. The growing protests by farmers, workers, and other marginalized sections, as well as the electoral defeats faced by the BJP in five regional elections in late 2018, suggest that these contradictions are becoming increasingly hard to contain.

Cultural nationalism also has an external dimension. Given its demographic weight and the presumed "moral example" of its Gandhian anti-colonial movement, India has always projected itself as a leader of the Global South, its founding role in the Non-Aligned Movement being a case in point. This position has evolved since its rapid economic growth and increasing attractiveness as a market, especially in the global instability of the post-2008 period. India's membership in the G20 and BRICS formations demonstrates a concern with economic and strategic power within the capitalist order; its campaign for a permanent seat on the UN Security Council is another instance of its demand for representation, not as a leader of the Global South, but in its own right as the largest "free-market democracy." It has moved closer to the US and its allies like Israel, increasing arms imports and carrying out joint security exercises, claiming shared interests as "democracies threatened by Islamic terrorism." This shift was authored by the centrist Congress Party as much as by the BJP, but the latter has sought to give it a cultural character. Modi is credited with having "made India great" on the world stage, especially by the economically powerful diaspora in the West that has been assiduously cultivated by the Hindu right wing; beneath the celebration of India's "arrival" and "recognition" lies a profound resentment of perceived slights and the actual experience of racism.

Conclusion

Analysis of right-wing populism informed by geopolitical economy can enrich our understanding of authoritarian populisms at both national and transnational levels. We have argued for the need to go beyond political economy to look at the ways in which nationalist discourses mobilize social identities around ethnicity, caste, religion, and sect to consolidate domestic support for a project of national assertion. By analyzing the positioning of "rising powers" in their respective regions and globally, we are able to see the contradictory nature of right-wing populisms and how they may simultaneously express deep international resentments and aspirations for national grandiosity.

Our analysis demonstrates the grave dangers posed by right-wing populism to equality, justice, democracy, and peace at national and international levels. Despite their critiques of Eurocentrism — or occasionally, of imperialism — "rising power" populisms do not challenge global capitalism or articulate alternatives grounded in anti-imperialist Southern solidarity. Rather, they participate in the game and fuel competition in it. The emphasis on "cultural difference" and the ideological attack on ostensibly monolithic Enlightenment values, on the other hand, often end up being used as ideological weapons to delegitimize divergent interpretations of "culture" and the political opinions of those who challenge populist claims to "the nation." Our analysis suggests that we organize not only against neoliberalism, but also against culturalism, national chauvinism, and a world order where empires and imperial aspirants vie for power.

References

Al-Azmeh, Aziz. 2012. "Civilization as a Political Disposition." *Economy and Society*, 41, 4.

Balagopal, K. 2011 [1987]. "An Ideology for the Provincial Propertied Class." In *Ear to the Ground: Selected Writings on Class and Caste*. New Delhi: Navayana Publications.

Bannerji, Himani. 2011. *Demography and Democracy: Essays on Nationalism, Gender and Democracy*. Toronto: Canadian Scholars' Press.

Brown, Wendy. 2017. "Apocalyptic Populism." *Eurozine*, 30. <eurozine.com/apocalyptic-populism/>.

Bruff, Ian. 2014. "The Rise of Authoritarian Neoliberalism." *Rethinking Marxism*, 26, 1.

Desai, Radhika. 2015. "Introduction: The Materiality of Nations in Geopolitical Economy." *World Review of Political Economy*, 6, 4.

Dirlik, Arif. 2002. "Interview." In Shaobo Xie and Fengzhen Wang (eds.), *Dialogues on Cultural Studies: Interviews with Contemporary Critics*. Calgary: University of Calgary Press.

___. 2003. "Modernity in Question? Culture and Religion in an Age of Global Modernity." *Diaspora: A Journal of Transnational Studies,* 12, 2.

___. 2015. "Twin Offspring of Empire, Neoliberalism and Authoritarian Neotraditionalism: Thoughts on Susan Buck-Morss' 'Democracy: An Unfinished Project.'" *Boundary,* 2, 42.

Finchelstein, Federico. 2017. *From Fascism to Populism in History.* Berkeley: University of California Press.

Giroux, Henry. 2018. "Neoliberal Fascism and the Echoes of History." *The Bullet*, August 20.

Hall, Stuart. 1979. "The Great Moving Right Show." *Marxism Today*, January.

Huntington, Samuel. 1996. *The Clash of Civilizations and the Remaking of World Order.* New York: Simon and Schuster.

Jaffrelot, Christophe. 2009. *Hindu Nationalism: A Reader.* Princeton: Princeton University Press.

Mamdani, Mahmood. 2004. *Good Muslim, Bad Muslim.* New York: Doubleday.

Mouffe, Chantal. 2005. *On the Political.* London: Routledge.

Prashad, Vijay. 2007. *The Darker Nations: A People's History of the Third World.* New York: The New Press.

Rancière, Jacques. 1998. *Disagreement.* Minneapolis: University of Minnesota Press.

Roediger, David. 1991. *The Wages of Whiteness: Race and the Making of the American Working Class.* New York: Verso.

Sud, Nikita. 2012. *Liberalization, Hindu Nationalism and the State: A Biography of Gujarat.* New Delhi: Oxford University Press.

Tokdoğan, Nagehan. 2018. *Yeni Osmanlıcılık: Hınç, Nostalji, Narsisizm* [New Ottomanism: Resentment, Nostalgia, Narcissism]. Istanbul: İletişim.

Urbinati, Nadia. 2014. *Democracy Disfigured.* Cambridge: Harvard University Press.

6. Migration "Crises" and the Left
In Search of the Political
Özgün E. Topak

The contemporary era has been described as the "Age of Migration" (Castles, de Haas, and Miller 2014), where global migration plays a major role in shaping public debates and policies. Throughout 2015, the migration "crisis" dominated the public agenda in Europe. Despite the complexity of reactions to the movement of migrants, we can discern two patterns in the mainstream response: criminalization and humanitarianism. The first pattern views migrants as criminals and potential terrorists who pose a threat to Western societies, while the second governs migrants as docile victims in need of charitable compassion. Despite the apparent differences between these two patterns, they share some fundamental similarities. Confining migrants within the "victim/villain" dichotomy (see, for example, Anderson 2008), both of these perspectives refuse to address migrants as political subjects or as displaced and dispossessed members of the global proletariat. In so doing, they strip "the political" in politics, reducing it to "post-politics" (Rancière 1999; Mouffe 2005; Žižek 2008).

Post-politics is a governing logic that eradicates the antagonistic field of the political, replacing it with "the sole interplay of state mechanisms and combination of social energies and interests" (Rancière 1999: 102). It promotes a technocratic-managerial approach to political issues that ignores antagonistic political identities. This form of politics refuses to acknowledge the root political causes of migration, or the political identity of migrants as the global proletariat. Instead it assembles a mixture of criminalizing and humanitarian policies to control and exclude migrants. This chapter critiques these two different but equally post-political responses to mass migration. It emphasizes the need to move beyond the two perspectives and advances a third approach whose principles are rooted in migrant social movements.

Global migration poses a major challenge for internationalist leftist politics in the twenty-first century and demands that the national question be taken seriously. The elision of the national question resulted in tragic failures for international working-class movements in the late nineteenth and early twentieth centuries, when nationalism created and then deepened divisions within the working classes (van Holthoon and van der Linden 1988). The European working classes were constructed as *homo nationalis* through ideological state apparatuses (Balibar 1991) and internalized the racial global hierarchies of capitalism at the expense of their international class positions.

How can the left avoid its past mistakes and rethink the relationship between migration, nationalism, and class struggle today? If the left aspires to confront the rise of an increasingly nationalist and authoritarian right, we must move beyond the dominant criminalization-humanitarianism nexus and articulate a form of politics that establishes international class solidarity with arriving migrants. This chapter has no pretense of providing a formula for a true leftist position in the age of mass migration. Rather, it attempts to search for the principles upon which a leftist politics-to-come could be built and argues that some of these principles can be found in migrant social movements. To that end, I examine the case of 300 Migrant Hunger Strikers (3MHS) in Greece, one of the major migrant protests held in Europe in recent years. Before examining this case, however, I critique the criminalization and humanitarianism frameworks. This critique is important because it is not only the right but also sections of the left, from nationalists to liberal leftists, that are caught up in the criminalization-humanitarianism nexus.

Governing Migrants through Criminalization

Criminalization is the main framework through which migrants are governed. It entails two intersecting processes: discursive and physical criminalization. Discursive criminalization involves constructing migrants as security threats in public discourse. In the post-9/11 context, the terms with which migrants — particularly those of Muslim origin — are described are subsumed under the ideological formation of the "War on Terror," which acts as a master category, defining what can be said about Muslim migrants and positioning them as dangerous security threats to Western societies. Following the 2015 refugee movements, another layer was added to the discursive criminalization of migrants: new discourses of migration "crisis" representing migrants not only as security threats (such as disguised terrorists) but as agents of destruction or "insurrection" (Soguk 2017) whose main objective is to destroy more than to terrorize. The headline of a centre-right newspaper illustrates this new discursive construction: "This migration crisis could test the European project to destruction." Migrants are portrayed as barbarians storming the gates of Western civilization or as hordes invading Europe. The construction of migrants as "barbaric others" follows the Orientalist logic lucidly identified by Edward Said (1979). This logic establishes a series of contrasts between West and East, positioning the East as "barbaric," "violent," "backward," and "irrational" while the West is its opposite: "advanced," "civilized," and "rational."

Discursive criminalization underpins and justifies physical criminalization. It assigns a different place for migrants and deems the violation of their human rights lawful. Indeed, the normalization of thousands of migrant deaths at the borders of Europe demonstrates that migrants belong to another level of humanity and are governed by a different set of laws. Despite being concentrated around borders, physical criminalization practices are spread throughout Europe, exercised through various forms of police surveillance and racist attacks against migrants.

The criminalization of migration is a post-political strategy in that the representation and treatment of migrants as criminals serves to hide the political root causes of migration. Migration is a complex issue that is influenced by various factors. However, similar to many other complex social issues, migration exists within the social totality of capitalism (Althusser 2005) and is shaped by capitalism's historical and contemporary processes. These processes include 1) capitalism's historical "core-periphery" divide as well as its race and gender hierarchies among the global proletariat (e.g., Balibar and Wallerstein 1991); 2) the contemporary activities of global multinational corporations that deepen capitalism's historical divisions (e.g., Delgado Wise 2013); 3) contemporary primitive accumulation processes, which create mass dispossession, proletarianization, and urbanization in the Global South, (e.g., Samaddar 2017) and which are furthered by the use of new technologies in agriculture, land grabs, neoliberal development, and privatization projects, as well as climate change; and 4) imperialist military interventions in peripheral societies, which can take the form of direct military interventions (as in the case of Libya) or proxy wars (as in the case of Syria).

The root causes of migration demonstrate that rather than being Islamist masses invading Europe, migrants are dispossessed members of a global proletariat who are fleeing from the violence and poverty created by capitalism and who challenge the global hierarchies of capitalism by means of fleeing. Yet, the post-political criminalization discourse refuses to acknowledge the political root causes of migration and denies migrants their global class identity, instead assigning them a cultural identity: Muslims. The culturalization of migration discourse has become particularly hegemonic since the eighties, with the decline of the socialist alternative and the rise of post-political parties in Europe. As Yılmaz (2016) demonstrates, during this period the right successfully intervened in public discourse to redefine the immigration debate in culturalist terms. The mainstream left's abandonment of class politics in favour of postmodern identity politics further created the suitable conditions for the right to relabel migrant workers from predominantly Muslim countries simply as Muslims. Once they were stripped of their class identity, migrant workers became targets of nationalist and racist discourses that accused them of disturbing the fictional cohesion of society. The decline of class discourse went hand in hand with rising xenophobia. As Rancière (1992: 63) puts it:

> Objectively, we have no more immigrant people than we had twenty years ago. Subjectively, we have many more. The difference is this: twenty years ago the "immigrant" had an *other* name; they were workers or proletarians. In the meantime this name has been lost as a *political* name. They retained their "own" name, and an other that has no *other* name becomes the object of fear and rejection.

Remarkably, some sections of the left also adopt elements of a post-political perspective. Statements by philosopher Slavoj Žižek about the 2015 migrant movements exemplify this position. While Žižek differed from the right by emphasizing the need to tackle the political root causes of migration, he joined the right by stating that "most of the refugees come from a culture that is incompatible with Western European notions of human rights" and calling for (further) restriction of their mobility rights (Žižek 2015). This leftist position similarly follows the two steps of post-political discourse identified by Rancière. First, it displaces the class character of migrants' mobility and reframes it in culturalist terms, using Orientalist language. Second, it supports, directly or indirectly, the development of criminalization measures to protect "Western values." (Interestingly, in his earlier writings, Žižek [2008] challenged the notion of "Western values" for its false universality and its effective justification of migrants' marginalization.) Abandoning the class perspective in favour of a culturalist one, Žižek's current position fails to see that class is an objective condition (based upon one's relation to the means of production) and that most fleeing migrants belong to the global working class. The fact that some of these migrants may not have "class consciousness" (a subjective class identity) does not mean that they are "barbaric Muslim others." It rather means that the left holds much responsibility in supporting the transformation of the arriving migrants from being a class *in* itself to being a class *for* itself. The solidarity efforts during the 3MHS event provide clues about this form of leftist intervention.

Governing Migrants through Humanitarianism

The humanitarian perspective views and treats migrants as passive subjects of compassion and is associated with the liberal left perspective. Unlike the criminalization perspective, it does not necessarily use inflammatory rhetoric about migrants, yet it also does not define them as political subjects worthy of solidarity and equity. Similar to the criminalization perspective, this perspective fails to account for the political root causes of migration and the class status of migrants, and it therefore contributes to the depoliticization of migration and migrants. While humanitarianism claims to be apolitical, it in fact mobilizes a particular form of politics, post-politics, to govern migrants. It operates "as a transnational system of governance tied to capital and labor even while purporting to be apolitical" (Ticktin 2006: 35). Ultimately, in dialogue with criminalization, humanitarianism serves to maintain the global hierarchies of capitalism.

The recent EU border policies provide a context for us to observe how criminalization and humanitarianism intersect and cooperate. Migrant tragedies involving mass deaths (such as the Lampedusa shipwreck in October 2013) and sensational images (such as the image of three-year-old Aylan Kurdi lying lifeless on a Turkish shore) served as catalysts for the "humanitarian turn" in EU border policies. Humanitarian practices included expressions of solidarity with migrants, mourning rituals, and Angela Merkel's "open-door" policy in 2015. Rather than challenging the post-political paradigm, these short-lived practices underscored the fact that, from the perspective of European governing elites, migrants are worthy of solidarity only when they are dead and thus beyond the possibility of becoming political subjects.

Ultimately a more instrumental form of humanitarianism took over, similar to the one that was previously mobilized to legitimize the imperialist military interventions in Afghanistan and Libya. The EU launched a number of border control operations and intensified cooperation with Libya and Turkey "to prevent more people from dying at sea" (Council of the European Union 2015). These efforts blocked migration routes out of Libya and Turkey, contributing to a violation of migrants' basic human rights and deepening their suffering. Thus, humanitarian concern for migrant lives was quickly translated into new policing and surveillance initiatives, showing how criminalization and humanitarianism go together.

Humanitarianism complements criminalization within the domestic context as well. It assigns migrants who are legally recognized as refugees abject subjectivity (Nyers 2006), which is characterized by docility, obedience, invisibility, and eternal gratefulness to host societies, no matter how exploitative the host societies' material conditions. Similar to criminalization, abjectification aims to suppress the political agency of migrants and serves to maintain social-order hierarchies.

Through governing migrants as abject beings, humanitarianism enacts what Derrida terms *conditional hospitality*, which involves the application of sovereign instruments (from surveillance technologies to repressive immigration laws) to keep tabs on the activities of the other. To the extent that conditional hospitality manages to control the other with these instruments, it succeeds in consolidating the national-self/foreign-other distinction. Therefore, the conditional hospitality of humanitarianism can be understood as a nationalist project. Like the hostility or outright exclusion that characterizes the criminalization perspective, the humanitarian perspective contributes to hierarchies among the working classes and silences important questions about the political root causes of migration and migrants' class status.

In Search of the Political

How can the left move beyond the hegemonic criminalization-humanitarianism nexus and articulate a political alternative? I now turn to the political principles that came out of a major protest, the 300 Migrant Hunger Strikers in Greece, to reflect upon the material conditions of possibility for a leftist politics-to-come in the age of mass migration. By their political protest, migrants rejected the post-political identities of the criminalization-humanitarian nexus (e.g., "criminals," "Muslim others," "abject beings") and constituted themselves as political subjects of the global proletariat. They also identified the political root causes of migration and formed class solidarity with Greek workers.

The hunger strike took place in 2011 within the context of the unfolding Greek economic crisis. The crisis and subsequent austerity measures resulted in the impoverishment of Greek workers and contributed to the rise of anti-immigration sentiments. Three hundred undocumented migrants staged a hunger strike in Greece to express their opposition to increasing racism, which scapegoated them for the economic devastation caused by austerity measures. Another motivating factor for migrants was the austerity measures themselves, which deepened their own exploitation and precarity. The hunger strike lasted for forty-four days and ended when migrants were granted better legal rights, including a path to status. Even though the government later did not keep most of its promises, the particular ways in which migrants articulated their political agency during the strike could still serve as a template for future politics (Topak 2017).

In contrast to the criminalization-humanitarian nexus, throughout the event, migrants emphasized the political causes of migration and clearly connected these causes to processes of global capitalism. They stated:

> We came here to escape poverty, unemployment, wars and

dictatorships. The multinational companies and their political servants left us no choice but to repeatedly risk our lives to journey towards Europe's door. The West that is exploiting our countries while benefitting from much better living conditions is our only chance to live decent lives, to live as human beings. (AMHS 2011a)

Emphasizing the root causes of migration enabled these migrants to politicize the activity of border crossing and refuse a criminal identity. Rather than an illicit act violating immigration laws, in these migrants' formulation, border crossing was an act of political resistance against the violence and hierarchies of capitalism. Their politicization of border crossing also challenged the humanitarian paradigm's representation of migrants as abject victims running away from unfortunate and inevitable disasters. They stressed the human-made nature of capitalism's violent processes and clearly identified the complicity of Western states and capitalist institutions in them. They further challenged the humanitarian paradigm by highlighting their own political agency: "We take our decisions by ourselves during the assemblies we hold, and we do not get influenced by external factors. Nobody is hiding behind our backs or fronts. And we do not receive 'guidance' by anybody" (AMHS 2011b).

Therefore, through their protest, migrants moved beyond the victim/villain dichotomy and constituted themselves as political subjects — as members of the global proletariat who have suffered and continue to suffer the injustices of capitalism. Despite the fact that all migrants were from Muslim-majority countries, they did not identify themselves through their religious/cultural identity. Rather, they opted for class identity and referred to themselves as *migrant workers.*

Following Rancière (1992, 1999), these migrants' appropriation of working-class identity could be understood as a practice of political subjectivization — a process whereby those who are not counted as part of a social order struggle to be recognized as political subjects. In other words, it occurs when those "who have no part" assert claims on the social order and demand equality. Rancière draws on the history of nineteenth-century workers' movements in France to illustrate how political subjectivization can be materialized. He demonstrates how workers, by politicizing the name *proletariat*, revealed and challenged the hierarchical social order, or what Rancière (1999: 38) terms the "regime of wrong." Migrant hunger strikers in Greece similarly contested the inequity of the dominant social order through political subjectivization. Constituting themselves as global proletarians, migrants protested against and even shaped the social order, succeeding in being recognized as political subjects with a politicized identity.

It is important to emphasize that in these migrants' formulation, working-class identity had less to do with being a member of the industrial and typically male working class than with being a subject of neoliberal globalization's violent and exploitative processes. This broad definition of working-class identity left room for the diverse groups who suffer the injustices of neoliberal globalization in different ways — from racialized female migrant domestic workers to white-collar workers who have lost their jobs due to austerity measures.

Political subjectivization is an interactional process. It requires that the groups involved are open to recognizing the political subjectivity of those who claim it. Indeed, the migrants' struggle would not have succeeded if it was not actively supported by various groups in Greek society. Some activist groups (including anti-racist, anarchist, and student activists) formed a solidarity network and supported the strike from its beginning to its end. They helped migrants find the spaces to stage the hunger strike, formed a medical team to monitor the worsening health conditions of the migrants, organized solidarity demonstrations, protected migrants from racist attacks, and helped the migrants to disseminate their political messages to the Greek and international public. Significantly, migrants' broad mobilization of working-class identity shaped the discourses of these solidarity groups, who argued that Greek civil servants, industrial workers, agricultural workers, migrant cleaners, and fishermen are all on the same side in their fight against "the multinationals and the bankers' mafia" (OSIT 2011).

More traditional segments of the Greek working class represented by trade unions and worker associations, while being hesitant at the beginning, gradually expressed their support. Migrants' political subjectivization as global proletarians similarly influenced the responses of these groups, many of which found common ground with the migrant workers (Mantanika and Kouki 2011). The letter of support from the Association of Translators/Editors/Proofreaders was illustrative in this regard:

> We feel the need to respond to the appeal for solidarity issued by the Assembly of Solidarity with the Hunger Strikers, by stating that within this misleading climate of polarised opinion that has been created these last few days we stand firmly on the side of the hunger strikers.... In the face of exploitation, poverty, misery, and persecution, we are all equal, we are all foreigners. (Cited in Mantanika and Kouki 2011: 486)

Notably, these acts of solidarity unsettled the existing host/guest divisions and disturbed the logic of nationalism. We could locate elements of what Derrida (2000) terms "unconditional hospitality" in these solidarity efforts, not because they exemplify an abstract openness toward the other, but because they entailed a deconstructive moment whereby host groups questioned their identity of hostness and opened themselves to the possibilities of "justice-to-come" or "the new international." These solidarity efforts stand in contrast with humanitarian ethics. Humanitarianism, even when it shows concern for the well-being of migrants, secretly reinforces the hierarchies between migrants and citizens, saviors and victims, hosts and guests, subjects and objects. The radical ethics that came out of the protest, while not succeeding in eradicating these distinctions, showed that there is an alternative way of responding to the migrants that respects them as equal agents who are worthy of solidarity. In order to avoid promoting a messianic ethical agenda, however, we must underline that the migrants' political subjectivization (as global proletarians) made this radical ethics possible in the first place. Groups who stood in solidarity with migrants did so not because they felt responsible to open themselves to uninvited, unnamed others but because they realized that those others in fact carry the same political name as them: proletariat.

The hunger strikers showed how things might be otherwise. However, the reach of their voices has been limited: Shortly after the hunger strike, there was a surge in xenophobic violence against migrants, orchestrated by groups affiliated with the neo-Nazi Golden Dawn party. Today, migrants in Greece and other countries in the West are still predominantly governed by the criminalization-humanitarian nexus at different levels. How can the political principles that came out of the 3MHS event be transformed into enduring political structures? Moving forward, this is a key question to consider.

References

Althusser, Louis. 2005. *For Marx*. New York: Verso.
AMHS. 2011a. "Statement of the Assembly of Migrant Hunger Strikers." January 23. <hungerstrike300.espivblogs.net/2011/01/23/statement-of-the-assembly-of-migrant-hunger-strikers/>.
___. 2011b. "Press Release: Decision of the Assembly of Migrants on Hunger Strike." January 28.
Anderson, Bridget. 2008. "Illegal Immigrant: Victim or Villain?" COMPAS *working paper series*, WP-08-64, University of Oxford.
Balibar, Étienne. 1991. "The Nation Form: History and Ideology." In Étienne Balibar and Immanuel Wallerstein, *Race, Nation, Class: Ambiguous Identities*. New York: Verso.
Balibar, Étienne, and Immanuel Wallerstein. 1991. *Race, Nation, Class: Ambiguous Identities*. New York: Verso.
Castles, Stephen, Hein de Haas, and Mark J. Miller. 2014. *The Age of Migration: International Population Movements in the Modern World*. New York: Guilford Press.
Council of the European Union. 2015. "European Union Military Operation in the Southern Central Mediterranean." *Official Journal of the European Union*, 2015/778, L 122/3.
Delgado Wise, Raúl. 2013. "The Migration and Labour Question Today: Imperialism, Unequal Development, and Forced Migration." *Monthly Review*, 64, 9.
Derrida, Jacques. 2000. *Of Hospitality*. Stanford: Stanford University Press.
Mantanika, Regina, and Hara Kouki. 2011. "The Spatiality of a Social Struggle in Greece at the Time of the IMF." *City*, 15, 3.
Mouffe, Chantal. 2005. *On the Political*. London: Routledge.
Nyers, Peter. 2006. *Rethinking Refugees: Beyond States of Emergency*. New York: Routledge.
OSIT. 2011. "Solidarity with the 300 Migrants on Hunger Strike, Open Solidarity Initiative of Thessaloniki." <allilmap.wordpress.com/2011/01/21/solidarity-with-the-300-migrants-on-hunger-strike/>.
Rancière, Jacques. 1992. "Politics, Identification, and Subjectivization." *October* 61: 58–64.
___. 1999. *Disagreement: Politics and Philosophy*. Minneapolis: University of Minnesota Press.
Said, Edward. 1979. *Orientalism*. New York: Vintage.
Samaddar, Ranabir. 2017. *Karl Marx and the Postcolonial Age*. Cham: Palgrave.
Soguk, Nevzat. 2017. "Migrants Unbound: Insurrectional Migrancy in a Globalized World." *Centre for Refugee Studies Seminar Series*, October 12. Toronto: York University.
Ticktin, Miriam. 2006. "Where Ethics and Politics Meet: The Violence of Humanitarianism in France." *American Ethnologist*, 33, 1.
Topak, Özgün E. 2017. "Migrant Protest in Times of Crisis: Politics, Ethics and the Sacred from Below." *Citizenship Studies*, 21, 1.

van Holthoon, Frits, and Marcel van der Linden (eds.). 1988. *Internationalism in the Labor Movement 1830–1940*. Leiden: E.J. Brill.

Yılmaz, Ferruh. 2016. *How the Workers Became Muslims: Immigration, Culture, and Hegemonic Transformation in Europe*. Ann Arbor: University of Michigan Press.

Žižek, Slavoj. 2008. *The Ticklish Subject: The Absent Centre of Political Ontology*. London: Verso.

_____. 2015. "In the Wake of Paris Attacks the Left Must Embrace Its Radical Western Roots." *In These Times*, November 16. <inthesetimes.com/article/continued/18605/breaking-the-taboos-in-the-wake-of-paris-attacks-the-left-must-embrace-its>.

7. Navigating Contemporary Struggles
Class Composition and Social Reproduction

Elise Thorburn and Gary Kinsman

Starting within Class and Social Struggles

In the fall of 2016, Inuit, NunatuKavut, Innu, and settler community members, collectively known as the Labrador Land Protectors, breached the fence at the Muskrat Falls hydro dam and occupied the worksite for six days. The Crown corporation of the Newfoundland and Labrador government, Nalcor, was billions of dollars over budget on the megaproject and refused to clear all vegetation from the flood zone. The Land Protectors insisted that without removing vegetation and top soil, the risk of methylmercury contamination in the Churchill River and the surrounding flora and fauna was inevitable (Brake 2018; Behrens 2018). Methylmercury is a neurotoxin that can damage the brain and nervous system and is especially damaging to fetuses and infants (Calder et al. 2016). The Cree Board of Health has warned that it takes up to twenty years for mercury levels to return to normal in smaller fish, and up to thirty-five years in larger fish that eat other fish (Michelin 2017).

The flooding of the lands around the dam will poison the water and animals that are the traditional food supply of the people of Nunatsiavut. Assisted by some of the workers at the Muskrat Falls site, the overall struggle over Muskrat Falls is therefore one of social reproduction, including the reassertion of people's control over water and land. In essence, it is a fight for the right to continue to exist. Issues of Indigenous rights, environmental justice, class, and social reproduction have all converged in this struggle, and there are connections to be made here with the long-term mercury poisoning and the struggle against it at Grassy Narrows in northwestern Ontario (Free Grassy Narrows n.d.; Behrens 2018) and with ongoing Indigenous-led struggles against the Trans Mountain and other pipelines, in defence of water and land. These are central struggles against the interests of capital and the Canadian state, and they raise crucial questions for the recomposition of left and movement organizing.

Some on the left do not see these as class struggles given their narrow understandings of "class." Rather, they simply slot such actions under "environmental struggles" or perhaps "Indigenous struggles." Yet the organized resistance in Muskrat Falls brought some settlers and workers into active solidarity with Indigenous struggles against colonialism while also raising crucial questions over social reproduction. Similarly, many on the "left" do not see the struggles of Black Lives Matter, Idle No More, and other anti-racist and anti-colonial organizing as crucial to current class struggles. For us, these movements are at the *cutting edge* of class struggle, in that they mediate relations between race, colonialism, gender, and class. We return to the significance of the struggles at Muskrat Falls later.

Our starting point for this inquiry is within class and social struggles, rather than within "the left" as it currently exists. In our view many of the conceptual tools currently mobilized by the left, including a reliance on political economy, prevent us from understanding what is going on in current struggles. But these aforementioned struggles remind us of the importance of the analytical resources coming from the autonomist Marxist and feminist traditions, which address struggles of class composition and social reproduction in a very different way. Autonomist Marxism highlights the need for working-class struggles to be autonomous not only from capital but also from political parties and union leaderships. In doing so, it foregrounds the need for those oppressed *within* the working class to engage in their own autonomous struggles (Cleaver 2000). By using a broader notion of class and class struggle that includes unpaid labour, and focusing on struggles over social reproduction, we also argue for the centrality of Indigenous struggles to "left" organizing within the Canadian state. Such struggles often centre on issues of social reproduction — primarily the defence of land and water.

We suggest that although the insights of autonomist Marxism have not often been extended to the struggles of Indigenous Peoples, they nonetheless reveal the centrality of these struggles against capitalist relations and state formation. This moves far beyond stressing the importance of struggles for national self-determination and against racism. As the Zapatistas have made clear, there are intrinsic connections between Indigenous and anti-capitalist struggles in that Indigenous struggles must by definition be anti-capitalist in character (Zapatista Army of National Liberation 2006). At the same time, Indigenous knowledge and struggles have the capacity to transform anti-capitalist struggles, provided there is a willingness to engage and learn.

In other words, we think of the diversity of contemporary movements, including what is often dismissed as "identity" politics by the mainstream left, as a reinvigorated class struggle — a struggle against capitalism at the reproduction points of its most valued commodity: the capacity to labour. We also reject the mainstream left's critical attitude toward "identity" politics, which fails to recognize the reality of identity-based oppression or hegemonic forms of identity (like Canadianness or whiteness). This leads to a narrow "class first" type of politics that does not adequately address the mutually constructed character of class, race, gender, sexuality, ability, age, and other relations (Bannerji 1995). Instead, *working class* comes to be coded as white, male, and heterosexual, and this must be actively resisted. As Kellogg stresses in this volume, class struggles are often highly racialized, and as Topak furthermore suggests, a broader notion of working-class struggle must centrally include migrants and the dispossessed.

We therefore draw upon insights from autonomist Marxism that make such class relations visible in contemporary movements. In particular, we highlight *class composition* and *social reproduction* — concepts that emerged as theoretical tools out of the Italian workplace and community rebellions in the sixties and seventies. Autonomist Marxism saw such struggles as having the potential to develop autonomy for oppressed sections *within* the working class and to break more generally from capitalist social relations. The concepts of class composition and social reproduction move forward our theorization of current movements as class struggles provided they are not understood as monolithic in character, are used in a concrete social and historical sense, and are integrated with analyses of gender, racialization, colonialism, sexuality, ability, and other mediated lines of social oppression.

Class Composition and Cycles of Struggle

Taking seriously capital as a social relation, early autonomists focused squarely on labour (broadly defined) as the primary, rather than dependent, variable in capitalist development. It is the struggles of the working classes that bring about crises, collapses, and changes in the composition of capital — including its modes of production and reproduction. In analyzing the struggles of workers in the 1960s, Mario Tronti (1964) wrote, "We too have worked with a concept that puts capitalist development first, and workers second. This is a mistake. And now we have to turn the problem on its head, reverse the polarity, and start again from the beginning: and the beginning is the class struggle of the working class."

From this turn comes perhaps the most distinctive theoretical contribution of the autonomist Marxist tendency: *class composition*, which focuses not on capital but on the working class (including unwaged reproductive workers as well as waged "productive" labourers). John Holloway follows this idea by suggesting that "we" (i.e., struggling workers and oppressed people) *are* the crisis of capitalism (Holloway 2005, 2010, 2016, 2019). Class composition seeks to describe the relation between labour and capital in particular historical moments (Notes From Below 2018). Unlike traditional Marxist perspectives, the "working class" here is not thought of as an object or a classification, but rather as always existing in struggle.

Class composition is the *relationship* between how the working class organizes against capital (the *political* composition of the class) and how capital organizes labour power (the *technical* composition of the class). The political composition of a class is determined by how it is organized, including its internal divisions and its modes of social reproduction.

Particular political compositions of the working class become expressed through certain forms of struggle. Capital's response to these struggles attempts to impose technical changes designed to restore discipline and authority. This new *technical* composition forces a "decomposition" of the class, which subsequently gives rise to new organizational possibilities and a new class composition (Negri 1991; Nunes 2007; Cleaver 1998). Working-class struggle is therefore internal to capital (both *within* and *against* capital) yet carries the possibility of moving *beyond* it (Holloway 2005, 2010, 2016; Kinsman 2017).

Capitalists actively struggle to decompose the political and social capacities of working-class composition by exacerbating and reorganizing internal divisions in the working class, ripping apart sources of working-class and oppressed people's power, fragmenting groups and struggles, and extending social surveillance and technological transformation against workers (Huot 2016). These attempts to weaken working-class struggles can also produce new conditions for their re-emergence and recomposition.

This continuing process of class composition, decomposition, and recomposition constitutes a cycle of struggle (Kinsman 2005; Dyer-Witheford 2006). Skilled craftworkers in the early twentieth century often fought for more control over their waged work, leading to an emphasis on workers' control of production. This working-class composition was in turn decomposed by the organization of "scientific management," "deskilling," and mass production. In response to the mass convergence of waged workers and outbreaks of class struggle, capitalists struggled to decompose and fragment these gatherings in part by dismantling the earlier Fordist organization of mass production (Kinsman 2005). These insights need to be extended to the struggles of the non-waged sections of the working class and collective struggles over social reproduction (Mohandesi and Teitelman 2017).

Understanding these cycles and our positions within them is crucial for evaluating our own sources of power. For autonomist Marxism, the notion of the circulation of struggles describes the ways in which different movements impact each other, sometimes circulating the most "advanced" forms of struggle across geographical locations and creating important ruptures with capitalist relations. For instance, in the global justice, Occupy, and occupation of city square movements in parts of Europe, assembly-based organizing spread quite rapidly around the globe. Since its reinvigoration by feminists in the seventies, struggles around social reproduction have also circulated and accelerated globally.

Social Reproduction as a Site of Struggle and Transformation

In relation to class composition, social reproduction has received less theoretical attention. The technical basis of capitalism lies not only in the constant capital of machines and the variable capital of "productive" workers, but also in the variable capital created and sustained through reproductive labour. Further, the political composition of the working class is found not only in movements of resistance but in those self-valorizing activities that reproduce struggle. "Self-valorization" is a term used within autonomist Marxism to describe how workers struggle not only against capitalist relations but also to create alternative ways of life that break with capitalist and oppressive relations — the movement *beyond*. Social reproduction influences both the technical and the political composition of the class. In line with Marxist feminist scholars Silvia Federici (2012) and Mariarosa Dalla Costa (2019), we highlight the unwaged and waged reproductive work at what Federici calls the "point zero" of capitalism.

Social reproduction is the everyday maintenance and reproduction of life. It designates the ways in which the physical, emotional, and mental labour necessary for the production of humanity is socially organized. We can think of the care we give to others, the regenerative activities that we participate in — the work of love, sexuality, friendship, sharing a home, a bed, a meal, child care, elder care, care for the disabled — as socially reproductive labour. Indigenous struggles have stressed the caring work involved in defending the land, water, and non-human creatures. Social reproductive labour has a dual role in the reproduction of labour power for capital but also in social life itself, including in possibilities of resistance. It is this dual character that allows labour power to be the unique commodity that can produce surplus value.

Social reproduction is therefore a key site for emerging resistances to capitalist domination and in augmenting struggles today. In fact, social reproduction has always been key. Contrary to popular belief, the long history of class struggle has not been primarily fought by waged workers in factory settings. Federici (2012) notes that the anti-systemic struggles waged by Indigenous, rural, anti-colonial, and feminist movements have been the planetary majority throughout history, and all have a broadly defined class character. These movements often centred on the possibility or impossibility of social reproduction. While the concept of social reproduction originates in Marx's *Capital Volume II* (1978), it was ignored in much Marxist analysis until recently (Federici 2004, 2006, 2012, 2018a, 2018b). This has meant that the struggles of Indigenous people, subsistence farmers, women and domestic workers, and students are often placed outside the purview of classical Marxism.

Recent scholarship has attempted to expand political economy approaches to explain social reproduction struggles (Bhattacharya 2017). Political economy approaches — unlike Marx's work, which was a critique of political economy and of how economics hides social relations between people behind the power of things and objects — are limited in their capacities to analyze social reproduction struggles. Instead, we argue that autonomist Marxist feminist approaches to social reproduction struggles are much more useful in establishing these reproductive realms as sites of resistance and relating this to class composition (Toupin 2018; Rousseau 2015, 2016).

A Recomposition of Struggle?

So, how do we use class composition and social reproduction in understanding contemporary landscapes of social and class struggles?

On *their* side, we are currently seeing a recomposition of the neoliberal pro-austerity right in state politics along with more racist and even fascist forces. While this is being disrupted by anti-austerity, anti-racist, and anti-fascist organizing, the resistance is often fragmented. On *our* side, after a period of decomposition of class and social struggles within neoliberal capitalism, we are beginning to see new forms of recomposition that do not always look like previous forms of recomposition.

Less "traditional" forms of class recomposition include struggles around race, colonialism, and gender, such as Black Lives Matter, Idle No More, and the Women's March following Donald Trump's inauguration. Many of these likewise address questions of social reproduction. But one example of a mediational (Bannerji 1995) and anti-colonial class struggle that suggests directions for recomposition in the present is the aforementioned resistance to the Muskrat Falls project.

We examine the Muskrat Falls struggle using the tradition of militant research central to autonomist Marxism. This includes workers inquiries, which have been central to how autonomist Marxists investigate and learn about compositions of struggle and social reproduction (Marx 1938; Haider and Mohandesi 2013; Notes from Below 2018). This research generally links working-class people with militant organizers and researchers to collaboratively develop knowledge and struggle-oriented theory. Militant research learns from working-class and oppressed people about how their experiences of oppression are organized and how they resist in their communities. Elise, who was involved in solidarity organizing with the land defenders at Muskrat Falls, also engaged in militant research.

First, we describe the broader social context for this struggle: Central to Canadian state formation is its character as a white settler state based on the colonization of Indigenous lands (Coulthard 2014; Estes 2019). Newfoundland and Labrador (NL), an oil-dependent "economy" that suffered a massive financial crisis with the drop in oil prices in 2015, now has the highest levels of income inequality in Atlantic Canada (Smellie 2018). Living off of the land and accessing "country foods" (wild game, fish, plant life) is integral to Inuit and Innu culture, but also to many of those in the settler communities of Newfoundland and Labrador, where fish is a dietary staple.

In 2016, as mentioned, with the help of workers at the Muskrat Falls site, Indigenous and settler land protectors occupied the worksite, demanding that methylmercury contamination be taken seriously, and at least three people engaged in a hunger strike. In response to the groundswell of protest in Labrador and Newfoundland, and as far away as Ottawa, the provincial government held all-night meetings with Indigenous leaders and agreed to "assess" the issue of contamination going forward. In a province with limited political organizing, the Muskrat Falls protests generated near-universal support. The government had proposed steep rate hikes on domestic energy use in Newfoundland in order to cover the thirteen billion-dollar project, but its plans were met with an explosion of demonstrations and opposition.

Settlers in Newfoundland, themselves accustomed to subsistence strategies partially based around fishing and hunting, commiserated with the Labradorians' fear of having their country foods contaminated by methylmercury. Workers at the Muskrat Falls site from the island quit in protest of the ballooning costs that would bankrupt an already fragile province and force even more people to bleed out from its shores and onto the rest of the continent. A security guard at Nalcor offices in St. John's left his position in disgust after overhearing the way executives talked about the Indigenous protestors. Workers inside the site provided blankets and food and even information to the land protectors who engaged in the workplace occupation. There were levels of Indigenous-settler and worker-Indigenous solidarity the likes of which have rarely been witnessed elsewhere.

At the time, Elise, in collaboration with the Labrador Land Protectors, was involved in forming Anti-Poverty NL, in St. John's, as a way of developing the struggle. In an effort to organize for poor and working-class communities, they tied issues of "fuel poverty" to the struggle against the Muskrat Falls megaproject and to demands for Indigenous sovereignty. They maintained that no one should be forced to choose between heating and eating — a way to connect the demands that provincial megaprojects not poison traditional Indigenous food sources with the insistence that fees for essential energy services in a chilly region must not impact the working classes' capacity to feed themselves. In this way, they tried to build a collaborative movement that learns from Indigenous cosmologies of building relationships beyond the human, works to develop solidarities across lines of colonization, and implicates settlers in processes of decolonization. This form of class composition importantly links Indigenous and non-Indigenous class struggles; it also demonstrates the centrality of struggles over social reproduction and against colonialism, as well as possible lines of support between settler and Indigenous struggles.

Social reproduction and anti-colonial struggles are now at the centre of class recomposition, reconfiguring class relations in radical ways that centre the socially reproductive. In general, though, these and other recompositions are still fragmented and limited, though, and need to be extended. The struggle over Muskrat Falls continues, even though the flooding of the reservoir started in August 2019. This and other struggles have not yet translated into broader struggles against the forces of neoliberal capitalism that finance and advance these environmentally and culturally destructive operations.

Recomposing Class Struggles with a Focus on Social Reproduction

In this chapter we hope we have shown the importance of class composition and social reproduction analysis for any recomposition of a left that is actively part of class and social struggles. Many of the struggles portrayed as "identity politics" by the mainstream left are now in the forefront of class and social struggles, and many of these are based on struggles over social reproduction and for the autonomy of oppressed sections of a broader working class. This is partly the result of how neoliberal austerity makes social reproduction more central to current racialized class struggles. In our view, any revitalization of left organizing needs to learn from the insights of autonomist Marxist and feminist organizing. This also leads to viewing Indigenous struggles as central to current class and social struggles. We hope others will take up these lines of investigation in theory and practice, adopting militant activist research to aid in the recomposition of struggles and movements for *radical* social transformation. This project of militant inquiry and resistance must be extended into all our terrains of struggle.

References

Bannerji, Himani. 1995. *Thinking Through: Essays on Feminism, Marxism and Anti-Racism*. Toronto: Women's Press.

Behrens, Matthew. 2018. "Mercury's Toxic Legacy from Grassy Narrows to Muskrat Falls." Homes Not Bombs, December 20. <homesnotbombs.blogspot.com/2018/12/mercurys-toxic-legacy-from-grassy.html>.

Bhattacharya, Tithi (ed.). 2017. *Social Reproduction Theory: Remapping Class, Recentering Oppression*. London: Pluto.

Brake, Justin. 2018. "'It's Cultural Genocide': Labrador Land Protectors in Court on Anniversary of Muskrat Falls Occupation." *APTN News*, October 23. <aptnnews.ca/2018/10/23/its-cultural-genocide-labrador-land-protectors-in-court-on-anniversary-of-muskrat-falls-occupation/>.

Calder, Ryan, Amina Schartup, Milling Li, Amelia Valberg, Prentiss Balcom, and Elsie Sunderland. 2016. "Future Impacts of Hydroelectric Power Development on Methylmercury Exposures of Canadian Indigenous Communities." *Environmental Science and Technology*, 50, 23.

Cleaver, Harry. 1998. "Zapatistas and the Electronic Fabric of Struggle." In John Holloway and Eloína Peláez (eds.), *Zapatista! Reinventing Revolution in Mexico*. London: Pluto Press.

___. 2000. *Reading Capital Politically*. Chico: AK Press.

Coulthard, Glen Sean. 2014. *Red Skin, White Masks: Rejecting the Colonial Politics of Recognition*. Minneapolis: University of Minnesota Press.

Dalla Costa, Mariarosa. 2019. *Women and the Subversion of the Community: A Mariarosa Dalla Costa Reader*. Oakland: PM Press.

___. 2006. "The Circulation of the Common." Paper presented at Immaterial Labour Conference, April 28–30. Cambridge University. <dlc.dlib.indiana.edu/dlc/bitstream/handle/10535/4519/circulation percent20of percent20the percent20common.pdf?sequence=1&isAllowed=y>.

Estes, Nick. 2019. *Our History Is the Future: Standing Rock versus the Dakota Access Pipeline, and the Long Tradition of Indigenous Resistance*. New York: Verso.

Federici, Silvia. 2004. *Caliban and the Witch: Women, the Body, and Primitive Accumulation*. New York: Autonomedia.
___. 2006. "The Restructuring of Social Reproduction in the United States in the 1970s." *The Commoner*, 11 (Spring).
___. 2012. *Revolution at Point Zero: Housework, Reproduction and Feminist Struggle*. Oakland: PM Press.
___. 2018a. *Re-Enchanting the World: Feminism and the Politics of the Commons*. Oakland: PM Press.
___. 2018b. *Witches, Witch-Hunting, and Women*. Oakland: PM Press.
Free Grassy Narrows. n.d. <freegrassy.net/learn-more/grassy-narrows/history/>.
Haider, Assad, and Salar Mohandesi. 2013. "Workers' Inquiry: A Genealogy." *Viewpoint Magazine*, September 27. <viewpointmag.com/2013/09/27/workers-inquiry-a-genealogy/>.
Holloway, John. 2005. *How to Change the World Without Taking Power: The Politics of Revolution Today*. London: Pluto Press.
___. 2010. *Crack Capitalism*. London: Pluto Press.
___. 2016. *In, Against and Beyond Capitalism: The San Francisco Lectures*. Oakland: PM Press.
___. 2019. *We Are the Crisis of Capitalism: A John Holloway Reader*. Oakland: PM Press.
Huot, John. 2016. "Autonomist Marxism and Workplace Organizing in Canada in the 1970s." *Upping the Anti*, 18.
Kinsman, Gary. 2005. "The Politics of Revolution Today: Learning from Autonomous Marxism." *Upping the Anti*, 1.
___. 2017. "Within, Against and Beyond: Urgency and Patience in Queer and Anti-Capitalist Struggles." In Alex Khasnabish and Max Haiven (eds.), *What Moves Us: The Lives and Times of the Radical Imagination*. Halifax: Fernwood Publishing.
Marx, Karl. 1938. "A Workers Inquiry." *New International*, 4, 12.
___. 1978. *Capital: A Critique of Political Economy, Volume II*. London: Penguin Books.
Michelin, Ossie. 2017. "The Mighty Fight for Muskrat Falls." *Briarpatch Magazine*, May 1. <briarpatchmagazine.com/articles/view/the-mighty-fight-for-muskrat-falls>.
Mohandesi, Salar, and Emma Teitelman. 2017. "Without Reserves." In Tithi Bhattacharya (ed.), *Social Reproduction Theory: Remapping Class, Recentering Oppression*. London: Pluto.
Negri, Antonio. 1991. *Marx Beyond Marx*. Brooklyn: Autonomedia.
Notes from Below (eds.). 2018. "The Workers' Inquiry and Social Composition." January 29. <notesfrombelow.org/article/workers-inquiry-and-social-composition>.
Nunes, Rodrigo. 2007. "Forward How? Forward Where? I: (Post)Operaismo Beyond the Immaterial Labour Thesis." *Ephemera: Theory and Politics in Organization*, 7, 1.
Rousseau, Christina. 2015. "Wages Due Lesbians: Queer Marxist Feminist Organizing in 1970s Canada." *Gender, Work and Organization*, 22, 4.
___. 2016. "The Dividing Power of the Wage: Housework and Social Subversion." *Atlantis: Critical Studies in Gender, Culture, and Social Justice*, 37, 2.
Smellie, Sarah. 2018. "Mind the Gap: St. John's Wage Inequality Worst in Atlantic Canada." CBC News, January 28. <cbc.ca/news/canada/newfoundland-labrador/

st-johns-highest-wage-inequality-atlantic-canada-1.4507110>.
Toupin, Louise. 2018. *Wages for Housework, The History of an International Feminist Movement, 1972–77*. Vancouver: UBC Press.
Tronti, Mario. 1964. "Lenin in England." <marxists.org/reference/subject/philosophy/works/it/tronti.htm>.
Zapatista Army of National Liberation. 2006. "Sixth Declaration of the Lacandon Jungle." In *The Other Campaign/La otra compana*. San Francisco: City Lights.

8. Class-Based Organizing in an Identity-Based World

Assya Moustaqim-Barrette

The left is disorganized and weakened at a time when left alternatives are needed most. Unionization in Canada has declined steadily since the 1980s and work has become more and more precarious. Since the austerity legacy of the Harper administration will not be corrected by Trudeau's government, Canada may next elect a leader even further to the right. Indeed, in Ontario, Canada's most populous province, the virulent right-wing populist Doug Ford has been elected premier.

In response to poor economic prospects and the interlinked crises of environmental degradation, resource scarcity, and increasing governmental austerity, more and more people are becoming politicized. While the far right has always existed in Canada, xenophobic and ethnonationalist forces have recently seized this opportunity to make huge popular gains, as demonstrated by the powerful "alt-right" movement, the rise of populist right-wing figures such as Jordan Peterson, a University of Toronto psychology professor and YouTube celebrity, and the re-emergence of white supremacist visibility as embodied by Richard Spencer, an American neo-Nazi.

The left has not been completely sidelined, though, with figures such as Bernie Sanders inspiring a level of political activism that has not been seen in the lifetimes of many of his previously uninvolved young supporters. Even still, Sanders' actual policies are best characterized as social democratic. In the absence of other prominent leftist leaders, many people are turning to small-scale political action and advocacy groups to address the crises jeopardizing their futures. There is a growing segment of people, especially of the younger generation, who are becoming politicized in some form. The swift ascent of Alexandria Ocasio-Cortez, the recently elected congresswoman backed by the Democratic Socialists of America, showed us that there are thousands who are open to being energized by leftist politics.

The question is: how might the left best recruit this segment, especially facing competition from the more hegemonic ideas of left liberalism? I explore this issue here through detailing my own progression from liberal to radical politics, beginning from the position that re-examining the radical left's recruitment strategy is more important than ever. Only a progressive, revolutionary movement can save humanity from the existential crises it faces.

The Process of Politicization

Looking back at the path that eventually led me to socialism may provide a few lessons for those of us trying to inspire people to build left capacities to take power and work toward a more equitable and just reorganization of society. My journey began with an interest in the environmental crisis, which was started after the passing of my father. Upon his death, my family and I were responsible for clearing away the apartment where he had lived alone for around two years. The sheer volume of clothing, furniture, books, gadgets, and other items that I had to dispose of (either by throwing away or donating) was deeply disturbing to me. It was a very alienating experience to have to discard something that a loved one had put so much time and money into acquiring. It got me thinking about consumerism and its effects on individuals in our society.

Although I was not equipped with the theoretical tools to contextualize these impressions, it had me questioning the spiritual and environmental sustainability of the average consumerist lifestyle today. As a result, I became a "zero-waste" activist. I started a green-living blog, hosted used-clothing swaps, and organized workshops on worm composting. I also undertook a personal challenge where I did not buy anything new for two hundred days, instead fulfilling my needs through purchasing used items, borrowing, or going without.

As I went through this process, I started to meet others who were engaged politically. This got me interested in joining a "formal" political organization, which is something I had avoided since graduating from university. It felt natural for me, as a religious Muslim woman, to find likeminded others in, and to support the causes of, the Muslim community. I joined a small group of grassroots Muslim activists associated with the National Council of Canadian Muslims and worked primarily on issues of Islamophobia and promoting Muslim visibility in politics and the media.

I accepted all the liberal bourgeois prescriptions for what had to be done to move humanity to a sustainable place; these revolved around lifestyle-based changes and activism. But the more I wrote on green living, the more I learned about the inadequacy of these lifestyle solutions. I would write articles on the benefits of veganism but would encounter works like *Should We Eat Meat?* (Smil 2013), which showed me that asceticism was a simplistic response to a much more complex and nuanced issue. I would write on purchasing used clothing only to discover how secondary used-clothing markets ravaged African community textile industries (Cline 2012). Finally, realizing that as a whole the economy was consuming more resources than the Earth could provide long term, I got around to reading about degrowth economics, which advocates for the reduction of production and consumption in the Global North and liberation from a one-sided paradigm of growth-based development (see also Ravensbergen, this volume).

I soon wrote a piece for *Quartz* on the necessity of degrowing the economy to save the planet. For this piece, I interviewed Dr. Nicolas Kosoy, a professor from McGill university studying ecological economics and advocating the conscious slowing and shrinking of the capitalist economy. I asked him a series of questions on the feasibility of his project and at one point, pressed him on whether it was truly realistic to degrow the economy since that would require some industries to take voluntary profit reductions. He responded, "If capital cannot serve the needs of humanity, then perhaps it shouldn't exist." This proposition caught me by surprise — like many others of my generation, I'd never considered a system beyond or outside of capitalism to be possible or desirable. This launched me into the process of studying Marxism, a journey I am still on today.

The identity-based politics I had been involved in, which focused more on forming exclusive political alliances than on building broad-based party politics, gradually lost their appeal. On one hand, this activism, which had once seemed universal, now appeared petty and tribalistic.

Identity politics can be very discourse-centred — how to say what and to whom were topics of conversation that would consume whole meetings and produce endless streams of WhatsApp messages. I started finding these conversations tedious, the displays of offense often no more than performance. Feeling that my time and focus could be better used, I started working more with left organizations. I can't claim that my time has necessarily resulted in more political gains, but it has at least allowed me to contribute my capacities toward an initiative that I feel will contribute to an eco-socialist future.

How Left Organizations Can Recruit Politicized Liberals

So, what lessons might I suggest from my experience? There are a few key elements that I think are important for those of us on the left seeking to grow our ranks.

First, it's important to target people who are already active in some way politically. To learn and understand left politics takes energy and time, and those who have already taken the step to affecting the world around them will be readier and more willing to devote this time. At first, this activism does not have to be very evolved — any small act, like attending a meeting or even writing posts on social media is a start. Since many people are active within identity politics, socialist organizations should try to create linkages between themselves and identity-based groups that can effectively redirect the diversity informing the political attitudes and beliefs of identity-based organizing toward broader critiques of class inequality and capitalism.

For instance, the Socialist Project in Toronto is working on a campaign to improve transit along a predominantly low-income bus route in the city. Encouraging identity-based organizations and activists to embrace socialist solutions could be as simple as inviting these groups to support the campaign, attend a canvassing, or distribute a petition. On the discursive level, seeing a socialist organization support and organize around a cause whose impacts cut through identity groups can be a powerful way of showing activists the limitations of identity-based organizing and the possibilities in expanding beyond them.

Second, we should not fear debating or challenging identity politics; many people get drawn into this type of political activism early on in their politicization process because it is simply the most widely available form of activism. Yet, identity politics and some aspects of left liberalism are very limiting and can be easily debated. A radical left should boldly challenge the liberal left, as the alt-right has done with much success. After all, left liberals, with their reification of identity, echo the soft side of the alt-right, further weakening their leftist position. While working with Muslim activists, I learned that many of my fellow co-activists were also dismayed and tired of the endless conversations around political correctness and were hoping for something more substantive.

Yet, the radical left critique of the liberal left is lacking or silent, perhaps for fear that we shall make enemies of would-be allies. I disagree with this position. The critique must be respectful, but people are yearning for a reasonable and wide-ranging response to the deepening crises of our time. As identity politics cannot offer such a position, the left must fill in these gaps by openly questioning liberal politics and offering rational critiques. Of course, action cannot be reduced to critique — it should also create spaces where people can "live" socialism through creatively addressing people's everyday needs. For example, by conducting a "needs survey" in a neighbourhood and creating a plan to address these needs, one may find that a particular locale requires child care. The role of left activists in this regard could be to organize the community to lobby government institutions to initiate this service, or even to work with the community to build it for themselves. This demonstrates the power of collectivity among the working class and can serve to show the limitations of reformism. It can also be coupled with recruiting people to make educational media for a leftist Facebook page — a tactic that has been applied by the alt-right, enabling them to grow their numbers and recruit whole new subsets of people.

At the same time, identity issues cannot be disregarded. We must create inclusive spaces for people to come, learn, and talk. I find many left "public" spaces to be overly intellectual and remind me of the alienation I felt when I was listening to people being chided for not using certain words during my time in more identity-based spaces. Across both approaches, there is a lack of empathy and a style of communication that is inaccessible to those who lack formal education. Our public talks and meetings shouldn't just be accessible to someone with an advanced degree in the humanities or social sciences. Nor should they require deep and intimate knowledges of complex classical political economy texts. They must create spaces where people feel as if they can ask questions, raise concerns, and voice their feelings and lived experiences.

Further, left activists tend to be male, white, and highly educated. The lack of diversity in left activism is a factor that deters many. What the radical left requires are efforts to diversify our members to reflect the material diversity of the working class. By recruiting on the basis of causes that appeal to working people everywhere, this will theoretically spark interest across a wide and diverse range of people. However, creating socialist spaces that properly welcome and include them in meaningful ways is a larger challenge. Ignoring the reality of identity-based oppression is not productive. I think the way to go about this is by making the linkages between identity-based oppression and class-based issues clear. This strikes a balance between ensuring that class-based issues remain a key vector for augmenting and organizing the left while also addressing the very real difficulties brought about by racism, sexism, transphobia, and other forms of institutionalized and embodied discrimination.

I would respectfully disagree, however, with the viewpoints of Kellogg, Thorburn, and Kinsman in this book. While I agree with their stances of seeing class, race, and gender in a more holistic sense, I do see a hierarchy of importance when it comes to socialist action. Racism and sexism are amplified after-effects of a politics that does not prioritize universal programs as a goal. In other words, these varieties of discrimination are secondary phenomena and not the primary cause of the oppression that women, people of colour, and other marginalized groups suffer. The fact that leftists' organizing spaces are unfriendly or unwelcoming to a wider diversity of people is an aesthetic and strategic failure that restricts the ability of the left to have a more extensive impact by reducing its numbers and penetration into the working class.

Bernie Sanders is a leftist politician who, in my mind, has touched on a possible means of overcoming the identity/class-based organizing divide in an effective way. Sanders, who is coming from a context where questions of racial discrimination are very significant, has been able to create a dedicated mass of racially diverse supporters. I believe that he has accomplished this by using effective populist rhetoric, redrawing the lines between racialized groups, and reorienting this antagonism toward the "millionaires and the billionaires." Just as the US alt-right has successfully redirected frustrations arising from the conditions brought on by neoliberalism toward a class of political elites, Sanders has effectively redirected these frustrations toward an identifiable segment of the elite capitalist class.

Ocasio-Cortez has also been effective by embedding struggles around identity-based issues into a deepened and broadened liberal discourse of human rights ("trans rights are human rights" or "disability rights are human rights"). This demonstrates how the radical left can approach issues of rights entirely within the purview of broader socialist organizing — these types of discursive moves bring siloed identity issues into a framework (of "human rights") that is easily understandable by working people. Just as we all need and are entitled to certain material affordances for survival, human rights are seen as a necessary common good.

What I think is most important among all these politicians — and something that socialist organizations should note — is their messaging consistency and populist character. Instead of pummelling the working class with difficult-to-grasp concepts such as class and the identity divide, politicians such as Jeremy Corbyn, Ocasio-Cortez, and Sanders simplify by framing class-based demands in an accessible "us versus them" dichotomy. Time and time again, these politicians communicate issues from health care to housing as the very rich taking an unfair share and depriving regular people of these essential goods.

Third, the left must invest in making accessible and contemporary learning materials available. When I started learning about Marxism, I was a fairly educated person, holding a bachelor's degree in electrical and biomedical engineering. However, I would not have been able to get to any level of understanding and agreement with left politics was it not for the YouTube videos I watched that broke down Marx's concept of the commodity, the graphic novels that explained capitalism's incompatibility with the environment, and the communist memes that, though simplistic, showed me the irrationality of bourgeois justifications of capitalism through humour.

While I agree that this is not always an ideal form to disseminate knowledge and do outreach, this is the reality of the information terrain as it exists. To gain momentum, the left must communicate in plain language that working-class people can understand and relate to.

This can come through blog posts, YouTube videos, podcasts, memes, and much more. Many leftist politicians have taken up the mantle and created engaging content on a wide variety of digital communication platforms.

Ocasio-Cortez routinely tweets messages and opinions alongside updating her Instagram stories with everyday events from the life of a democratic socialist in Congress. Jeremy Corbyn has a YouTube channel that features short updates and talking points. However, no leftist politician (or any leftist at all) has yet to rival the online presence of the right, which makes it even more important that the left invest in producing and distributing this type of media. Indeed, momentum may be growing as several contemporary progressive and left-leaning interest groups and NGOs (such as The Leap and 350.org) now have dedicated digital communications staff and even departments.

Marx (1957: 42) said, "Criticism has plucked the imaginary flowers from the chain not so that man will wear the chain without any fantasy or consolation but so that he will shake off the chain and cull the living flower." The world urgently needs to deliver this criticism and free people of the illusions keeping them ignorant and subservient. The radical left cannot afford to fear offense, because that is not its goal, as Marx explains — the goal is to expose the lived realities of capitalism. Frustration and anxiety are coming to an apex, and the task of the left today is to leverage this strategically to empower the working class to build something better.

No one knows how socialism will come about. Previous revolutions happened in many stages, when conditions for these revolutions were in place. However, materialist analysis offers us a roadmap to at least envision — if not create — a world with a more healthy and empowered working class, the result of universal access to essential services, including health care, child care, and education. These considerations also point to a need to give people more access to time through the progressive socialization of labour and the shortening of the work week. By creating these improved conditions and continuing to democratize aspects of society, the working class can lead the way to a better future.

References

Cline, E.L. 2012. *Overdressed: The Shockingly High Cost of Cheap Fashion*. New York: Penguin.

Marx, K. 1957. "Contribution to the Critique of Hegel's Philosophy of Right." In Karl Marx and Friedrich Engels, *Marx and Engels on Religion*. Moscow: Foreign Languages Publishing House.

Smil, V. 2013. *Should We Eat Meat? Evolution and Consequences of Modern Carnivory*. Hoboken: John Wiley & Sons.

Section 3

Building Parties or Movements?

9. Experiences on the Socialist Left
Winning, Losing, and Continuing

Herman Rosenfeld

My experiences with various iterations of the socialist left enterprise raise a rather vast and complex field of issues and challenges. Rather than attempt to summarize a yet-to-be-written book in ten pages, I'd like to describe some of my personal experiences with building socialist left experiments (for the most part, in my post-Maoist life) during the period from the late 1990s to the present. What I want to convey here is that we need to combine a number of things: participation in bourgeois democratic electoral institutions, through a socialist party, to both popularize socialist ideas as well as bring socialists to power through democratic means; work to transform and engage with the state; develop deep roots across the working class in all of its diversity and segmentation; and foster ongoing popular mobilizations, both as a form of democratic institution building and as a way to challenge the power of capital and its use of various forms of state power against us.[1]

My Maoist years — from roughly 1974 to 1984 — involved working to build a Marxist movement in Montreal and later Toronto. The political orientation was mixed. While it was horribly sectarian, class reductionist, rooted in the ideology of the Stalinist deformation of the Russian revolutionary experience, and furthermore tailed behind the comings and goings of the Chinese "anti-revisionist" orientation, it also developed roots in a number of centres of working-class life and combined fighting capital with initiating concrete tactical struggles and coordinating socialist education. In 1976, while I was a member of one of the Maoist groups, the

Canadian Communist League/Workers' Communist Party (CP), I moved to Toronto and got a job working in a General Motors plant. However, within the span of a few months in the early 1980s, the groups, parties, and organizations associated with that movement, including the Workers' Communist Party, all literally disappeared.

After the end of the CP and some all-too-short and abortive attempts to resurrect its essential political core, I dropped out of socialist political experimentation for a while. When David McNally and others initiated the broad and non-sectarian Rebuilding the Left project, though, I joined. That was around 1999.

Rebuilding the Left (RTL) was a project that sought to bring in anyone who considered themselves on the left of social democracy in the political spectrum and "anti-capitalist." There was an initial public meeting at a University of Toronto auditorium with almost seven hundred attendees. Occurring in the midst of the anti-globalization protests, the session felt like the beginning of something exciting. But the feelings were deceiving: beneath the promises of a new left project were very few common perspectives or understandings.

In the attempt to create an organization of sorts over the ensuing months, it became clear that we had huge differences. And, since this was literally the first time that veterans of the socialist left from earlier decades had spoken with each other and younger progressives engaged with these activists, the situation was not surprising.

Many of the participants were people who saw themselves to the left of the Liberals and were essentially social democrats; many considered themselves to be "anti-capitalist" without any real clarity about what that meant. (A number of colleagues from the RTL who styled themselves as anarchists and socialists of different stripes had no idea about really challenging capitalism in any serious way.) Many considered the definition of working class to be limited to the poor on the one hand, or to organized labour on the other — and that narrowness reflected deeper political implications that would become apparent over time. Some would argue that the working class was irrelevant or bought-off, and it therefore could be discounted as an agent of social transformation. There were a number of activists who retained the allegiances and narrow baggage of earlier, more sectarian political projects (such as various Trotskyist incarnations) and others who did not (including former Trotskyists, Maoists, CPers, and anarchist groups).² But there was little common political language and even less common experience.

The RTL did create a non-sectarian environment where those who stuck around with the project did talk, work together, and interact on a respectful basis. But it did not prove a space for debates or efforts to reach political clarity on anything. Over time, people drifted away or moved toward other political projects. Some supported the activities of the Ontario Coalition Against Poverty (OCAP) as their main project; others were excited by the so-called "New Politics Initiative" within the New Democratic Party (NDP); and some of us found ourselves somewhat disenchanted with the RTL. But the core of people who kept it going didn't just dissipate. Interestingly enough, it became a space for people of like political orientations to "find themselves" and get engaged in another generation of political projects. In this way, I began working with a group of Marxists who were geared toward common aspirations to build a political movement based on the working class (in all of its segmentation) and looking to contribute to developing socialists in workplaces and communities.

Socialist Project, First Incarnation

Out of the ashes of the RTL project, a number of us found a common level of experience and built around it, developing a set of principles that remain today. We started a movement that would be organized around the need for a socialist — not only "anti-capitalist" — orientation and geared toward building socialists across the various components of the working class, as well as being feminist, anti-racist, and anti-homophobic. We wrote a statement and recruited individual socialists from various activist communities, specifically from the working class. From our common experience in and around the RTL, we argued that a socialist movement grounded within the Marxist tradition really was the only way of providing a solid analysis of current capitalist society and, critically, we looked toward the working class as a necessary instrument for an alternative, socialist society. Too often, "anti-capitalist" reduced itself to a rejection of the effects of capitalism and neoliberalism without any notion of how to move beyond our dependence on private capital accumulation as the driving force of society. (Interestingly, syndicalists — many of whom were associated with the IWW — often became our closest allies, as they, too, were working to build an alternative based in the working class.) Socialism, at the very least, would mean collective ownership and democratic control and planning of the key elements of economic life, along with democratization of the state and political institutions. As well, the need to move away from fossil fuel dependence and address the emergency of climate change would require dramatic reorganization of social production and reproduction (Gindin 2018).

We decided that we certainly weren't ready to create a political party, but instead an organization that saw itself as a node for the development of socialists and a magnet to provide education and mobilization for working-class activists, hoping to recruit them to socialism. In the spirit of Sam Gindin's famous article from *This Magazine* (1998), we looked to build an organization that was "more than a movement, but less than a party." We decided to call ourselves the Socialist Project (SP).

It included quite a few workers from auto plants and radicals who politically agreed with our statement. The gender breakdown of the workers meant that there were quite a few women members. We created a number of committees, such as recruitment/membership, education, and labour.

The Socialist Project also spawned similar initiatives across Ontario, as well as in Winnipeg. But again, at a certain stage, the SP began to stagnate and lose members. This reflected a number of errors we all made:

- We were unable to give leadership to the worker-activists in the auto plants and the local communities. We lacked organizers able to work with the activists in Windsor and Ingersoll so that socialist and class-struggle approaches could be applied in ongoing struggles. As a result, the activists were left unarmed to challenge the growing corporatist approaches that came to dominate local unions and the CAW at the time. A base in these workplaces and communities could not be built without full-time organizers fostering a challenge to the powers-that-be in the local unions and workplaces.
- Our work in the labour committee was the centre of a lot of this weakness, even though we ended up recruiting some excellent young socialist union activists in the Toronto area. As well, we did not develop work with the more precarious

segments of the working class in Toronto and the activists in our group felt isolated from those who were working in those areas. It also meant that we did not really build a class-wide base but concentrated on the unionized sectors.
- We were impatient about getting bigger in a short time frame. This led to the rather ill-fated creation of the Greater Toronto Workers' Assembly (GTWA). With its creation, which emanated from the labour committee of the SP, the Socialist Project essentially ceased to exist, dissolving itself into the GTWA.

Greater Toronto Workers' Assembly

The GTWA tried to combine incompatible projects: uniting the anti-capitalist left and building a larger anti-neoliberal movement. In the end, it couldn't do either. The various anti-capitalist groups once again had major differences, but we never really debated those differences in a systematic (or even a casual) way. While the former SP members liquidated our independent organizational work, none of the other left groups followed suit with their projects. We thought that we were working together to find a new form of unity, but while the others worked together and with us in the Assembly, they continued to meet, develop their collective approaches, and recruit. We (different socialist groups) never debated whether unity was a goal, or what our collective roles or approaches were. It seemed like the various groups went into the assembly process with their particular ideological and political approaches and never adjusted them. It wasn't quite the same as the "entryism" practised by various Trotskyist groups inside the NDP (such as Socialist Action Forward and Fightback) — they weren't necessarily only there to recruit members to their organizations or to take over the RTL. It was more that the lack of any real fundamental discussion about different political goals simply meant that groups saw the GTWA as a space to argue for their various projects — or, just as crucially, to maintain their fundamental stances, policies, and approaches without adjusting them in their interactions with others.

One of the ongoing bones of contention was the level and significance of sexist practices in the Assembly — an issue we never resolved. Another central issue had to do with the role of leftists in mass protests, particularly around our collective experiences in the G-8 demonstrations. While some argued that we should support the adventurist activities of a small number of street protesters, others argued that radical tactics do not necessarily translate into radical outcomes. Many of us saw our role as educating working people about issues of neoliberalism and imperialism rather than somehow demonstrating a greater "radicalism" through forms of violence against stores and small businesses. While we all agreed on the need to oppose the massive police repression and defend protesters from criminalization, there were large gaps between Assembly members on how to assess the G-8 experience. Although there were some interesting and quite creative forums and debates, the political differences around the protests were never properly summarized, much less resolved. In many ways, it reflected differences between socialists and certain forms of anarchism that were part of the larger project.

When considering how to actually enliven collective resistance to the austerity attacks on working people, here, too, we had difficulties. Some members were only interested in working with poor and precarious people, and they saw unionized workers as somehow privileged. Others, tied to better-off groups of unionized workers, refused to respect the more daring and challenging tactics and strategies organized by the former and saw them as a threat. When then-Toronto mayor Rob Ford's attacks began to affect people's lives, a whole section of the Assembly left the organization to start their own movement against the cuts. We were left with an organization that couldn't fulfil either of its goals, and it ended up falling apart.

The failure of the Assembly raised a number of questions. What movements should we be building and how should we develop common approaches in doing so? Was it impossible to build a common movement between socialists and certain anarchist movements and traditions? The differences between various political currents clearly remained, although transposed to a new era. These differences made working together highly problematic on a variety of issues, such as how to integrate anti-oppression and class struggle; the lack of seriousness and refusal to work toward building a common socialist organizational space; and whether or not working to develop a socialist current within the working class was necessary. Throughout, there also remained the key problem of various segments within the working class having different approaches, subcultures, and material differences (as well as different movements attached to each of them), which needed to be bridged but weren't in the GTWA era.

Second Incarnation of the Socialist Project

Many of the SP members came together after the Assembly's demise to rebuild the space we had originally created and update its analysis and organization in the light of our experiences with the Assembly. Clearly, we were now working in a political environment where we were small — part of a universe of small left/socialist currents. After a couple of years of floundering, we have finally begun to reorganize ourselves and have attracted a modest number of younger people to the Socialist Project.

The past issues and challenges we faced remain with us, leaving a long agenda of necessary undertakings:

- Carving out political positions on critical issues: NAFTA; the role of the state and how to transform it; how to deal with the rise of the populist right; demands for democratic sovereignty; environmental transformation; challenging the power of capital; and how to analyze the current international conjuncture.
- Building the movement outside of the New Democratic Party (NDP) and differentiating ourselves from social democrats, all while sometimes fighting for similar reforms, often in alliance with them.
- Building political parties, whether a larger anti-neoliberal grouping left of the NDP where socialists can work (à la Québec Solidaire)[3] or an independent socialist party.
- Bringing socialist ideas and orientations to spaces of working-class life and struggle. (Note that this presupposes a vision of "bringing socialism into the working class from the outside.") In doing this, we must address our lack of materials and educational spaces.
- Developing an alternative agenda. How can we present a socialist critique of centrist and right-wing neoliberal capitalism without an alternative agenda? How can we present a political frame of reference that can translate these ideas into a language that working-class people from across diverse segments can relate to?
- Figuring out how to approach the issue of electoral participation.

- Engaging in both mass movement building and electoral politics — but how? Too many excellent activists influenced by certain forms of anarchism either drop out or inexorably drift toward social democratic parties like the NDP, because the latter provides the only electoral vehicle that currently has a chance of entering the government.
- Moving beyond socialist political strategies that hope to replace the state with radical alternative institutions through insurrection and eschew efforts to engage in electoral politics or to democratize existing state institutions. Obviously, alternative institutions and collective movements are necessary, and these need to both supplement and play a key role in challenging capitalist state structures. But the latter can't be smashed and replaced holus-bolus.
- Developing a socialist method for organizing with ongoing working-class and broader movements — for instance, around public transit or housing — that require a class-struggle orientation.
- Addressing the diverse discourses and political opinions of the many segments of the working class and building on elements of class commonality.
- Integrating eco-socialist approaches in everything we do and bridging the gap with the environmental movement.
- Creating a solidaristic and supportive relationship, as socialists, with Indigenous struggles for democratic rights and self-determination.
- Supporting anti-oppression struggles while also supporting a socialist perspective within them. Challenging racism, sexism, and heterosexism within the working class.

How I See Socialist Movement Building Today

First, there is the issue of navigating differences. We have to be able to theorize and respectfully discuss and debate the aforementioned issues. Second, we must establish the need for political parties and the role of socialists in building and working inside them. Third, we must root socialist ideas within the working class, recognizing that we have almost no materials that talk about socialism, capitalism, or educational spaces for working-class constituencies, while the right, liberals, and social democrats certainly have ways of reaching workers. We have to build capacities to do this now. Fourth, we must support struggles against forms of oppression while building a class-oriented movement. Those movements are often varied and have activists who are not necessarily oriented to building an alternative to capitalism. We need to learn to work in alliance with them and over time to learn how to challenge these different forms of oppression both within our ranks and beyond. Finally, class-based leaders must come from their ranks and become important components in the struggle for socialism.

Notes

1. State power generally refers to the material forms of the state (especially the military, police, and administrative departments present across a national territory, from courts to border control) and the state's ability to use such forms and its overall dominant position to shape the political, social, and economic life of a nation.
2. CPers refers to members of the Communist Party of Canada. See the chapter by Jordan House for extensive discussion of the meaning of sectarianism.
3. Québec Solidaire is a leftist party formed in 2006 that emphasizes a range of progressive issues, from equality and inclusion to the environment, and is also oriented toward Québec's independence.

References

Gindin, Sam. 1998. "The Party's Over." *This Magazine*, November/December.
___. 2018. "Socialism for Realists." *Catalyst,* 2, 3. <catalyst-journal.com/vol2/no3/socialism-for-realists>.

10. What's Left after the Breakup of the CPGB?

Bruce Curtis and Justin Paulson

This chapter examines the lessons that might be drawn from the later history of the Communist Party of Great Britain (CPGB). The party's confrontation with Thatcherism raises a question that remains with us: How is an "augmented left" to pursue a principled politics in a period in which rational politics mobilizes support but does not win elections? Such a question today concerns the performance of politics in a digitized media environment, where messaging strategies and the emotive and aesthetic dimensions of appeals are quite different from those reigning in the heyday of the CPGB. Yet the fundamental issue for an augmented left strategy persists: What line, if any, is a principled left politics to draw between the popular and populism? How are political energies to be excited by progressive popular projects rather than by populist fantasies?

With some momentary upticks, membership levels in the CPGB declined from the end of World War II until its dissolution as a political party in 1991. Decline accelerated in the 1980s, even though the party-run Communist University of London (CUL) had attracted large numbers of participants over the previous decade and despite the fact that the party's sociology study group produced several widely read collections of papers on topical political issues. Most striking, the party's "theoretical and discussion journal," *Marxism Today,* was growing dramatically in subscribers, readership, and political influence as the party itself collapsed. All three of these entities had been intended to forge a broad democratic alliance capable of leading to socialist transformation.

A number of contributors to the literature on the CPGB have highlighted this irony (including Eaden and Renton 2002; Andrews 2004; Samuel 2006;

Worley 2016). Worley remarked that the party's early 1970s debates over the political possibilities of youth culture "revealed the party capable of motivating and hosting intellectually vibrant discussion even as it headed for dissolution. It remains something of a paradox that *Marxism Today* became ever more effervescent as the party fell deeper into decline" (515).

But Raphael Samuel (2006: 32–33) wrote in the mid-1980s that "it may be no accident that the meteoric rise of *Marxism Today* ... has coincided with a sharp decline in Party membership." In his analysis, a large part of the problem was that the CUL and the journal were centripetal, not centrifugal forces. They created spaces where party members could work free from party direction and, instead of drawing on and developing the party's intellectual capacities, they were "largely parasitic or ... dependent on intellectual and cultural energies generated outside" (Samuel 2006: 39).

Indeed, key sections of the CPGB reacted to the late 1970s floundering of the Labour Party and the subsequent triumph of Margaret Thatcher's authoritarian populism with the declaration of "New Times" (Hall and Jacques 1991), calling for new strategies to deal with changed political economic and class-cultural conditions. Discussion with social democrats and left liberals was understood to be a tactic to broaden the influence of socialist ideas. Some party sections were more interested in colonizing the left of the Labour Party, in order to push it in the direction of socialist policymaking, than in (re)building the party. Yet by the middle of the 1990s, the CPGB was gone and the Labour Party it sought to influence had moved right rather than left. If we think of an "augmented left" as a "big tent" political movement, tendency, or grouping able to advance socialist or social democratic policy and practice, the fate of the CPGB may thus be instructive.

The CPGB had not always tried to mobilize such a large tent. At *Marxism Today*'s inception in 1957, the journal insisted on orthodoxy: for party members, it was to be a source of "vigorous Marxist polemic against non-Marxist views" (Durkin 1959). The need to connect with and to organize within the Labour Party was understood as a means to show it the correct path, while issues concerning women and people of colour in Britain were initially excluded from the pages of *Marxism Today*. Matters changed dramatically in the 1970s, particularly in *Marxism Today* and at the CUL, both of which began making the party's discussions and debates more relevant to a broader swath of party militants, readers, and scholars — including many non-Communists. Ultimately, it was an activist intellectual wing of the party, rather than organized labour or the party's Central Committee, that set this tone. And it was this section of the party that grappled most directly with the strategic implications of changing social and political-economic conditions.

The move from polemicizing against non-Marxists to dialoguing with them attracted a great deal of interest and gave much greater currency to socialist critique. There were, at times, sharp divisions between "traditionalists" in the party and those questioning the substance and meaning of political-economic change. The 1977 version of the *British Road to Socialism* stressed the importance of feminist and anti-racist social movements in the struggle for socialism, promoted the construction of political alliances between the labour movement and intermediate social strata, and pushed for critical engagement with the Labour Party. Its adoption led to the establishment of a rival party by a breakaway faction. Calls from within the party for greater democratic participation and accountability were refused by the CPGB executive in 1977.

Similar divisions were evident in the debate that surrounded the publication of Eric Hobsbawm's 1978 "The Forward March of Labour Halted." Hobsbawm sided with those critical of an older language of labour militancy, in which a disciplined proletarian army was undertaking an irresistible campaign to conquer political power. Against this position, some traditionalists saw the devastating defeat of the left by Thatcherism simply as another Tory interlude (reminiscent of the German Communist Party's former slogan, "After Hitler, us!") and opposed the creeping Eurocommunist tendencies of party intellectuals. But the party leadership did not — and, in several instances, could not — successfully discipline the membership. When leadership did succeed in moulding editorial lines and keynote addresses in its own image, it appeared heavy-handed and out of touch.

The broad left strategy was a response to structural changes in Britain itself. For most of its existence, the party understood itself to represent the interests of what it saw as its natural constituency: wage earners in the industrial, manual working class. But the industrial manual working class was in decline, along with the power and credibility of the industrial unions. The growth in numbers of workers in the service sectors and in the public service heightened the visibility of groups with ambiguous class interests. The unionization of public-sector workers changed the dynamic of labour politics. Their militancy was susceptible to being cast not as a struggle of class against class, but as one of (privileged) unions against the public — and decades of such cynical discourse left its mark on common sense. The influx of women into the paid labour force and the rise of feminism challenged the party's historical focus on male wage earners supporting dependent wives and children. Post-Fordist production techniques were also invading British industrial sectors, accompanied by the increasing mobility of capital. Such technologies threatened the position of key constituents of the CP, such as engineers. Post-Fordist changes were read by many party intellectuals as creating a "new worker," one forced by the conditions of work and employment to be increasingly "flexible" and "adaptable," but who also experienced new kinds of freedom, new tastes and needs. In terms of both class structure and cultural understandings, the decline of the CP's "natural" constituency forced a reconsideration of the strategy and tactics that had been based on the interests of a white, male industrial working class.

Added to these structural changes in the British political economy were the postwar demographic transition, immigration from parts of the old empire, and an increase in domestic living standards — a "capitalist abundance" — which both increased levels of commodity consumption and increased possibilities for young people especially to "stylize" their lives and personae. As Marx and Engels had themselves stressed, capitalism could revolutionize habits and tastes, popular beliefs and practices. Some in the party, and fellow travellers such as Stuart Hall, pointed to the ways in which the constituency of socialism was always (and always had been) broader than a mostly white, male working class. That that fraction of the class was, however, the core of the party rank and file and of its leadership was significant in the membership decline, as the intellectual, political, and cultural life of the party moved in new directions.

It might have been possible in the late 1970s to engage organized labour in the discussion of "New Times," and to work to expand the constituency of organized labour itself, but by and large this did not happen. As a consequence, organized labour not only lost its agency in theoretical analysis, but it rapidly lost its seat at the table in shaping the direction of the CP's debates and discussions. Unionized workers ceased to be the primary audience of *Marxism Today* (*Marxism Today* 1984; Samuel 2006).

Ultimately, the debates spurred by these party organs encouraged the recognition that the connection between class and political party is not one of simple identity. It eventually even became accepted that while class struggle is the structuring force of capitalism, that struggle does not necessarily take the form of direct conflict between class actors — it can be mediated in all kinds of ways. The "new social movements" of the 1960s and 1970s pursued demands that had class resonances but were often not directly class demands. Political parties represented, in the technical sense of re-presenting, class and other interests and might indeed better be seen as creating or hailing (or "interpolating") the constituencies for which they claimed to speak. This rethinking was facilitated by the rejection of economism and led to various reconceptualizations of the working class.

The strategic thinking of many party intellectuals was influenced here by their reading of Antonio Gramsci (1971 [1929–1935]), who, in their understanding, argued that the struggle for socialism was a struggle for cultural hegemony. The success of socialism was seen to be bound up with cultural and educational work to make socialism into a kind of "common sense" shared by the great majority of society. Although the party did not pursue cultural politics as vigorously as some of its competitors, it did attempt to engage with some sociocultural transformations by sponsoring popular festivals that appealed to large cross-sections of youth. *Marxism Today* moved in the 1980s toward a cheeky, tabloid-style magazine focused more on British culture than directly on politics. It was widely read and very popular, but less and less focused on Marxism. Thus, while the party's intellectuals had an appreciation of the necessity of bringing aesthetic, emotional, and cultural pleasures into politics, their version of "common sense" lacked the bite it provided when refashioned by right-wing and populist initiatives.

The Gramscian influence also worked to counter the traditionalist dismissal of the bourgeois state as a simple organ of class domination. Bourgeois democracy, it was argued, had substantive as well as formal democratic features. The lesson drawn by Marx (1986 [1871]) from the experience of the Paris Commune — that it was not sufficient for the proletariat to seize the state apparatus and thereafter attempt to rule — encouraged reflection on how socialists and communists might work with and against the state at the same moment. Gramsci's argument — that capitalist domination was deeply entrenched in culture and needed to be combatted there, and not through the tactics either of coup d'état or of anarchist terror — had an added impact in the face of ultra-left terrorism, in Italy and Germany especially. Yet while the proponents of the CPGB as a vanguard party were much in retreat, in theoretical circles at least, the role and necessity of the party were growing less clear.

While *Marxism Today*, the Communist University, and the publications of the sociology group produced penetrating analyses of the strategies that brought the Thatcher government to power, documented the vicious nature of her regime, and fashioned a new constituency among academics and youth, the broad left strategy failed to reinvigorate the party. Nor did it push Labour to the left. Nor did it lay the groundwork necessary to roll back Thatcherism after the fact, nor to prevent the re-emergence of right-wing populism at a later date. (We are reminded that the Thatcher campaign's effective slogans included "Make Britain Great Again" and, in the wake of a wave of strikes earlier in the 1970s, "Labour's Not Working.")

To the contrary: the party collapsed and Labour enthusiastically embraced neoliberalism. But how much responsibility should be borne by the broad left strategy, with its related attempts to bring culture into politics?

One common criticism of the analysis of "New Times" from within the CP was that this exploration and the resulting strategy abandoned the party's natural constituency (Sivananden 1990; Hall and Jacques 1991; Samuel 2006). By this line of reasoning, open debate and broad analysis of a range of topics designed to appeal to a new audience had the unintended effect of dissolving the unity of the industrial proletariat as a political subject destined to the play the role of the leading revolutionary force in society. While it is true that the critical work conducted under the rubric of "New Times" did challenge the party's prior unity, the analysis did grasp real changes in British society. The implications were clear both to proponents and opponents: If the revolutionary proletariat was not a unitary force, then the grounds for the CPGB's existence as its natural guide, theoretician, and spokesperson were undermined. Yet there is no reason to believe that the converse was true: that by not adopting the *British Road to Socialism*, by not opening up theoretical and political discussion to those outside the party, that it would have miraculously survived the 1980s and led a vanguard in the fight against Thatcher (much less that it would have survived the collapse of the USSR

— the final blow that led to the dissolution of the party and its various activities at the end of 1991).

More damning, however, has been the received wisdom that the critical political and social analysis presented by *Marxism Today*, the sociology study group, and the reshaped CUL caused the CP to lose focus, invented an easily co-optable language for a new kind of politics with a new constituency, and thus contributed directly to New Labour and, with it, the collapse of the left. We are less convinced than others that there is any clear line of causation. It is too easy, we think, to take up a position of left purity that says one must take a line and hold to it or else be co-opted. The particular way in which the CPGB declined may have been the result of the broad left strategy, but this does not mean that New Labour was its inevitable result.

Marxism Today expended much ink at the end of the 1980s advocating for a New Labour for New Times. Yet far from being impressed by Tony Blair's resurrection of the Labour Party, the editors put together a special issue in 1998 for the sole purpose of distancing their work from New Labour's government. Blair's "New Times" was, of course, a bastardization of Stuart Hall's. There was nothing particularly remarkable about Blair's own connection to *Marxism Today*; when he wrote his vacuous piece for the journal in 1991, he was only the last in a long line of Labour leaders and MPs who had written for and otherwise engaged with *Marxism Today* since the 1970s. The journal's editors saw potential in those connections — and not without reason. At the same time, Labour turned out to be able to get as much out of *Marxism Today* as *Marxism Today* was able to influence the direction of Labour. Although the CUL ended in 1980 (its legacy continued with publications that would get reviewed in *Marxism Today*), *Marxism Today* continued sponsoring its own annual weekend conferences, usually featuring Stuart Hall, Labour leaders such as Tony Benn, cultural workshops and sessions, and so on. Conferences such as "The Great Moving Right Show," "Left Alive," and "Left Unlimited" brought many of the debates and discussions from *Marxism Today* to a larger audience and helped identify concerns and themes, especially those previously absent from CP or Labour politics, that, they felt, could be productively taken up by a future politics (whether of a Communist, an Old Labour, or an as-yet-undetermined New Labour flavour). The goal was to make left ideas more mainstream, not to blunt them: when

Labour leaders saw themselves as part of a big-tent left rather than a "Third Way," this goal was less of a problem than it became in the 1990s. Thus, the failure may have been not in the party's attempt to reshape a new constituency, but rather its failure to stitch the new one with the old and to conceptualize the political subjectivities, the hopes and dreams, that such stitching would require. The party intellectuals could make sense of Thatcher incisively on a theoretical terrain but could not organize effectively to stop her.

The experience of the CPGB teaches that augmenting the constituency of the left is fraught. Real questions remain about the nature of a "left" constituency, particularly about the political issues, the day-to-day matters, and the political utopia that may activate it. Many CPGB intellectuals had argued that party and class are two different entities, that the party did not simply speak for or embody the interests of the working class, but rather that the work of a party was to fashion a constituency. If this is the case, then what is the constituency of an "augmented left"? Is it ready-made, out there, and waiting for us? Or must it be created? What are the practical devices, techniques, and tactics that are required to fashion such a constituency? And, crucially, how does one fashion a broad constituency without losing political focus? How and in what form are the cultural, the aesthetic, and the emotive to be articulated with principled positions to produce political energy and excitement?

The CPGB's fashioning of a broader constituency treated it as something of a zero-sum equation: the shift away from concerns with organized (and organizable) labour, including to whom the leading party publications and debates were designed to appeal, was deliberate, and it accelerated following the miners' strike. As the target audience shifted, scholarly pieces were read by intellectuals (of all parties) rather than campaigners. Theoretical debate was no longer required to be accessible, even though it was becoming much more nuanced and rigorous. A magazine or journal such as *Marxism Today* can only ever *talk* about resistance (in this case, to Thatcherism), but — here we come back to the role of the party, or a party-like apparatus — the resistance itself must be built by people doing the resisting. Who are the agents, if not organized labour? Today, in the US, "the resistance" is promoted on social media and late-night talk shows as something of a cathartic, ritualistic set of utterances and denunciations by liberal commentators, while actual resistance activities are taking place in

Black Lives Matter, at Standing Rock and pipeline blockades, etc. — rarely, unfortunately, taken up by organized labour — and not yet coalescing into any kind of a party (the Democratic Socialists of America's efforts notwithstanding).

The question of articulation — brought into CPGB-sponsored discussions by Stuart Hall — continues to be one that any left needs to grapple with, particularly if it seeks to expand its reach. How to engage with the working class writ large, especially at a time when it is so much larger than its self-identified component and when many of its professed members are so easily seduced by the right? The answer is surely not to engage in the cynical variant of a politics of articulation that Tony Blair may have gotten from *Marxism Today*, but which rightly infuriated its editors — that is, the strategy of accepting the political landscape as a given and appealing to the self-described interests of people one thinks will vote, even if that means accepting what may be their basest instincts (nationalism, markets, racism, and so on). But a proper politics of articulation does have to take everyday misery seriously. An anti-racist, anti-nationalist politics still can — and should — appeal to people's needs as well as to their hopes and dreams. Is this a discussion that can or should be led by a party? (How much longer could *Marxism Today* have continued if it had always been independent of the CPGB, rather than folding in 1991 — potentially right when it might have exerted the most pull on Labour?)

Another lesson that can be taken from the CPGB experience, one which leaves us with further queries, is that open debate and dialogue did not create politics on their own. In the short term at least, it mattered little how much more correct and inclusive the perspectives in *Marxism Today* were in contrast to a party line that insisted on the primacy of the industrial labourer as both the subject and object of politics. *Marxism Today's* columns on Gramsci did not themselves foster political struggle any more than did their columns on fashion and wine. It is not a zero-sum game, of course, and one can and perhaps should do both; it is also not entirely out of the question that the broad left strategy lost the political war against Thatcherism but may have won a long-term "culture war" that made Jeremy Corbyn's renewal of the Labour Party possible. On that score, there is surely cause for optimism. Yet the left cannot content itself with winning in the long term. The suffering and misery caused by right-wing policies are also often felt quite quickly.

If the left — perhaps uniquely — needs clear principles, democratic and inclusive debate, and nuanced analysis, there is no obvious line from here to political strategy and certainly not to political clout. The left often understands its political task to be the articulation of diverse social and economic struggles. Meanwhile, the right builds its constituencies by articulating its agenda to a set of fantasy narratives and appeals to self-interest. As the CPGB recognized, some of the work of the left must also then be in relation to the fantasy work of the right. The legacy of *Marxism Today* includes the most incisive critiques of the tropes of Thatcherism, its moral panics, images, and slogans; however, a strategy for producing an augmented left capable of defeating Thatcherism politically never materialized.

We are left, then, with a query about modes and means of communication, about the organizational grounds for using them, and about the substance of issues and demands that might fashion an "augmented left" not on paper but in the streets and at the ballot boxes. These questions are urgent, given the intensification of "personality" or "charismatic" politics in many parts of the world, the volatile nature of digital communication technologies and the simplification of political messaging that helps fashion populist politics. Populism, too, fashions broad constituencies, often by disregarding established norms of conduct and claiming to attack a political-economic order that indeed creates real misery for huge numbers of people. Is this, as Laclau (2005) suggests, a terrain on which an augmented left should seek to engage? Or are populism's chains of equivalent signifiers more suited to a politics of the right? What sorts of transgressive political initiatives could fashion a populist broad left constituency without abandoning either its principles or a class politics? (We notice here the ways in which Bernie Sanders's 2016 political campaign invoked what for a great many Americans are the transgressive concepts of "socialism" and "revolution" to great effect — despite the social democratic substance of his "socialism.") With whom should the left's ideas be popular, and how can they be made popular without recourse to populism?

The last decade and a half of the CPGB offers a case study of a modestly successful attempt to augment the constituency for the ideas of the left, but at the expense of part of its traditional base. Most crucially, it failed to augment the left politically against an ascendant Thatcherism, despite having crafted the most rigorous analyses of it. Nor could it prevent the

Labour Party from appropriating some of its analyses for that party's own rightward march. Against a newly ascendant xenophobic and nationalist populism in Europe and North America, the question for the left is, again, not merely one of growing the constituency for socialist ideas and critique, but how to augment its power and compete more effectively against the performative spectacles of the right.

References

Andrews, Geoff. 2004. *Endgames and New Times: The Final Years of British Communism, 1964–1991*. London: Lawrence and Wishart.

Durkin, Tom. 1959. "Marxism Today Discussion Circles." *Marxism Today* (December).

Eaden, James, and David Renton. 2002. *The Communist Party of Great Britain Since 1920*. New York: Palgrave.

Gramsci, Antonio. 1971 [1929–1935]. *Selections from the Prison Notebooks*, eds. Quintin Hoare and Geoffrey Nowell Smith. New York: International Publishers.

Hall, Stuart, and Martin Jacques (eds.). 1991. *New Times: The Changing Face of Politics in the 1990s*. New York: Routledge.

Laclau, Ernesto. 2005. *On Populist Reason*. London: Verso.

Marx, Karl. 1986 [1871]. "Drafts of 'The Civil War in France.'" In *Marx & Engels Collected Works*, vol. 22. London: Lawrence and Wishart.

Marxism Today. 1984. *Marxism Today Colour Supplement*.

Samuel, Raphael. 2006. *The Lost World of British Communism*. London: Verso.

Sivanandan, A. 1990. "All That Melts Into Air Is Solid: The Hokum of New Times." *Race and Class*, 31, 1.

Worley, Matthew. 2016. "Marx-Lenin-Rotten-Strummer: British Marxism and Youth Culture in the 1970s." *Contemporary British History*, 30, 4.

11. Building Political Infrastructure for the Present

Lina Nasr El Hag Ali

In light of the current legitimacy crises of liberal democracies to truly represent the people, how do we as leftists avoid the fate of having our political efforts reduced to nothing more than a spectacle? Captured in transitory protests, how we do address those who seek to "have their voices heard" but end up frustrated by the lack of responses? And how do we prevent parties that emerge as radical forces from getting trapped in compliance with the existing political terrain? Given the complexity of the current political moment, the project of state capture cannot remain the only end goal of today's left movement.

The Marxist left accepts the fundamental presupposition that the transformation of our current structures in both base (as in the system of production) and superstructure (the state and its institutions) is the ultimate goal of revolutionary politics. But this macro-level analysis often misses the critical elements of building transformational infrastructure here and now. Key forms of organizing and resistance can affect the terrain of politics both immediately and in the "long run." Sustaining the mass "non-hierarchical" organizing called for broadly on today's left compels us to address the inadequacies of our current political infrastructure — including the stated left alternatives — and begin to envision what is necessary for sustaining transformative change in the aims of a socialist future. This chapter is an attempt to draw out the possibilities for alternative forms of political infrastructure. It will do so by exploring developments in Toronto, Canada.

Curtis and Paulson, in their examination of the lessons of the Communist Party of Great Britain (CPGB), emphasize the challenges of moving away from a traditional support base and subsequently losing political influence. Relatedly, I ask, if an identifiable working class exists, where can it be found today? And if the working class has changed, how can we understand the changes it has undergone? How do we move forward in developing a political platform without the defined characteristics of a target base? What are our alternatives, other than building a party? And how do we break with the routine reliance on existing infrastructure — particularly the political — for transformation? For those interested in these questions, a consideration of how societal change unfolds, how it mutates into "new" and divergent categories and practices, is the task at hand. Change, in the form of *mutations*, will help us better understand the "catalytic moment" in achieving the ends of a socialist society. My aim in this work is to contextualize *augmentation* as the process of *mutation*.

Mutation is typically used to refer to permanent *errors* that arise from the process of replication in sequencing. So, in attempting to *do the same*, you are left with a permanent alteration in the sequence (Nei 2007). What the concept of mutation does for us, in this context, is clarify the tenuousness of understanding linear time as progressive, as well as the flaws in an *inherent rationality* associated with both biological and social transformation.

Mutation serves as an interesting departure in our theorizing. In what ways does society, politics, or economics mutate? In what ways can thinking of change as mutational provide us with insight into transforming contemporary institutions and practices, including the political party? von Bargen suggests to readers that multiple conceptions of "civil liberties" exist as a way to tease out different means of developing equality in rights. How do we begin to think of alternatives regarding anti-capitalist political infrastructure in this more varied and multidirectional way? How can the concept of mutation open up analysis of contemporary radical political practice?

The Current Context

The starting point here is the uncertain world of the in-between described in Latham's chapter. Under such circumstances, the need for political infrastructure beyond the traditional elements — institutionalized elections, the structure of the party, and the system of representative government as the authoritative spaces for political participation — is urgent because what we have been working with so far has not created the context for broad-based anti-capitalist movements. While some on today's left, taking up Simone Weil's (2013) argument against the "trap" of political parties, believe that the political party itself is insufficient because of the slow crawl of progressive change, this has not inspired much dialogue on what we should then understand to be viable left strategies. Many, like Rosenfeld in this volume, still believe in the party. He is not alone, as participation in parties across Europe shows. But relative to decades ago, there has been a shift. The decline of the CPGB throughout the 1980s, as Curtis and Paulson remind us, occurred as activists focused on issues such as disarmament, race, gender, and immigration in an increasingly "decentralized" fashion.

What can we learn from this shift, and what possibilities does political decentralization open up for us? On the one hand, the issue-focused and anti-globalization movements in the end opened few avenues for radical anti-capitalist transformation. On the other hand, leftists relying on a party-centric political infrastructure tend to hope that it will not be undermined by the constraints of the current capitalist society and that it will garner electoral success. On the assumption that radical revolution led by vanguard parties is not in the cards for the foreseeable future, the question is whether something can point us to different avenues for building mass support. This has become especially important as the continued and further deepening of political, economic, and social inequality has both frustrated the general population and aroused right-wing populist sentiments.

Toronto: Sites of Mutation

The decentralization of the left could in fact be a strategic advantage for addressing the complex concerns of people today. Some authors in this book might disagree with this approach and prefer developing a more singular way forward together. Rosenfeld rightly points to the recurrent descent into sectarianism that divergent strategies bring about. The question to ask here is: can the various divergent energies among different groups be gathered and developed in a way that is effective for fostering a movement toward radical left transformation? After all, not all political or economic gains are the result of long-term organizing; there are those that seem to develop through error. I do not believe, as Rosenfeld suggested at times, that we need to view our differences as a hindrance; if anything, we can clearly articulate corresponding end goals. For example, much of the left would agree that we need a return to public ownership, workers' self-management, and other forms of popular control. Also, old words like these can perhaps take on new meanings with a left that is keen on the adaptation of these concepts to our complex societies today. If our past efforts have taught us something, it is that achieving these aims should not only rely on the direction of a party. We need perspectives on political infrastructure that don't simply encourage the handing off of issues to "higher powers" in the transition from protest to governance. There needs to be room for makeshift processes, through trial and error, that eventually become organized processes of intervention. This is one way to think again about dual power — that is, power organized by the masses directly versus power organized to use the state for progressive ends.

Processes of mutation have transformed the multiple failures of left responses to the housing crisis in Toronto. The Parkdale Neighbourhood Land Trust, for example, is a project aimed at tackling a variety of issues, from food insecurity and housing to political participation and poverty, through the model of a "community land trust" (Goodmurphy and Kamizaki 2011). This model allows for members of the community to purchase and hold land in common, in the form of a trust, managed by members of the community itself. Again, this concept of community ownership is not necessarily new, but we can see the community land trust as emerging because of the failures of the existing, more traditional infrastructure to redress community concerns. The land trust, in order to be sustained, has embedded itself in a web of community projects in Parkdale, including community centres, food co-ops, residents' associations, and shelters (Goodmurphy and Kamizaki 2011). This network of "community organizations" can form the basis of political infrastructure needed to move forward as well as play a key role in community politicization because of their direct and democratic structures.

Another example of the emergence of new political, social, and economic structures is the popular governance of the Toronto Harm

Reduction Alliance (THRA), which, with the help of a dispersed community of health-care workers, peer workers, and labour activists, formed the Toronto Overdose Prevention Society (TOPS). Almost immediately, this group was able to meet the needs of those overdosing while simultaneously pressing for the overdose crisis itself to be recognized (Arnone 2017). Acknowledgment of the crises on the part of our health institutions came after the presence of a challenge to their decision-making power. The Ontario health ministry approved safe injection sites that would double as overdose prevention sites. In the end, people preferred to use the makeshift services of TOPS, located in Toronto's Moss Park, rather than switch over to government-mandated sites. The outcome of THRA's organizing efforts has yet to be fully realized, but in the wake of renewed interest in the health and safety of drug users, the ability of people and their organizing efforts to shape terms of service remains a real possibility.

The lesson to be gleaned from the TOPS project is not simply in the legislation that will surely follow (Edwards 2017), but in the direct political and material infrastructure it has provided to activists and organizers in the city. Rather than aiming for the provincial and federal governments to create spaces and sites that address the needs of drug users, THRA created its own sites, articulated its own narrative of the opioid crisis, and others were forced to follow suit. This kind of change should be highlighted, analyzed, and given the weight afforded to strategic conversations of institutional capture. Mutation in this instance has not yet shown itself. But the potential shift in the views and policies concerning drug use/users remains.

Of course, the political party as a site of participation will not be eclipsed by these moments of community-driven change, but these forces need not be pitted against each other, either. In the spirit of augmentation, and reflecting on the more entrenched positions that divide the left, we can imagine an approach to political infrastructure that reconfigures existing avenues for political participation. The party as the site of most impactful change, as the end of the left's political intervention, is insufficient. But the methods of change do not need to, in themselves, represent a fundamental shift. Change as driven by mutation represents an openness and a willingness to experiment with the variety of methods and tools at our disposal. The change is the result of the popular support of that effort; its institutionalization can come in the form of the state's attempt at capturing those methods or practices, or the groundwork itself can be set by the actions themselves, as is the case in the aforementioned examples.

Conclusions

In order to move toward the radical anti-capitalist transformation that left augmentation seeks, perhaps we should reconfigure our approach to change itself. In the long-standing tension between the search for new methods and clinging to old methods, those actions fostering political engagement are even momentarily lost or forgotten. We lament the ephemeral qualities of the protest and yearn for the stability of the political organization, all the while ignoring the spaces of engagement created in between to deal with serial crises. Such a position continues to be self-defeating, with a left that has failed to fundamentally change the ways in which people engage socially, economically, and politically, and it misses the "transitory" mechanisms of engagement that might emerge in a given political moment. Rather than only looking to the party with hopeful fervour, we can look to those working daily to provide responses to the inadequate means of participation, whether it's through pop-up safe injection sites or reconfiguring a model of neighbourhood tenants' associations to win rental strikes (Parkdale Organize 2017). One of Rosenfeld's decisive lessons is that showing up for other people's efforts and recognizing and supporting their work is central to building working-class power, and this point needs emphasis now more than ever. We need a twofold approach: supporting those projects actively developing alternative infrastructures *and* amplifying them via traditional institutions. Political infrastructure beyond the party does not allow us to postpone change to the "ripe moment"; it requires us to build political infrastructure in and for the present.

Given this, we need to focus on rethinking the ways in which change takes place and how to incorporate an understanding of changes, shifts, and failures that results in the possibility of creating new avenues for transformation. I offered the notion of mutation here as a way of thinking about changes and how they develop, not out of new practices, but rather from errors typically seen in the repeating of old approaches. These errors create new openings in our process and ultimately new paths for developing our methods of organizing, action, and politicization. If the transformation of our present institutions remains the goal, then a recognition and assessment of how that change is created becomes a necessary task. The concept of mutation can help us understand better the need to break with the routine reliance on existing infrastructure as the only road to transformation.

References

Arnone, Annie. 2017. "Overdose Prevention Society Scrambling for Proper Safe Injection Sites." *Toronto Star*, November 5. <thestar.com/news/gta/2017/11/05/overdose-prevention-society-scrambling-for-proper-safe-injection-sites.html>.

Edwards, Peter. 2017. "Health Canada Approves Immediate Opening of a Safe Injection Site in Toronto." *Toronto Star*, August 20. <thestar.com/news/gta/2017/08/20/health-canada-approves-immediate-opening-of-a-safe-injection-site-in-toronto.html>.

Goodmurphy, Brendon, and Kuni Kamizaki. 2011. "A Place for Everyone: How a Community Land Trust Could Protect Affordability and Community Assets in Parkdale." Parkdale Community Land Trust. November. <pnlt.ca/wp-content/uploads/2015/04/a-place-for-everyone-parkdale-community-land-trust-november-20111.pdf>.

Nei, Masatoshi. 2007. "The New Mutation Theory of Phenotypic Evolution." *PNAS*, 104, 30.

Parkdale Organize. 2017. "Parkdale Rent Strike Ends in Victory!" August 3.

Weil, Simone. 2013 [1957]. *On the Abolition of All Political Parties*, trans. Simon Leys. New York: New York Review of Books.

12. Class Struggle in the Marketplace of Ideas
Toward a Leftist Framework of Civil Liberties

Julian von Bargen

Another week, another "panic" concerning free speech. Another grifter, be it Lindsay Shepherd, Milo Yiannopoulos, Alex Jones, or someone else, banned from social media. Another "controversial" speaker, usually a code word for bigoted, gives a talk at a university to "trigger the libs" and decries the counter-protest organized to deplatform them. Another right-wing politician takes power and at least threatens to legislate that all publicly funded universities implement the University of Chicago free speech principles on their campuses or risk losing funding.

These are recurring phenomena, but the free-speech "crisis" is a canard. These "crises" are part of a political strategy deployed by right-wing, counterrevolutionary economic and political forces in the US and Canada. Their goal is to narrowly redefine civil liberties in a way that makes free speech paramount and likewise to curtail the collective rights of unions, political parties, and social movements to criticize, strike, assemble, organize, picket, and boycott. These collective rights are seen as a threat by conservative (and liberal) politicians who seek to protect the status quo. The question posed to those on the left is: what is our response?

This chapter aims to lay out the stakes of civil liberties and connect the importance of a *collective* set of civil liberties to the left's capacities to win power. When considered in a broader historical context, the changing substance of civil liberties can be seen as part of a historical struggle over the substance of freedom and citizenship. This history reinforces the importance for the left not only to defend civil liberties, but also to augment them to serve a left project.

With historical struggles over civil liberties in mind, the frequent leftist dismissal of civil liberties as liberal or bourgeois is troubling. The argument is usually as follows: Because civil liberties are defined in narrow, political terms and do not address systemic economic inequalities, they are insufficient for left projects. Or, worse, civil liberties are not only insufficient, but weaponized by right-wing forces to stir up hate, discredit social provisioning, and attack left organizations and movements. There is truth to both claims. The second one in particular poses a major threat to women and people of colour, two groups that suffer a disproportionate amount of harassment online from trolls, bots and coordinated campaigns by right-wing organizations. But does this mean we should stop supporting civil liberties? The answer is not to discard them; rather, I propose an augmentation of civil liberties, a redefinition based on a history of movement building through the protection and extension of collective action.

What Are Civil Liberties?

Civil liberties are usually defined as fundamental rights granted to "the people" as part of a social contract — often embodied in a constitution — that underpins a free, democratic society. These rights include the freedoms of speech, thought, assembly, association, worship, and conscience. They also include key provisions such that the law applies to all, and all have a right to a fair trial. These are believed to be fundamental and therefore worthy of special protections because without them, a society cannot be either free or democratic.

The ascendance of the new right has shattered two illusions about civil rights: one, that the expansion of equal political and economic rights to the working class was a *fait accompli*; and two, that their achievement was a universally shared desire. The second point is the larger challenge: a contest over the substance and extension of civil liberties has been inherent to their history because reactionary movements have arisen consistently to oppose the extension of civil liberties to the working class and subaltern.

Put another way, political rights to assembly, association, expression, running for office, and making law are often limited by the economic rights afforded to private owners of business, property, money, and production.

Whose rights ought to be prioritized is not the result of some appeal to a platonic set of discovered civil liberties, but rather the result of a contest between competing segments of society. The US constitution was designed to protect the few from the many. This was because Madison (1961), among others, feared that in an unequal country, a democracy without certain protections could be susceptible to takeovers by the impoverished classes, who might redistribute wealth and property. This does not mean that civil liberties are useless or unimportant. What it suggests, rather, is that a single platonic set of civil liberties does not exist. Instead, multiple conceptions exist. The dominant understanding of "civil liberties" is the outcome of social contests over the substance of particular *sets* of civil liberties.

Conceptions of Civil Liberties beyond the Marketplace of Ideas

The histories of civil liberties are flush with proof that multiple conceptions exist. The Whig narrative of free speech tells the story of enlightened progressive judges who saw the truth. Justice Oliver Wendell Holmes Jr. in particular is credited with reinterpreting the first amendment to blend free speech and the free market.

> When men have realized that time has upset many fighting faiths, they may come to believe ... that the ultimate good desired is better reached by free trade in ideas — that the best test of truth is the power of the thought to get itself accepted in the competition of the market, and that truth is the only ground upon which their wishes safely can be carried out. That, at any rate, is the theory of our Constitution. (Quoted in Cohen 2013)

This was a novel interpretation, at least for the US Supreme Court, and to some commentators (Cohen 2013), Holmes' dissent in *Abrams v. United States* was the discovery of a universal concept. This chapter asserts a different reading. Holmes's dissent reflected an ascendant conception of civil liberties in its time. Lost in the Whig history of an unfolding liberal conception of civil liberties is that in the period following World War I, Justice Holmes was not the only one offering a radical reinterpretation of the first amendment. Galvanized by the use of the Sedition Act of 1918 to prosecute five Russian-born men for "provoking and encouraging" resistance through anti-capitalist pamphlets, the American Civil Liberties Union was founded in 1920 to defend American civil liberties. As will be discussed, though, the ACLU had a different conception of civil liberties.

Analytically, civil liberties are the key component for making sense of and evaluating so-called free societies because what is meant by *free* is revealed in the ways a society legally conceptualizes and limits freedom through rights. Freedom is not and has never been a singular, self-evident, or coherent concept. Nor have almost any of the people who have deployed the concept over its long history meant total, unrestricted freedom for the individual. It's not hard to figure out why. Total freedom means individuals have the freedom to do whatever they want, but almost everyone agrees there are some things that individuals are not allowed to do, and to restrict individuals from doing these things does not mean a society is unfree. More sophisticated questions of freedom, therefore, start with an understanding that prioritizing some freedoms means limiting others. The question free societies must ask is: what's a fair way to decide which limits will be placed on freedom to assure liberty for all?

The ACLU's conception of civil liberties was both concurrent with and substantively different from that of Justice Holmes. Their starkly partisan conception of civil liberties was a response to a very different climate for civil liberties prior to and just after World War I. In the US in this era, the capitalist class and the state collaborated to prevent workers from contesting their economic subordination. They pushed a conception of civil liberties designed to improve the leverage of the capitalist class and undermine the collective power of labour. Corporate interests worked with legislators to develop laws that would "open shops" by allowing workers in a unionized workplace to avoid union membership. Importantly, this argument was justified with an appeal to the fundamental civil liberty of an individual to engage in contracts. The idea is that all workers should have the right to enter willingly into a contract without the state or anyone else intervening to stop them. Enforcing this right was a catalyst to America's "deadliest labour war" in the coal fields of Colorado in 1913–14. This war was ended by the Rockefeller-owned Colorado Fuel and Iron Company when their militia attacked and destroyed a workers' camp, killing eleven children and two women in the attack, as well as an estimated eight to twenty labourers (Andrews 2010).

This business-friendly model of civil liberties was also key to judicial decisions issuing thousands of injunctions against non-violent workers organizing to reduce the working day, improve wages, improve labour's position at the bargaining table, and improve working conditions. The most defining example of this is probably the Pullman Strike of 1894, which was ended when the US attorney general, Richard Olney, and the president, Grover Cleveland, stepped in to override the governor of Illinois, issue an injunction to block the strike, deploy two thousand troops to enforce the injunction, and arrest the labour leaders behind the strike. A year later, the US Supreme Court upheld the right of the federal government to do so.

Though their conception changed over time, at the founding of the ACLU in the 1920s, the organization saw itself as "a frank partisan of radical labour" (Weinrib 2016). What they sought to protect was not the marketplace of ideas but the right of labour to agitate. This is an entirely different conception of civil liberties, meant to secure fundamental economic and social change by asserting labour's absolute right to picket, boycott, and strike. Moreover, these rights would be extended up and down the supply chain. The idea was that if a small manufacturer were underselling a unionized factory by underpaying employees, a secondary strike would allow the union to fight back. Their right to agitate would also allow other unions to prohibit their members from purchasing these non-unionized products, a secondary boycott. This is an excellent example of the importance of political infrastructure, of the sort that Nasr discusses in this volume. Prior to World War I, the state and courts intervened on behalf of the capitalist class to prevent labour's exercise of their collective power. But with the help of the ACLU, starting in the 1920s, a definition of civil liberties that protected and extended the right of collective organizations to assert their demands was part of later successes to extend political and economic rights to the working classes. This was galvanized by the Palmer raids, which saw the attorney general, A. Mitchel Palmer, and the FBI target politically radical immigrants and domestic trade unionists.

In Canada, something like the partisanship of the ACLU existed as well. Following the lead of the Communist Party of the US, and with a nudge from the Soviet Comintern, the Communist Party of Canada (CPC) helped to set up the Canadian Labour Defense League (CLDL). During its existence, from 1925 to 1940, the CLDL raised money in large part to help defend over six thousand individuals targeted by law enforcement agencies enabled by the censorious provisions of the War Measures Act (Petryshyn 1982). These provisions, falling under section 98 of the act, had little to do with World War I and were only made law in response to the Winnipeg General Strike of 1919, specifically to repress radical labour organizing. Section 98 attacked members of "unlawful organizations," defined as organizations that advocated the "use of force" in promoting economic or governmental change (although "force" was left open to interpretation). Specifically, it attacked new immigrants from eastern Europe, including Finland, Ukraine, and Russia, with the threat of deportation. This was no idle threat: throughout the 1930s until the repeal of the act in 1936, about four thousand Canadians of eastern European heritage were deported.

Section 98 was notable because although it was written as a general law about all organizations, it was adopted to destroy the CPC specifically. As Ontario Provincial Police commissioner Victor Williams put it, "Gentlemen, we are going to strike a death blow at the Communist Party." Once the legislation was in place, it was used widely and aggressively. In the early 1930s, Toronto's Board of Police undertook a massive anti-communist campaign. This included legislation that forbade public addresses at all public meetings not in English, as well as legislation that allowed the chief of police to cancel all licences to "public halls and other places of public amusement" that rented their premises for "communist or Bolshevik public meetings." It led to raids across the country on union organizers, charges of sedition against newspaper editors, and the possible murder of Finnish-born labour organizers in the logging industry in northwestern Ontario. As the state's attacks on labour increased, the CLDL worked harder to protect its members and this led to raids on the CLDL itself (Petryshyn 1982).

In both the US and Canada, there was a shared commitment of the ruling classes to attack the civil liberties of working-class people who were engaging in collective action. The character of the repression was slightly different in the US, however, where it centred on upholding the rights of individuals and corporations. This approach was more nuanced and successful precisely because it framed its opposition to collective action by defending a contending vision for civil liberties. The case for a left conception of civil liberties remains.

Contemporary Challenges to Civil Liberties

Today, increasingly, the "common sense" on civil liberties is that they should be designed to protect individual or corporate rights over the rights of collective labour. That's why recent protests over the right of right-wing provocateurs to give public talks on university campuses across North America has led to a "free-speech panic" in some liberal and leftist corners. The right of speakers to contribute, unfettered, to the marketplace of ideas is paramount. Yet the rights of protesters are hardly as sacrosanct. In other words, the free-speech panic is a canard, a deception from the bigger issue. What limits, if any, should be set on constitutional or charter freedoms?

Recent scholarship on the American right is instructive in making sense of this canard. Corey Robin's *The Reactionary Mind* (2011) contextualizes the specificity of differing conceptions of civil liberties in North America. He argues that what makes a conservative a conservative is not a commitment to preserve traditions or established institutions, nor a concern over rapid change, though conservatives often espouse these positions. For Robin, what makes a conservative is that they oppose the extension of political and economic rights — that is, civil liberties — to everyone. Conservatives are not opposed to changing society, and in many recent cases they have pursued intense attacks against the very traditions and institutions one would expect a democratic conservative to defend, including markets, the courts, the military and intelligence apparatuses of the state, the rule of law, the media, elected representatives, and the electoral system itself. Why? According to Robin, it is because those institutions have been susceptible to pressure from mass movements that possess collective civil liberties — liberties that apply beyond male plutocrats and their allies.

Contemporary conservativism is an uneven, contradictory formation, so it's worth examining influences on the dominant vision of rights that has come to define the "common sense." In *Democracy in Chains*, Nancy MacLean (2017) argues that one of the most influential architects of right-wing politics in North America today is James Buchanan. Buchanan came of age as a conservative during the civil rights movement. At the time, the right had no response to the strategy of civil rights organizers to build popular movements through strikes, pickets, boycotts, demonstrations, marches, and other non-violent collective action. These movements were full of powerless people who realized they could use strength in numbers to make demands on politicians, parties, and government officials. The integration of schools demonstrated the extent to which collective action could compel the federal state to force wealthy individuals to pay for an increasing number of public goods and social programs they had no personal say in approving. Here, Buchanan saw a great threat to America coming from social movements. For Buchanan and many other Southern elites, the civil rights movement was a time of defeat from which they would learn and recover.

Of course, Buchanan was but one economist and professor. No doubt his public choice theory was highly influential for the Chicago school, which in turn was highly influential in training economists who went on to work with governments around the world to promote the "common sense" of individual and corporate rights. But he was also influential because he helped legitimize a larger strategy pursued vigorously by some segments of the GOP, including the presidential campaigns of Goldwater and Nixon's second campaign in 1968. Another central figure in the development of the current "common sense" was Republican electoral strategist Kevin Phillips, who helped to design the Southern strategy. He understood that for Republicans to win the American South, they had to appeal to middle-class whites protective of their social status and concerned about taxes and social provisioning. This white middle class was used to occupying a rung on the social ladder well above that of the average Black working-class citizen. In recent decades, rates of home ownership had surged, largely in suburban neighbourhoods, generating a trend of geographical and class division that accelerated with the white flight episodes of the late sixties (Kruse 2007). Since then, this dynamic has only grown more pronounced, making the strategy all the more responsive to the underlying currents of resentment circulating among the middle and upper classes across the US.

Some years later, fossil fuel magnates Charles and David Koch borrowed from this playbook to combat what they saw as the tyranny of the majority. Their strategies included emphasizing states' rights, implementing a poll tax, manipulating voting rules, election spending, and threatening dissenters with economic boycotts. These tactics became part of a package of "civil liberties" that claimed to protect the role of the individual from "the coercive powers of the collective" (MacLean 2017: 45). As MacLean traces, this conception had precedents in American history: the paranoid politics of plantation owners who knew exactly what they had to lose if the slaves were offered democratic and economic rights. But it was not just a phenomenon of the Southern aristocratic class, even if the libertarian conception of civil liberty found its near perfection in Virginian oligarchy. Instead, the Southern propertied class found common cause with Northern capitalists who had long insisted on the economic rights of the propertied over the collective rights of labour.

Today a conservative tendency shaped by Buchanan, Nixon, Phillips, and the Kochs has developed strong roots. Libertarian conservatism, free markets, and states' rights are now central planks of the Republican Party (though not exactly represented in the policies of Trump). This conservative conception of civil liberties has a long history in the US, emphasizing individual liberties as the highest principle. It is clear by this point that advocates like Buchanan and the Kochs know that the inequalities underlying the so-called "marketplace of ideas" are more likely to aid the powerful than the disenfranchised or the downtrodden. This is an advantage Buchanan and the Kochs worked hard to extend, so as to further exploit it. The history of reactionary libertarian conservatism in the US shows how a coherent vision animating years of research, lobbying, organizing, and reform can affect substantive political change. Leading this transformation was a set of weaponized civil liberties meant to undermine opposing social forces and enhance the position of the oligarchic capitalist class fragment funding the Republican Party.

Augmenting the Left

To this point, right-wing and liberal defenders of free speech have managed to characterize left protests and opposition to bigoted speech on campus and elsewhere as "regressive" and even "fascist." This characterization needs to be countered. Assembling to protest and challenge bigoted speakers are acts protected by rights to freedom of expression and should be defended as such. The same is true for the boycott, divestment, and sanctions (BDS) campaign to defend Palestinian human rights. Even if activists and organizers do not agree with BDS targeting Israel, the principle that civil rights include the right to boycott, assemble, picket, and strike are essential to the left's repertoire of contentious politics.

The right-wing idea that there should be no limitations on free expression — including hate speech or online harassment — needs to be opposed. New techniques deployed by powerful forces are using troll armies, reverse censorship, and flooding to weaponize free speech and attack dissenters (Wu 2018). In this context, opposing censorship on the principle that it might be used to censor the speech of the left ultimately leads to the left's censorship by other means.

Last, social media companies should not be allowed to (or applauded for) censor(ing) their cyberspaces. Laws should protect intermediaries from being held to account for what is said on their platforms and should assert specifically what is and is not acceptable speech in advance. Targeted harassment is not acceptable speech. Social media platforms should be held to account for the ways in which they incentivize harassment and polarization in their algorithms and on their platforms. These changes, among many others, might provide the political infrastructure for the left to regain its dynamism in Canada and the US.

References

Andrews, T. 2010. *Killing for Coal: America's Deadliest Labor War.* Cambridge: Harvard University Press.

Cohen, A. 2013. "The Most Powerful Dissent in American History." *The Atlantic*, August 10. <theatlantic.com/national/archive/2013/08/the-most-powerful-dissent-in-american-history/278503/>.

Kruse, K. 2007. *White Flight: Atlanta and the Making of Modern Conservatism.* Princeton: Princeton University Press.

MacLean, Nancy. 2017. *Democracy in Chains: The Deep History of the Radical Right's Stealth Plan for America.* New York: Viking.

Madison, J. 1961. "Federalist No. 10." In Clinton Rossiter (ed.) *The Federalist Papers.* New York: New American Library.

Petryshyn, J. 1982. "Class Conflict and Civil Liberties: The Origins and Activities of the Canadian Labour Defense League, 1925–1940." *Labour/Le Travailleur*, 10 (Autumn).

Robin, C. 2011. *The Reactionary Mind.* New York: Oxford University Press.

Weinrib, L. 2016. *The Taming of Free Speech: America's Civil Liberties Compromise.* Cambridge: Harvard University Press.

Wu, T. 2018. "Is the First Amendment Obsolete?" Columbia Public Law Research Paper No. 14-573. <scholarship.law.columbia.edu/cgi/viewcontent.cgi?article=3080&context=faculty_scholarship>.

Section 4

Advancing Eco-socialism

13. The Anthropocene and Us
Grounds for an Augmented Left?

David Ravensbergen

If the challenge of augmenting the left entails overcoming sectarian divisions and finding new ways of articulating a common political project, then climate change presents both an opportunity and an imperative for such a synthesis. Over the course of the coming decades, our current global emissions trajectory will push the climate into a state that will fundamentally alter the familiar features of life on Earth, as cities and ecosystems that developed under stable climatic conditions find themselves unable to cope with rapid and non-linear change. Yet even as this already unfolding future erodes the ecological conditions of possibility for Holocene politics, some models of emancipatory thought treat the deepening crisis of the biosphere as merely an addendum to the standard repertoire of left concerns. Against this tendency, I argue that the central task of the contemporary radical left must be to promote new modes of organizing socioecological life capable of staving off the worst effects of the climate crisis and equitably adapting to those impacts that can no longer be avoided. This will require re-examination of some of the core claims of political agency and social transformation that have traditionally animated the left — in particular, the thesis that the working-class majority can take control of the scientific, technological, infrastructural, and productive apparatus of capitalism and repurpose it for egalitarian, emancipatory, and ecological ends. As climate change throws both capitalist and anti-capitalist utopias radically into question, parsing out plausible left futures from those that can no longer be realized is key to the project of augmentation.

In contrast to the prevailing mainstream diagnosis of climate change as an externality or by-product of civilizational progress, the radical left offers a more precise explanation that sees climate change as the historical outcome of the social structures of fossil capitalism and imperialism (Malm 2016). Burgeoning scholarship in left ecology has underscored the ecological dimension of the critique of capitalism, forming the basis for an analytical framework that can meaningfully address poverty, inequality, and oppression, on the one hand, and ecological degradation on the other, as intertwined outcomes of the same socioeconomic system (see, for example, Bookchin 1982; Mies and Shiva 1993; Burkett 1999; Foster 2000; Moore 2015). What remains contested is how the analytical clarity of the critique of fossil capitalism and imperialism can be translated into a political project capable of both arresting ecocidal capitalist development and building new forms of social production and reproduction within the ecological limits of a degraded biosphere. As Naomi Klein (2014) has argued, climate change changes everything, and perhaps more than any other issue, it has the capacity to unite the disparate strands of the left in a bid for a better socioecological future than the variants of authoritarianism and eco-apartheid currently on offer (Parenti 2011). But as the atmospheric concentration of greenhouse gases continues to rise, urgent questions around the goals and strategies of a climate-based left augmentation remain open.

Among the numerous difficulties with augmenting the left by centring the climate, two particularly inconvenient truths stand out. The first is a broad disagreement between two contrasting normative visions of what a left climate strategy should entail. On one side are the ecomodernists — those who advocate technological solutions such as renewable energy and geoengineering as means of halting ecological breakdown and creating a green form of socialist abundance.[1] Exponents of the contrasting degrowth position emphasize redistribution coupled with an equitable downscaling of energy and material throughput (primarily in the energy- and resource-intensive advanced economies, with a corresponding increase in the periphery) as well as a shift toward new models of collective provisioning capable of promoting well-being without the pursuit of economic growth as an end in itself (Kallis et al. 2018). On the ecomodernist side, the argument is typically grounded in the traditional Marxian claim that the development of the means of production under capitalism creates the technological conditions of possibility for a sustainable socialist society (e.g., Huber 2019), whereas degrowth and other green anti-capitalists argue that a socialist revolution must do away with industrial agriculture and other ecocidal capitalist technologies if it is to have any chance of success (e.g., Bernes 2018). Given that these two positions invoke diametrically opposed visions of a post-capitalist socioecological future and propose radically different strategies for getting there, resolving this debate is an immediate priority for building an augmented left climate politics.

The second obstacle to forming an augmented left climate politics is the fact that the ecological crisis is not reducible to climate change. While climate change has captured the world's attention as the primary ecological issue of the twenty-first century, ecologists emphasize that what is often described as a climate crisis is best understood as a convergence of crises in interdependent Earth systems (Rockström et al. 2009; Steffen et al. 2015). The findings of Earth system science have been articulated through the concept of the Anthropocene, which has come to function as a kind of shorthand for the urgency and uncanniness of living in a planetary moment in which the basic characteristics of the Holocene world — its richness in plant and animal life, its biogeochemical cycles that sustained a stable climate — are undergoing rapid and unprecedented transformation as a result of capitalist development (Moore 2017). While deployments of the term in the arts, humanities, and social sciences are the subject of much ongoing debate, the core message of the Anthropocene should not be in dispute: the planet has entered a "no-analogue state," as the integrated functions of the Earth system that make this planet a suitable home for humanity are being pushed into conditions that are without precedent in human history (Angus 2016). Likewise, the implications for the radical left should be clear. As long as our political imagination remains grounded in the terrestrial stability of the Holocene, the rapid and unpredictable transformation of the planet's basic life-support systems will render many of the left's political assumptions obsolete.

Untenable Futures: From Ecomodernism to Green Social Democracy

Part of the difficulty in building a politics adequate to the ecological crisis lies in the fact that a frank assessment of the prospects for planetary life is likely to have a demobilizing effect on the political constituencies central to any left project. Forecasts of doom have little chance of competing with politics that promise direct and tangible increases in security and quality of life. As Sasha Lilley et al. (2012: 32) put it, "an awareness of the scale or severity of catastrophe does not ineluctably steer one down the path of radical politics." While I agree that there is nothing ineluctable or even probable about awareness of the extent of the ecological crisis translating into a principled militancy, the obverse *can* be claimed with certainty: failing to understand the scale and severity of the catastrophe *will* ineluctably produce a radicalism that is utterly inadequate to the challenge of building an equitable life within the biophysical boundaries of a degraded biosphere. In addition to developing new strategies for mobilization and organizing in the face of ecological despair, an augmented left must work through the implications of Earth system science and move beyond a vision of the good life premised on a more equitable extension of the profoundly unsustainable form of life enabled by the "imperial mode of living" in the core capitalist countries (Brand and Wissen 2012). Articulating such a politics necessarily involves confrontation and conflict between incompatible visions of the future promoted by different elements of the left. As Swyngedouw (2010: 228) puts it: "There is an urgent need for different stories and fictions that can be mobilized for realization. This requires foregrounding and naming different socio-environmental futures and recognizing conflict, difference and struggle over the naming and trajectories of these futures."

Looking to the stories of possible futures currently in circulation on the left, I argue that a prevailing imaginary of limitlessness impedes efforts to grasp the lines of political contestation that are being drawn by the socio-ecological crisis. While the unjust and immoral level of wealth, resource, and energy inequality between and within nations is central to anti-capitalist critique, the larger context of the planet's biophysical limits often does not register, despite clear evidence that a political vision premised on generalizing the high rates of resource and energy use in the nations of the industrialized core is an ecological impossibility (O'Neill et al. 2018). As a result, despite a shared desire to transform or overcome capitalism, sections of the left place the actual stakes of the ecological crisis beyond the boundary of what is considered politically admissible. We can see this dynamic at work in the case of Pink Tide governments like those in Brazil and Ecuador, where pluralist coalitions of unions, Indigenous movements, and parties of the radical left invoked a socialist horizon but were unable to meaningfully address the socioecological destruction wrought by deepening extractivism. With media and parliamentary discourse still dominated by the normative frames of the Holocene, most parties of the left continue to accede to the parameters of economic growth, accepting continuous increases in resource use and energy consumption as the acceptable cost of building redistributive politics.

Against this calculation, the degrowth position argues that further growth has become both socially and ecologically untenable, and that the left's political project must foreground the need for a reduction in material and energy use and the creation of alternative metrics for prosperity without growth (Jackson 2016). How such a project could be taken up by unions and other organizations of the left as a revolutionary strategy is a key question, particularly in light of the accommodation to capital by previous iterations of the ecological movement, including green parties. Before looking in more detail at the degrowth alternative, I consider ecomodernism and green social democracy as two variants of left limitlessness in what follows.

Written with all the stridency of a modernist manifesto, Nick Srnicek and Alex Williams' *Inventing the Future* (2015) exemplifies the ecomodernist position, as it exhorts its readers to reinvigorate the left by embracing two core demands: the full automation of production and the provision of a universal basic income. While acknowledging the menacing convergence of socioeconomic and ecological crises as a background condition for contemporary politics, the authors point to the emergence of a set of technologies that embody the conditions of possibility for a utopian future: the Internet, 3D printing, automation, clean energy, and biotechnology (Srnicek and Williams 2015). They argue that these technologies possess the latent potential to revolutionize society as soon as the obsolete social relations restraining that potential are abolished. Their argument hearkens back to the basic historical materialist vision of social transformation in the *Contribution to the Critique of Political Economy*, where Marx argues that the development of new forces of production has the capacity to throw the social organization of production into crisis, creating the conditions for social revolution (Marx 1978). For Srnicek and Williams, it is not only capitalist class relations that stand as a fetter on progress, but also the left itself that shares responsibility for failing to accelerate social change. The authors identify what they see as a pervasive left malaise, rooted in what they term "folk politics": horizontally organized and local in orientation, folk politics focuses on prefiguration, ephemeral moments of political contestation like Occupy Wall Street or summit protests, and building experimental small-scale infrastructure like local currencies, community gardens, and cooperatives rather than building hegemony and creating new institutions at scale (Srnicek and Williams 2015). By contrast, the left future they envision involves creating think tanks, new institutions, and harnessing technology for planned production and ecological management.

Aaron Bastani's promotion of the paradigm "fully automated luxury communism" (FALC) rests on the same set of premises. Like Srnicek and Williams, Bastani sees technology as the harbinger of an emancipated social order beyond work and scarcity, which he boldly terms "communism" in contrast to Srnicek and Williams's more innocuous "postcapitalism." The three authors agree that advances in robotics and artificial intelligence point to the potential for automation to liberate all of humanity from the drudgery of wage labour, provided control over technology is democratized and wrested from the hands of tech monopolists. Bastani's technological optimism extends beyond that of his counterparts, as he promotes the claims of companies like Planetary Resources, who contend that near-Earth asteroid mining will soon put an end to mineral scarcity, enabling a limitless boom of interstellar extraction free of any terrestrial consequences (Bastani 2018). Bastani also takes up the themes of folk politics, although his approach is more conciliatory. He acknowledges that radical green politics have been meaningful in their focus on "self-transformation, experimental togetherness and immediacy," but argues that the scale of the climate crisis is such that only bold and transformative action at the state level is capable of an adequate response (Bastani 2017).

For Bastani, intervention at the state level means supporting the UK Labour Party's bid under Jeremy Corbyn to implement the most robust package of social-democratic reforms since the end of World War II, as a kind of transitional program on the way to a fully automated future. In Bastani's case, trade unions, social movements, and an engaged party membership function as the key organizational vehicles for the campaign to elect a Labour government. Once in power, the task of the left would be to coordinate the emancipatory, post-scarcity future promised by emerging technology — which would free economic development from its dependence on material constraints, including living labour. The notion that the construction of a fully automated yet sustainable future might require any reduction in energy use, material throughputs, or rates of growth is dismissed, given that developments in solar technology mean that the sun will be able to supply the planet with "limitless energy" within the coming decades (Bastani 2017).

Both iterations of ecomodernism invoke climate change as a clearly delimited challenge to be solved, and they propose new technology as the means for arriving at a solution. What is clearly absent in both approaches is an appreciation of the profound transformation of the basic conditions of human existence that the climate crisis represents, or any recognition that the crisis extends beyond the climate and into the interdependent processes of the Earth system. There is no discussion of the ongoing sixth mass extinction and its implications, either from a non-instrumental standpoint that values the lives of non-humans for their own sake or in practical terms that recognize the importance of biospheric integrity for human life (Dawson 2016). In terms of organizing strategies, the bulk of the heavy lifting is done by new technologies. Similar shortcomings are on display in the varieties of green social democracy that have proliferated since the global financial crisis. Whereas ecomodernists emphasize automation, technology, and a post-work future, green social democrats highlight the need for coordinated state expenditure to create green jobs. Advocates of a Green New Deal propose green investments of 1 to 2 percent of GDP per annum in order to build out the necessary infrastructure for a decarbonized economy while providing a major boost to employment (UNEP 2009; Pollin 2018). Alongside sections of the US Democratic Party (led by Alexandria Ocasio-Cortez), green, and social democratic parties, the labour movement is a key element in the Green New Deal scenario, with proponents including the One Million Climate Jobs campaign and groups such as the BlueGreen Alliance of labour and environmental organizations in the United States (Kenis and Lievens 2015). While some advocates of this view see a Green New Deal as a one-time stimulus to build the infrastructure necessary to avert catastrophic climate change (Cohen 2017), most variants of the deal envision a harmonious coordination of employment and economic growth extending beyond the horizon — a revival of the discredited paradigm of sustainable development.

Embracing a Contingent Future

Against the scenarios of left limitlessness premised on a vision of technological development within the arc of industrial progress, the degrowth variant of a left politics for the Anthropocene proposes a more contingent historical narrative. First, it begins with a careful consideration of the details so often omitted in growth-centric politics: the lack of any evidence for the possibility of globally decoupling economic growth from growth in material and energy consumption and their associated destruction of the Earth system (Wiedmann et al. 2015); the imperial structure of the world system that enables luxury consumption in the core while offloading the socioecological costs onto the periphery; the low relative yields of renewable energy, and the mineral, metal, and land-use implications of creating a global wind and solar grid for an economy undergoing perpetual compound growth (Hall, Lambert, and Balogh 2014); and the simultaneous disruption of the interdependent Earth systems and myriad environmental justice struggles over the impacts of resource extraction and industrial development. (A comprehensive global list is available at <ejatlas.org>.)

Second, degrowth perspectives seek to integrate the details of the foregoing analysis into the foundation of a political project as opposed to including them post-hoc as secondary considerations. Rather than simply assert the superiority of socialist rationality and the possibility of overcoming the ecological challenge through democratic planning, degrowth begins from a position of attentiveness that seeks to understand the social and ecological harms caused by capitalism's relentless growth and then build a corresponding politics of liberation. As the growing body of left ecological literature alluded to at the beginning of this chapter makes clear, both the social and the ecological ills of capitalism are expressions of the same structural organization of planetary life. In order to address those ills, a web of new technologies deployed through a massive Green New Deal will not be sufficient; the fundamental structure of socioecological relations must be transformed (Foster 2017).

The basic contours of a degrowth politics can be found across a wide range of left traditions, from the Andean Indigenous philosophy of *Buen-Vivir* and feminist ecologies to eco-socialism and social ecology. In its best articulations, eco-socialism stands as a sharp rebuke to the productivist and Promethean strains of Marxist thought, proposing a model of revolutionary transformation that makes genuine ecological sustainability a central priority. Eco-socialism seeks to reorient the aims of economic life away from abstract, fetishized calculations of exchange value as recorded in metrics such as the GDP, instead bringing it in line with the "nonmonetary and extraeconomic criteria of social needs and ecological equilibrium" (Löwy 2015: 20). Social ecology similarly recognizes the need to reorient social relations around their dependence on living ecosystems as the primary aim of a revolutionary politics. Building on the Marxian critique of capitalism, social ecology deploys a broader anthropological scope, examining the domination of nature as the historical consequence of the emergence of hierarchical forms of social organization (Bookchin 1982). There are important differences in emphasis between the two frameworks: Eco-socialism tends to focus on the capture of state power as the key site of political struggle, whereas social ecology seeks to relocalize power through the creation of community council-based governance and proposes a more immediate politics around projects like transforming food production. But the shared emphasis on the need for a revolutionary ecological politics provides fertile ground for left collaboration.

While these degrowth-compatible formations of ecological thought are useful systematizations of viable futures, the challenge ahead remains how these paradigms can be translated into near- and medium-term political strategies and meaningfully inserted into the existing terrain of political struggle. The role of labour is particularly crucial here: what happens to working-class agency in a transition away from a growth economy based on wage labour? (See Barca 2017.) Can the labour movement be decoupled from the capitalist growth model to fight for a reconfiguration of work and material provisioning within planetary boundaries? For left parties and movements contesting politics at the national scale, an immediate challenge is determining how to exit the political framing dominated by GDP and growth ideology, instead working to articulate concrete proposals in ways that emphasize their efficacy in meeting human needs rather than providing the basis for renewed growth (Kallis 2017). Jeremy Corbyn's warning to the UK financial sector that it will be brought back into the service of the public good is one of many faint intimations of such a shift, but the Labour Party continues to articulate its vision in terms of its positive effect on long-term economic growth (Piper and Schomberg 2018).

There remains much work to be done to break the stranglehold of growth on our political imagination, and to begin to build infrastructure for collective life that casts aside the hyper-individualized forms of conspicuous consumption that were made to seem necessary under capitalism. As we reach the limits of a growth model that subordinated human needs and ecological integrity to the expansion of abstract value, an augmented left must face up to the challenges of strategy and building power without succumbing to the promise of a familiar Holocene politics premised on intensified extraction and endless growth.

Note

1. Ecomodernism is a variant of "post-environmentalist" thought that emphasizes technological development as the primary solution to the ecological crisis. Whereas the environmental justice movement seeks to empower Indigenous groups, peasants, and other communities on the front lines of extraction to stop ecologically destructive development, ecomodernism argues that development can be "decoupled" from its harmful effects on vulnerable populations and the natural world. Through technologies like genetic modification and nuclear energy, ecomodernism claims that human activity can be concentrated in dense urban areas and liberated from its dependence on the biosphere, thus freeing up large tracts of land for rewilding.

References

Angus, Ian. 2016. *Facing the Anthropocene: Fossil Capitalism and the Crisis of the Earth System*. New York: Monthly Review Press.

Barca, Stefania. 2017. "The Labor(s) of Degrowth." *Capitalism Nature Socialism*, September 11. <doi.org/10.1080/10455752.2017.1373300>.

Bastani, Aaron. 2017. "Fully Automated Green Communism." *Novara Media*, November 19. <novaramedia.com/2017/11/19/fully-automated-green-communism>.

___. 2018. "Interplanetary Gold Rush." *London Review of Books*, October 26. <lrb.co.uk/blog/2017/10/26/aaron-bastani/interplanetary-gold-rush/>.

Bernes, Jasper. 2018. "The Belly of the Revolution: Agriculture, Energy, and the Future of Communism." In Brent Ryan Bellamy and Jeff Diamanti (eds.), *Materialism and the Critique of Energy*. Chicago: MCM Publishing.

Bookchin, Murray. 1982. *The Ecology of Freedom: The Emergence and Dissolution of Hierarchy*. London: Cheshire Books.

Brand, Ulrich, and Markus Wissen. 2012. "Global Environmental Politics and the Imperial Mode of Living: Articulations of State-Capital Relations in the Multiple Crisis." *Globalizations*, 9.

Burkett, Paul. 1999. *Marx and Nature: A Red and Green Perspective*. New York: Springer.

Cohen, Daniel Aldana. 2017. "The Last Stimulus." *Jacobin*, 26.

Dawson, Ashley. 2016. *Extinction: A Radical History*. New York: OR Books.

Foster, John Bellamy. 2017. "The Long Ecological Revolution." *Monthly Review*, November 1. <monthlyreview.org/2017/11/01/the-long-ecological-revolution>.
___. 2000. *Marx's Ecology: Materialism and Nature*. New York: Monthly Review Press.
Hall, Charles A.S., Jessica Lambert, and Stephen B. Balogh. 2014. "EROI of Different Fuels and the Implications for Society." *Energy Policy*, 64.
Huber, Matt. 2019. "Ecosocialism: Dystopian and Scientific." *Socialist Forum* (Winter). <socialistforum.dsausa.org/issues/winter-2019/ecosocialism-dystopian-and-scientific>.
Jackson, Tim. 2016. *Prosperity Without Growth: Foundations for the Economy of Tomorrow*. New York: Routledge.
Kallis, Giorgos. 2017. "Socialism Without Growth." *Capitalism Nature Socialism*, September 12. <doi.org/10.1080/10455752.2017.1386695>.
Kallis, Giorgos, Vasilis Kostakis, Steffen Lange, Barbara Muraca, Susan Paulson, and Matthias Schmelzer. 2018. "Research on Degrowth." *Annual Review of Environment and Resources*, 43.
Kenis, Anneleen, and Matthias Lievens. 2015. *The Limits of the Green Economy: From Re-inventing Capitalism to Re-Politicising the Present*. New York: Routledge.
Klein, Naomi. 2014. *This Changes Everything: Capitalism vs. The Climate*. New York: Simon and Schuster.
Lilley, Sasha, David McNally, Eddie Yuen, and James Davis (eds.). 2012. *Catastrophism: The Apocalyptic Politics of Collapse and Rebirth*. Oakland: PM Press.
Löwy, Michael. 2015. *Ecosocialism: A Radical Alternative to Capitalist Catastrophe*. Chicago: Haymarket Books.
Malm, Andreas. 2016. *Fossil Capital: The Rise of Steam Power and the Roots of Global Warming*. New York: Verso Books.
Marx, Karl. 1978. "A Contribution to the Critique of Political Economy." In Robert Tucker (ed.), *The Marx-Engels Reader*. New York: W.W. Norton & Company.
Mies, Maria, and Vandana Shiva. 1993. *Ecofeminism*. Black Point: Fernwood Publishing.
Moore, Jason W. 2015. *Capitalism in the Web of Life: Ecology and the Accumulation of Capital*. New York: Verso Books.
___. 2017. "The Capitalocene, Part I: On the Nature and Origins of our Ecological Crisis." *Journal of Peasant Studies*, 44, 3.
O'Neill, Daniel W., Andrew L. Fanning, William F. Lamb, and Julia K. Steinberger. 2018. "A Good Life for All within Planetary Boundaries." *Nature Sustainability*, 1.
Parenti, Christian. 2011. *Tropic of Chaos: Climate Change and the New Geography of Violence*. New York: Nation Books.
Piper, Elizabeth, and William Schomberg. 2018. "Corbyn Warns Bankers: Finance Will Serve Britain under Labour." *Reuters*, February 19. <reuters.com/article/us-britain-politics-corbyn/corbyn-warns-bankers-finance-will-serve-britain-under-labour-government-idUSKCN1G402M>.
Pollin, Robert. 2018. "De-Growth vs. a Green New Deal." *New Left Review*, 112.
Rockström, Johan, et al. 2009. "Planetary Boundaries: Exploring the Safe Operating Space for Humanity." *Ecology and Society*, 14, 2.
Srnicek, Nick, and Alex Williams. 2015. *Inventing the Future: Postcapitalism and a*

World Without Work. New York: Verso Books.
Steffen, Will, et al. 2015. "Planetary Boundaries: Guiding Human Development on a Changing Planet." *Science,* 347.
Swyngedouw, Erik. 2010. "Apocalypse Forever?" *Theory, Culture and Society,* 27, 2–3.
UNEP (United Nations Environment Programme). 2009. *Global Trends in Sustainable Energy Investment.*
Wiedmann, Thomas O., et al. 2015. "The Material Footprint of Nations." *PNAS,* 112, 20.

14. Environmental Contradictions
The Need for an Eco-socialist Paradigm on the Brazilian Left

Sabrina Fernandes

Climate change poses a global challenge to human development and sustainability in the twenty-first century. There is scientific consensus that our current mode of production, consumption, extraction, and waste creation has placed untenable burdens on the planet. The majority of demands for systemic change to avert catastrophe come from leftist social movements and grassroots collectives, with some political parties also taking up the issue (Reitan and Gibson 2012). The movements behind the *Buen-Vivir* philosophy in Bolivia (as highlighted in this volume by Javier Cuestas-Caza, Rickard Lalander, and Magnus Lembke) have inspired those involved with environmental struggles throughout Latin America, including in Brazil, yet the environment overall remains a secondary issue for political parties. One reason for this is the way these state actors insist on the environment as a separate struggle rather than an issue connected to every single aspect of an emancipatory politics. The other reason has to do with our economic paradigm.

The Global South faces constant pressure to catch up to the development of the North after centuries of exploitation and colonization. As a result, long-standing leftist actors often set aside climate action challenges in favour of large-scale extractivist and neo-developmentalist policies in their countries (Hogenboom 2012; Reitan and Gibson 2012), and so their development paradigms focus on mining and fossil fuels in addition to strengthening the industrial sector.

Brazil provides an outstanding example here: While the moderate left government of the Workers' Party recognized the reality of climate change, it nevertheless approached it as a distant problem in order to promote aggressive fossil fuel exploitation and agribusiness growth, despite these policies' contributions to carbon emissions and deforestation. Even much of the leftist opposition to the "Pink Tide" (PT) governments between 2003 and 2016 was still entrenched in the developmentalist/industrial extractivist paradigm (Fernandes 2017a), which proposed that Indigenous Peoples and the environment should make sacrifices in the name of progress. The Pink Tide refers to a series of left-wing government experiences in Latin America that were inspired by mass movements at the end of the twentieth century and in the early twenty-first century. Some of these experiences were more radical, while others may be considered centrist, including the Brazilian Pink Tide under the Lula and [Dilma] Rousseff Workers' Party governments. With far-right Jair Bolsonaro now in charge of Brazil, things are already worsening for Indigenous and leftist environmental groups across the country.

This chapter will show how left-wing considerations of environmental issues as secondary to ensuring workers are in control of the means of production in fact weakens the left's ties to important social groups, fosters a limited and instrumental relationship between parties and social movements, and fails to acknowledge the connection between working-class and environmental issues. An augmented left must move beyond this limited dynamic to integrate environmental considerations at every level, especially if it is to avoid contributing further to the global environmental crisis.

My argument is divided into three parts. First, I briefly summarize why both the PT experience in Brazil and the leftist alternatives to it have turned such a blind eye to more radical environmental concerns. Second, I look at the need for a new paradigm by exploring the potential of eco-socialism. And third, I look at how civil society organizations and grassroots movements have continued to resist these policies and propose new paradigms, and how the organized left (political parties, labour unions, and other social movements) ought to promote an inclusive political project that takes seriously the challenges created by twenty-first century capitalism. This augmented view is something the left, following the PT, should consider more carefully.

The Brazilian Pink Tide's Ecological Record

Fabio Luis Barbosa dos Santos, speaking of the Brazilian left, argues that twenty-first century socialism must face the problematic notion of progress, given that experiences around economic growth in Latin America have only deepened a state of underdevelopment. This, he writes, must be done by subordinating development to the "imperatives of equality and ecology" (dos Santos 2016: 238). Dos Santos refers to two strong contradictions of the PT experience in Brazil under the Workers' Party. First, although poverty has diminished, the capitalist class has also profited from the state's increasing financialization, which initiated class concessions and large development projects that kept Brazil safe from the global economic crisis a few years longer than the Global North. Second, these large projects proceeded despite environmental concerns and with a continuous reduction in environmental protections, thereby alienating environmental social movements — a dynamic that pervaded the PT (Fernandes 2017b). This contradiction must not be taken lightly just because the right may inflict more damage now that it is in power.

Although the Brazilian left has taken the lead in rhetorically opposing climate change, its practices lag behind. It is not uncommon to hear labour unions insisting on the maintenance of "dirty" industries such as coal mining and oil extraction for the sake of the workers involved, going as far as advocating public subsidies to ensure the economic sustainability of these sectors (Klein 2014). The support for industrial neo-extractivism on the left is justified on the basis of development, economic growth, and employment, even though there has been much greater leftist progress by Indigenous and environmental groups in Brazil on issues of pollution, deforestation, and general ecological damage.

Beyond this, most state action regarding climate change under Lula and Dilma involved alliances and partnership building with corporations and the market. In promoting both fossil fuels and renewable energy like ethanol, the governments were unable to move Brazil into a less oil-dependent and carbon-intensive scenario.

The Radical Left's Own Environmental Contradictions

One segment of the non-PT left is closer to the centre. However, the other part of the non-PT left, which I refer to elsewhere as the radical left (Fernandes 2017b) and whose aspirations bend toward socialism and communism, also contains its own contradictions regarding the environment. The three main parties of the radical left — the Socialism and Freedom Party (PSOL), the Unified Socialist Workers' Party (PSTU), and the Brazilian Communist Party (PCB) — have provisions that consider the environment from an anti-capitalist perspective and favour environmental sustainability (Barros 2015). However, the extent to which environmental politics are capable of swaying the parties' general political demands in one direction or the other is another matter.

While the three parties are fierce opponents of large-scale agribusiness and have stood in defence of peasants, Indigenous Peoples, and traditional communities, they are not generally directly involved in land-based social movements and struggles. This difference is reinforced through the radical left's relative focus on urban spaces, by the difficulty it encounters in building strong political relations on the PT's turf, and by its inadequate efforts to connect with rural and agrarian environmental movements. Thus, while parties on the radical left generally see the environmental crisis as a problem, they justify their lack of engagement in terms of their smaller size, structure, and inability to be everywhere. In contrast, an augmented left — one that perceives environmental concerns as core to every struggle — would see these connections as a precondition for growth in strength and numbers. This would require not only an alliance with other social movements, but also work directed at growing the whole of the left by inviting new subjects into the eco-socialist paradigm.

In general, the current paradigm advanced by the radical left is one in which progress and the environment must be reconciled through workers' control of resources. In many left proposals, the environment appears as a side issue that can be considered and summoned whenever it fits into the central agenda. While this may have positive short-term results, it does not comprehensively address how workers' immediate economic interests might be at odds with the ecosystems affected by their industries. This is often the case when a labour union would rather keep an open-pit mine in operation to guarantee employment than push for green jobs and transition initiatives through political activism. When it comes to environmental issues, the radical left's mitigated approach is problematic in the long term, since the impacts of the environmental crisis will be borne disproportionately by the working class.

Even the Green New Deal proposal in the US, which is limited and awfully ecomodernist, looks very radical next to the Brazilian left's weak environmental considerations. However, ideas connected to the Andean Indigenous *Buen-Vivir* ("good living") and degrowth movements show up in official speeches and, indeed, efforts to translate such ideas through the government have resulted in legislative changes in Bolivia and Ecuador. As discussed in this section, though, the practice of entrenching the rights of nature into constitutions and declarations actually does very little in initiating the radical material change necessary to develop and promote alternative ecological praxis.

In Brazil, where bold legislation of this nature is lacking, there is a fundamental need for the left to augment its conceptualizations of the environment, climate change, and the impacts of ecosystem disturbances that will be inordinately felt by the working class it claims to represent. As the contradictions of capital and the environment meet the paradoxes in the leftist vision of progress and ecology, the left is being forced to reconsider previous notions of environmental politics that would either fall into a technocratic trap or simply treat the environment as secondary to working-class demands.

Although this chapter focuses more on surveying the state of the Brazilian left on these issues, it would be fruitful to explore the potential for leftist growth in Brazil through the development and integration of eco-socialist demands. Eco-socialism is key here, because it encompasses enough of a paradigm shift that it can end the left's habit of circling back as it tries to integrate environmental concerns. By moving from left-wing environmentalism to eco-socialism, the left will be able to see how the environment and nature should have been treated as core to the leftist project all along.

The Brazilian Left Needs a New Paradigm

The anti-capitalist left in Latin America has been very accepting of the continued exploitation of natural resources, provided they are under a state-based model of socialized control. In the case of Bolivia, for example, neo-extractivism is paired with foreign mining investment despite the socialist government's own environmentally friendly discourse and its role in initiatives such as the Cochabamba Protocol (Foster, Clark, and York 2010; Pellegrini 2016). This gap between discourse and action confirms Eduardo Gudynas' thesis that leftist politics in these countries is often subordinated to a "new extractivism" that is justified on the basis of the royalties and jobs it provides toward social development under state control (Gudynas 2010; Veltmeyer 2013). Indeed, leftist governments and organizations, despite claiming environmental justice movements as part of their legacy, have a much more complicated relationship with climate change.

Despite the growing relevance of nature as a legitimate subject of Marxism, analyses that inform concrete action tend to be filtered to focus on immediate economic needs rather than on the long-term effects of the spoliation of nature and its consequences for life on Earth. Questions over the social, environmental, and economic consequences of carbon-intensive production may have made their way into Marxist circles, but these continue to be crucially absent from important mobilizations that are informed by Marxist analysis on other matters.

Michael Löwy (2005: xi) defines eco-socialism as a radical proposition because it "distinguishes itself from the productivist varieties of socialism in the twentieth century … as well as from the ecological currents that accommodate themselves in one way or another to the capitalist system." This balance is a matter of praxis — the eco-socialist left must be coherent in the perspective it upholds and the mobilizations it promotes. However, this concern is currently at the margins of the global left, including in countries where the left is responsible for impactful ecological discourse but has failed to adapt and change at the policy level.

One important way to handle this fissure between the left and ecology is to conceptualize eco-socialism as a major paradigm shift. This requires emphasizing how eco-socialism means more than adding some green to socialism; it demands the building of an ecological perspective *within* socialism. This entails, for example, expanding on Löwy's (2002: 131) view that eco-socialism "proposes a strategy of alliance between the 'reds' and the 'greens,' the labor and ecological movements, and of solidarity with the oppressed and exploited of the South." It means that to overcome the dichotomy between humans and nature, as eco-socialism demands, we also need to overcome the dichotomy between red and green — that is, labour and environmentalism. To move beyond the productivist paradigm, eco-socialism must be understood as a paradigm of its own. That is why our approach must be not simply environmental, but ecological — integrating human society as part of nature, not as separate from it.

John Bellamy Foster (2000) argues that there is room for the Marxist left to overcome its contradictions and selective approach to the environment in order to devise new ways of organizing our societies and economies toward sustainability, environmental consciousness, and low-carbon systems. Marx did not propose a productivist paradigm as homogeneous; in fact, his analysis of industry pointed to the inherent contradictions between humans and nature, as much in terms of the latter being the property of the former as the unsustainability of the continuous exploitation of the planet if one indeed desires to see future generations live well in an alternative society under a new economic system.

A careful reading of Marx's life work and his materialism evinces his denunciation of this toxic and unbalanced relation (Foster 2000), producing important debates in what has been labelled "second-stage" eco-socialism. Whereas at first, eco-socialism grew out of confronting socialism with newly formed "green theory," the second stage moves beyond "adding green to red" in order to search for a green basis within the red politics of historical materialism. For Löwy, who actively engages in both first- and second-stage debates, Marx's thought was not complete and sometimes produced uncritical positions regarding capital's use of nature (Löwy 2002). This is why eco-socialist theory had to evolve beyond Marx's writings and other contributions from Marxist orthodoxy to develop a unique philosophy that uses the main Marxian vision of emancipation to consider the conditions for total transformation of life on Earth, resource limits, and the importance of challenging anthropocentrism through promoting human stewardship rather than domination.

Third-stage eco-socialist research, as considered by Foster and Burkett, is germinating today and its "goal is to employ the ecological foundations of classical Marxian thought to confront present-day capitalism and the planetary ecological crisis that it has engendered" (Foster in Burkett 2014: xii). Hannah Holleman (2015) defines this as a commitment to Marx's eleventh thesis on Feuerbach: theorizing the world in order to change it. Through this task, it is important to consider how grassroots approaches from the Global South offer a unique opportunity. The Latin American left needs eco-socialism to grow its perspective and capacity, and without South-based epistemologies and actors, eco-socialism will not move, dialectically, from research to action.

Grassroots Resistance and Eco-socialist Proposals

There are currently a few opportunities to investigate the use of eco-socialist praxis to augment the left in Brazil, even if most of the action being taken is still perceived as simple left-wing environmentalism by those involved. Beyond the leftist parties and their contradictions, environmentalism is well and alive today — but not always leftist. It is very common to find strong environmental groups in Brazil whose critique hardly escapes a localist or conservationist logic. It is no wonder that the largest political parties dealing with the environmental agenda fall into the green capitalism spectrum — both Rede Sustentabilidade and Brazil's Green Party. Because of this, the grassroots groups and social movements that promote both a socialist view and integration with environmentalist demands tend to focus on their struggles, with few expectations that the parties will be involved long term. Since most of the movements tied to the Vía Campesina network have a relationship with the PT, they do not always interact directly with the radical left parties, although this is becoming more common whenever there is a dispute between the movement's base and the leadership. One such example is at selected MST (Landless Workers' Movement) occupations throughout Brazil, where part of the base has opted to work with radical left parties such as the PSOL, despite the PT orientation of the MST's national coordination.

Overall, the deteriorating situation within particular communities around specific environmental issues has drawn the radical left parties closer while also creating fruitful ground for leftist collaboration beyond radical left divisions. This has been visible in struggles around water: In 2015, the state of São Paulo went through a serious water crisis under the administration of a right-wing PSDB (Social Democracy Party) government; it forced most of the left to fight together for the right to water in poorer communities, which experienced disproportionate water rationing versus rich neighbourhoods. Other states have gone through similar situations, in which campesino communities, right-to-the-city movements, local leaders, and leftist militants have come together to pressure their governments toward a new paradigm of water management that considers the surrounding ecosystems. These initiatives demonstrate that this is not simply about better water distribution and avoiding waste, but it also involves preserving water springs, reorganizing cities, and fighting agribusinesses' control over water sources.

With the corporate World Water Forum in Brazil in 2018, the Brazilian left worked together to organize an Alternative World Water Forum. Although most of the conflicts during the forum's organizing reflected the fragmented dynamics of the local left and internal disputes, the event itself presented an array of examples of eco-socialist thinking at the grassroots level. The forum lasted five days, and thousands of organizations and activists representing political parties, collectives, social movements, labour unions, local communities, and NGOs met to think of strategies not just around water rights, but also many other issues related to an integrated eco-socialist perspective: feminism, Indigenous struggles, territorial conflicts, corporate greed, racism, radical democracy, leftist unity, permaculture, agroecology, energy alternatives, climate action, elections, arts, union tactics, and veganism.

During the forum, activists expressed with frustration that it generally requires a crisis or tragedy, such as the Samarco destruction of the Doce River or the brewing water wars in Brazil, to alert the left of the need for more coordinated action around environmental protection. When it comes to climate change, the direct results of which are not yet immediately acknowledged in Brazil, local collectives pushing for climate action have to exert a lot of pressure to even get supportive statements from institutions within the organized left.

Outside of traditional leftist circles, where environmental concerns are still perceived as just a niche struggle, eco-socialism presents itself as a way to renew the left. This is important, especially when trying to mobilize around environmental issues with people who otherwise feel repelled by the contradictions of twentieth-century socialism; eco-socialism holds potential for augmenting the left because it requires a paradigm shift that can appeal to those who identify with leftist struggles but have felt frustrated with the dominant left-wing dogma of the past. Further, the more people begin to identify with eco-socialism, the greater their need to organize around these struggles — a dynamic we have seen in the recent creation of the Latin American Eco-socialist Alliance in Brazil. Eco-socialism is reverberating across more conversations throughout the country, with growing interest from organizations inside of PSOL and from collectives inclined toward ecofeminism. Indigenous organizations, such as Brazil's Association of Indigenous Peoples (APIB), have been actively organizing and their work pushes the left to acknowledge their rights and connection to nature as matters that affect the whole of society.

The elements of the Brazilian left engaged with environmentalism are still minor compared to the left that favours industrial extractivism and neo-developmentalism. While this shows that the current paradigm is indeed narrow and lacks due emphasis on nature and ecology, it also points to windows of opportunity to communicate precisely what is needed. It is not enough to expand the conversation about the environment throughout the left, since the issues are known but the effort and focus required are absent. Rather, it is necessary to augment it through a paradigm shift that will overcome the current contradictions by no longer separating demands as red and green but integrating them as part of the same eco-socialist struggle.

References

Barros, Antonio Teixeira de. 2015. "Política partidária e meio ambiente: a adesão dos partidos políticos brasileiros à agenda verde." *Opinião Pública,* 21, 3.

Burkett, Paul. 2014. *Marx and Nature: A Red and Green Perspective.* Chicago: Haymarket Press.

dos Santos, Fabio Luis Barbosa. 2016. *Além do PT,* 2nd edition. São Paulo: Editora Elefante.

Fernandes, Sabrina. 2017a. "Assessing the Brazilian Workers' Party." *Jacobin,* 25.

___. 2017b. "Crisis of Praxis: Depoliticization and Leftist Fragmentation in Brazil." PhD thesis, Carleton University, Ottawa.

Foster, John Bellamy. 2000. *Marx's Ecology: Materialism and Nature.* New York: Monthly Review Press.

Foster, John Bellamy, Brett Clark, and Richard York. 2010. *The Ecological Rift: Capitalism's War on the Earth.* New York: Monthly Review Press.

Gudynas, Eduardo. 2010. "The New Extractivism of the 21st Century: Ten Urgent Theses about Extractivism in Relation to Current South American Progressivism."

Americas Program Report, January 21. Washington, DC: Center for International Policy.

Hogenboom, Barbara. 2012. "Depoliticized and Repoliticized Minerals in Latin America." *Journal of Developing Societies*, 28, 2.

Holleman, Hannah. 2015. "Method in Ecological Marxism: Science and the Struggle for Change." *Monthly Review*, 67, 5.

Klein, Naomi. 2014. *This Changes Everything*. New York: Simon & Schuster.

Löwy, Michael. 2002. "From Marx to Ecosocialism." *Capitalism Nature Socialism*, 13, 1.

___. 2005. What Is Ecosocialism? *Capitalism Nature Socialism*, 16, 2.

Pellegrini, Lorenzo. 2016." Resource Nationalism in the Plurinational State of Bolivia." In P.A. Haslam and P. Heidrich (eds.), *The Political Economy of Natural Resources and Development*. New York: Routledge.

Reitan, Ruth, and Shannon Gibson. 2012. "Climate Change or Social Change? Environmental and Leftist Praxis and Participatory Action Research." *Globalizations*, 9, 3.

Veltmeyer, Henry. 2013. "The Political Economy of Natural Resource Extraction: A New Model or Extractive Imperialism?" *Canadian Journal of Development Studies*, 34, 1.

15. Andean Intercultural Eco-socialism in Times of *Buen-Vivir*?
A Red-Green-Culturalist Approach

Javier Cuestas-Caza, Rickard Lalander, and Magnus Lembke

From the 1990s onward, amid an increasingly rejected neoliberalism, nationally organized and internationally connected Indigenous movements strengthened their political positions in Bolivia and Ecuador. Against this backdrop, newly elected left-leaning Andean governments had to invent new formulas for how to bring Indigenous Peoples, speaking with their own voices, under their banner — that is, incorporating them into a unified force. A dominant reorientation was to introduce a radical model of resource governance, sometimes equated with eco-socialism (Löwy 2014), that arguably respects the rights of nature and Indigenous Peoples and challenges traditional notions of development understood as economic growth. This approach was incorporated in the new constitutions of Ecuador (2008) and Bolivia (2009) and was applauded worldwide by eco-activists and other advocates of social justice and group-differentiated rights. Some observers projected an eco-socialism with a new twist, one that overcame the dichotomy between red and green (see Fernandes, this volume), merging not only class struggle and environmental concerns, but also Indigenous knowledges and the Indigenous moral-philosophical conceptualizations of *Sumak Kawsay/Buen-Vivir*.[1] For some years, *Buen-Vivir* evolved into a red-green-culturalist epistemic-ontological platform and consequently became an attractive political, strategic, and potentially unifying asset for the left.

This chapter examines how the historical dilemma of creating a unified leftist force has been addressed in contemporary Ecuador and, to a limited extent, in Bolivia — that is, in settings marked by politically influential Indigenous movements. In our view, the new constitutions, and particularly the rise of *Buen-Vivir* as a political buzzword, fostered a historical opportunity for the left to create a common platform giving equal recognition to both universalist and particularistic identities. The new constitutional texts demonstrated that traditional generations of citizenship rights (civil, political, and social) had finally coalesced into a uniform call that also included the specific rights of nature/*Pachamama* and the collective rights of Indigenous Peoples (Lalander 2014, 2017; Lalander and Lembke 2018). At the discursive and institutional levels, at least, the stage was set for leftist unification.

As it seemed at the time, a common leftist-Indigenous agenda with strong ecological overtones had thus emerged, emphasizing the mid- and long-term ambition to leave "the oil in the soil, the coal in the hole, and the gas under the grass." A window of opportunity had been opened for *Andean intercultural eco-socialism*, a notion we chose to portray a red-green-culturalist project brought to fruition by means of a common adherence to *Buen-Vivir*.

Nevertheless, within a few years it was apparent in both countries that the prospect for a unified agenda was not within immediate reach. What primarily ended this historical opportunity, however, was not the revitalization of long-term ideological contradictions among and between the principal actors. The upshot was rather a deliberate governmental political turn to policies that would jeopardize the prospect for a red-green-culturalist liaison: neo-extractivism[2] and the advancement of the so-called Citizens' Revolution (*Revolución Ciudadana*), both of which were accompanied by a seeming governmental unwillingness to turn the country in a pluri-national[3] direction.

A Hobsbawmian Approach to Particularism-Universalism

Eric Hobsbawm (1996) wrote a short text on the challenge of identity-politics for left-wing political movements. Although a great number of identity groups had been historically supported by the left, their particularistic worldviews clashed with the universal ambition of the leftist project.

> The political project of the left is universalist: it is for all human beings. However ... identity politics is essentially not for everybody but for the members of a specific group only. This is perfectly evident in the case of ethnic or nationalist movements.... The nationalist claim that they are for everyone's right to self-determination is bogus. That is why the left cannot base itself on identity politics. It has a wider agenda. (Hobsbawm 1996: 43)

According to Hobsbawm, the universalist principle is thus paramount within the overall leftist project. In other words, the project cannot be defined as the sum of multiple identity-based groups giving priority to their own particular rights and cultural expressions. Although such groups frequently have joined the left, such alignments have often been made for short-term tactical reasons. Since their collective identities are negatively defined (us versus them), these groups are accordingly not ready for an unconditional submission to universalism (Hobsbawm 1996).

We take issue with this claim, arguing that certain universal rights hinge on forms of particularism that should enjoy a priori recognition. Indigenous Peoples across the world know that universalism is a double-edged sword. On the one hand, they may adhere to the principle of respecting and defending universal human values, thus accepting that any order aiming at upholding equal rights must be culturally neutral. On the other hand, their experiences tell them that universalism is rooted in a specific historical hierarchy known to them as neocolonialism. For an Andean left that has taken on the mission of rolling back the heritage of colonialism, aligning with Indigenous movements thus requires some form of particularization of universalism. In our study, the particularization of universalism refers to the process in which the state and dominant non-Indigenous society increasingly promote the recognition of Indigenous collective rights as a necessity for guaranteeing equal right for all citizens.

Similarly, for Indigenous movements that aspire to join forces with the left, a universalization of particularism is warranted. Here, the universalization of particularism refers to the process through which ethnically defined peoples include the universal dimension of equal citizenship rights on their political agendas. At stake is not the triumph of universal unity over particularistic diversity or vice versa, but unity in diversity. Moving in that direction not only requires a dismantling of coloniality; it requires constructing a new social contract, forged within intercultural arenas where top-down state policies intersect with bottom-up societal calls for change.

Universalist and Particularist Perspectives of *Buen-Vivir*

As mentioned, the rewriting of the Ecuadorian (and Bolivian) constitutions gave legitimacy to a project based on universal and particularistic ideals, on the one hand, and a confluence between leftist, ethnic, and environmental ideas, on the other. More concretely, what took place was a rapprochement between leading Indigenous organizations and the leftist governments of Rafael Correa (Ecuador) and Evo Morales (Bolivia). Because of that alignment, the notion of *Buen-Vivir/Vivir Bien* evolved into an important aspect of the new constitutions and national politics. *Buen-Vivir* is a difficult term to define; in fact, it is a concept in permanent construction and dispute (Le Quang 2017).[4] This fact has given rise to at least three currents of thought on *Buen-Vivir*: Indigenous-culturalist, post-development ecologist, and statist-socialist (Cubillo-Guevara, Hidalgo-Capitán, and Domínguez 2014; Le Quang and Vercoutére 2013; Le Quang 2017; Villalba-Eguiluz and Etxano 2017). Despite the evident differences that exist between each current, there is a certain consensus in understanding *Buen-Vivir* as an umbrella concept that brings together a set of knowledge and practices that imagine and pursue life forms other than Western modernity, the capitalist system, and the discourse of development. *Buen-Vivir* is inspired by the cosmo-visions of the original peoples of Latin America, with special emphasis on the communion between human beings and nature (Walsh 2008). At the same time, *Buen-Vivir* suggests that the ideal life is "in harmony with oneself, with society and with nature" (Cubillo-Guevara, Hidalgo-Capitán, and García-Álvarez 2016: 36). Under a social change approach, *Buen-Vivir* can be understood as an intercultural political project (Vanhulst 2015) where, theoretically, three principles can converge (Cubillo-Guevara et al. 2016): sustainability, demanded by ecologists (green); identity, demanded by Indigenous Peoples (culturalist); and equity, demanded by the less-favoured classes (red). For governments, the notion was ambitiously defined, encompassing red, green, and culturalist ambitions. In the Ecuadorian case, this convergence was further accentuated in the *National Development Plan for Buen-Vivir* (PNBV) for 2013–17.

Some stressed that the rapid ascendance of the notion had turned *Buen-Vivir* into an ambiguous political term (Bretón-Solo, Cortez, and García 2014). The PNBV, for example, advocated a mix of individualism and collectivism/communalism, thus signalling a shift away from the strictly Hobsbawmian version of universalism. At the same time, the plan put forth a rather traditional view in which communalism was essentially equated with Western ideas of nationalism and socialism. Accordingly, many soon began to question the initial post-constitutional impression that the government and the Indigenous movement would approach each other by means of a double discursive transformation — a particularization of universalism and a universalization of particularism. As it seemed, critics argued, the governments had simply brought Indigenous terminology into the day-to-day political jargon, adapting it to a model still largely constructed on universalism above particularism.

We argue that *Buen-Vivir* gradually developed into a "floating signifier" (Laclau 2005): a sign used, interpreted, and defined differently by various rivalling political actors in their endeavours to (re)construct identities, struggles, and antagonisms — a signifier floating between contrasting dominant political projects that are seeking to determine how society ought to be structured. Indeed, this elasticity even convinced the government that it could stick to it while simultaneously encouraging an incremental turn toward a "highly extractivist and modernist model based on bureaucratic and technocratic logics" (Alonso-González and Macías-Vázquez 2015: 315). Accordingly, in the aftermath of the constitutional enactments, interpretation of *Buen-Vivir* went down different pathways, causing increasing polarization between universalistic and particularistic interpretations. For the Indigenous movements, the governments had turned *Buen-Vivir* into a concept roughly equal to welfare policies for the poor. In their view, the governments had inserted it into a discourse that propagated a continued attack on nature. It seemed *Buen-Vivir* had lost its galvanizing potentiality.

In our view, the problem was *not* that *Buen-Vivir* increasingly came to serve as a floating signifier. Many political concepts acclaimed by the left have first emerged in floating forms. Only with time have concepts like *democracy* and *citizenship* acquired more fixed meanings, through popular resistance and governmental reforms. In fact, floating signifiers may possess an important and adequate function when it comes to joining apparently contradictory epistemological-ontological perspectives into a common political movement. *Buen-Vivir* had that capacity, particularly after having been incorporated into central paragraphs of the new constitutions.

The problem was instead that the leftist Ecuadorian and Bolivian governments, in their political practice and rhetoric, started to abandon the project of *Buen-Vivir*. As an immediate counter-response, the Indigenous movements in turn largely abandoned their efforts to approach the government. From being an open-ended concept with great potential to serve as a tool for leftist unification and for Andean intercultural eco-socialism, *Buen-Vivir* bifurcated into two diametrically differing interpretations: one emphasizing universalism over particularism, one stressing particularism above universalism.

The Citizens' Revolution and Neo-extractivism

As argued in the introduction, a window of opportunity for a unified left had opened as a result of the constitutional incorporation of Indigenous moral-philosophical conceptualizations and traditions. However, only a few years after the triumphant ascendance of *Buen-Vivir* as the leitmotif for a red-green-culturalist project, the concept had seemingly lost its unifying potential. Focusing on Ecuador, we argue that the loss of strength of *Buen-Vivir* is associated with a dual governmental reorientation: toward a political novelty known as the Citizens' Revolution and toward an increasing focus on progressive extractivism.

The Citizens' Revolution emerged as the centrepiece of the political program of the PAIS (Proud and Sovereign Homeland)-Correa administration. It rested on the duality of class and individual citizenship (citizenization)[5] and called for social de-sectorization — that is, the identification of everybody as citizens by means of abolishing social stratifications along the lines of ethnicity, religion, gender, et cetera. With its individualist and modernist ambitions, the revolution aimed to construct state-society relations that were not rooted in ethnic, religious, or gender-based cleavages (see Ospina and Lalander 2012). In this sense, it collided with the constitutional affirmation of the pluri-national state and the recognition of the collectivist practices and traditions of ethnically defined peoples. An important purpose was also, allegedly, to weaken an Indigenous movement that had acquired significant mobilizing capacity and discursive coherence. With its attack on collectivism, pluri-nationality, and local autonomy, the Citizens' Revolution added to an already infected relationship between the Correa administration and the Indigenous movement. Leading representatives of the Ecuadorian Indigenous movement interpreted citizenization as an attempt by the Correa-PAIS government to divide their organizations and co-opt their leaders (Ospina and Lalander 2012). For them, the new and progressive ethno-ecological vocabulary had largely turned into cosmetic constitutional adjustments, including the notion of *Buen-Vivir*.

Turning to the second reorientation of the Correa administration, toward progressive extractivism, it is worth repeating that the constitution was initially celebrated worldwide for recognizing the cultural particularities of Indigenous communities and for its commitment to protect nature, even declaring nature a subject of rights. It soon became evident, however, that the implementation of the red-green-culturalist agenda was severely circumscribed by powerful economic and political interests related particularly to key strategic sectors of the national economy, such as hydrocarbons and mining. Elsewhere, this contradiction has metaphorically been referred to as a straitjacket for progressive governments. Although the constitutionally recognized ethnic and environmental rights may have been anchored in good intentions and serious political commitments, they were increasingly perceived as, at best, long-term political visions. The ostensible message was instead that their immediate realization would hamper the ability of the government to carry out necessary and progressive welfare policies by means of revenues derived from extractive industries (Lalander 2014). Today, Indigenous movements, energized by constitutional promises, are increasingly placing themselves at loggerheads with the *realpolitik* of extractivist-based welfare policies that, in their view, not only threaten fragile biosystems but also local cultures and societies.

As this exceedingly extractivist reorientation proceeded, Indigenous movement representatives began asserting that *Buen-Vivir* and other

Indigenous principles, such as pluri-nationality and interculturality, had been symbolically appropriated (co-opted) by the government (Ospina and Lalander 2012) to serve as developmental neologisms in a discursive apparatus that legitimized extractive policies and citizenization. As the route toward pluri-nationality and intercultural eco-socialism became increasingly truncated, two separate interpretations of *Buen-Vivir* surfaced. Whereas the Indigenous movement turned to connotations rooted primarily in particularistic and ethnically centred understandings of political relationships, nature, and mankind — simultaneously somewhat downplaying welfare universalism and Hobsbawmian leftism — the government preferred to interpret *Buen-Vivir* as a mere appendix to social rights. *Buen-Vivir* became, in the official discourse, something that could be achieved, at least in the short run, by an extractivist reorientation.

The marginalization of traditional Indigenous grievances as a result of the Citizens' Revolution being financed by expansive progressive extractivism is perhaps best exemplified by looking at the conflicts that emerged between the government and its transnational allies, on the one hand, and Indigenous communities, on the other. In the table below, we have selected three well-known cases to exemplify these conflicts (Table 1).[6]

For our purposes, it is important to repeat that the notion of *Buen-Vivir*

Table 1. Cases of conflict due to extractive policies in Ecuador

Public Policy	Constitution 2008	Cases (Examples)	Conflicts
Mining	Arts. 57, 71–74, 317, 408	*Quimsacocha* Project, *Mirador* Project	Collective/Indigenous rights, agricultural degradation, human displacement, water degradation, diseases
Hydrocarbons	Arts. 57, 71, 74, 317, 407–408	*Yasuní*-ITT (oilfields)	Rights of nature, rights of Indigenous Peoples and peoples in voluntary isolation, biodiversity, environmental pollution
Agribusiness	Arts. 60, 281–282, 318, 411	Monocrops of banana, sugar cane and African palm, floriculture	Land-grabbing, access to water, small-scale versus large-scale agriculture

Prepared by the authors

was, following the constitutional rewriting, inserted in two distinct lines of argument, the first seeing it as the end goal of policies that prioritized extractivism, the second associating it with the very resistance to such policies. A demarcation had emerged between the universalist, citizenship-based and the particularistic, ethnicity-based versions; in *Mirador*, *Quimsacocha*, *Yasuní*, and various sites of agribusiness expansion, the left was divided, as was the notion of *Buen-Vivir*.

Concluding Reflections: *Buen-Vivir* as Andean Intercultural Eco-socialism

We have argued here that *Buen-Vivir* represents a concept and discourse that seemingly managed to capture the idea of a harmonious red-green-culturalist coexistence. To a certain degree, it also captured the optimistic idea that a window of opportunity had finally opened for true and meaningful post-liberal politics. Still, as soon as *Buen-Vivir* gained broader public legitimacy, it was thrust into a particular statist reorientation toward citizenization and extractivism. Hence, what eventually ended the historic opportunity for leftist unity was not inherent ideological contradictions but a deliberate governmental turn to policies that undermined the red-green-culturalist agenda. Closing the circle between theory and practice has been a weakness for the Ecuadorian left in terms of interculturality,[7] since both the political project of *Buen-Vivir* as well as state action have been coexisting under restrictions in a modern/colonial capitalist system. The challenge is to learn from the experience of the last ten years and to continue to improve theoretically the concept of *Buen-Vivir* as well as the discussion of revolutionary ecological politics (see Ravensbergen in this volume).

Drawing on a Hobsbawmian approach, we identified two current interpretations of *Buen-Vivir*. The first stresses that its agenda must be inserted into a general framework prioritizing universalism above particularism, while the second claims that the road toward universalism and societal equity requires a recomposition of state-societal relations in accordance with a formula giving initial preference to particularism above universalism. In our view, neither of these interpretations truly answer the call for unity in diversity — an ambition that must be at the forefront of leftist unification.

Before the partition of *Buen-Vivir* into two distinct senses (unity above diversity and diversity above unity) the notion offered a potential symbiosis. Today, the initial vision of a joint, harmonious, red-green-cultural project has been torn apart by increasing state-societal animosity. This essay does not give preference to either the universalist or the particularist version of a red-green-culturalist agenda, though it suggests that the division into two distinct *Buen-Vivir* interpretations assisted in closing a unique window of opportunity for leftist unification.

A central problem with *Buen-Vivir* is accordingly that it has so far floated too much. At the same time, some degree of floating is unavoidable and even necessary, considering the different epistemic-ontological standpoints of the actors involved. In a previous study, Mathieu Le Quang and Tamia Vercoutère (2013) proposed a beneficial fusion of *Buen-Vivir* with eco-socialism. We hold that acknowledging the complexity of the red-green-culturalist quandary requires a systematic juxtaposition of eco-socialism and *Buen-Vivir/Vivir Bien*, paying attention to both tensions and compatibilities between them (Lalander and Lembke 2018).

Our idea of Andean intercultural eco-socialism follows this line of reasoning. It proposes a way to overcome the polarization between universalism and particularism through a vision anchored in eco-socialism and a position rooted in two processes: 1) a decolonial reconstruction of universalism, moving away from monocultural, Eurocentric and neoliberal understandings of state and nation; and, simultaneously, 2) a universalization of particularism — that is, an expansion and de-indigenization of *Buen-Vivir*. Moreover, in combining class, ethnicity and ecologism, Andean intercultural eco-socialism is perceived as a societal project rather than a statist one.

The inclusion of *Buen-Vivir* into the constitutional text could have been a step toward a redefinition of universalism, thus fuelling the possibility of a new national identity from below.

Such an interpretation of *Buen-Vivir* would still embody a certain elasticity (it would float); but it would be neither an empty concept nor a tool to co-opt and disarm an Indigenous movement.

In this context, some questions remain. Could diversity be an element in a project seeking the re-construction of national identity? How much should a concept like *Buen-Vivir* float or be elastic in order for it to serve as a unifying notion within such a project? Our conviction is that a floating signifier may serve opposing political doctrines as a tool, but that it may also be used as a vehicle for bringing former combatants into a broader (leftist) political movement.

Finally, for such a movement to materialize in Ecuador, we argue, *Buen-Vivir* must be inserted into an overall project seeking unity in diversity. In adhering to such a project, the state and the Indigenous movement may jointly address the complex process of inclusive nation-building from below.

Notes

1. *Buen-Vivir* (Spanish) and *Sumak Kawsay* (Kichwa) are the conceptual labels used in Ecuador, whereas in Bolivia, the corresponding concepts are *Vivir Bien* (Spanish) and *Suma Qamaña* (Aymara). Regarding the translation of *Sumak Kawsay* into *Buen-Vivir*, we should mention that several academics and Indigenous intellectuals have criticized this simplification. For more detail of the semantic differences between *Sumak Kawsay* and *Buen-Vivir*, see Lalander and Cuestas-Caza 2017; Cuestas-Caza 2018.
2. In this text, we define extractivism as "the extraction of natural resources, in large volume and intensity, mainly to be exported as raw materials" (Gudynas 2015: 13).
3. In this text, pluri-nationality refers to a concept that seeks to overcome the condition of racism, exclusion, and violence that characterizes the modern nation-state. Pluri-nationality seeks recognition and extension of the rights of ethnic minorities (self-determination, collective rights, territory, self-government) while seeking the redefinition of the social contract, through unity in diversity (Chuji 2008).
4. For further interpretations of the different versions of *Buen-Vivir*, see, for example, Cubillo-Guevara, Hidalgo-Capitán and Domínguez 2014; Bretón-Solo, Cortez, and García 2014; Domínguez, Caria, and León 2017; Lalander and Cuestas-Caza 2017; Lalander and Lembke 2018.
5. In this chapter, *citizenization* refers to the establishment of a political order in which individuals — not collectives — are key political subjects and primary recipients of state-distributed rights.
6. Due to space limitations, we will not go into detail on the empirical cases (see, for example, Ospina and Lalander 2012; Sánchez-Vázquez, Leifsen, and Verdú-Delgado 2017; Silveira et al. 2017).
7. In this text, interculturality refers to the construction of harmonious inter-ethnic relationships in societies characterized by diversity, while simultaneously acknowledging the historical and current existence of racism and discrimination. Such inter-ethnic coexistence is perceived as something that in the long run strengthens society (Walsh 2008).

References

Alonso-González, P., and A. Macías-Vázquez. 2015. "An Ontological Turn in the Debate on Buen Vivir — Sumak Kawsay in Ecuador: Ideology, Knowledge, and the Common." *Latin American and Caribbean Ethnic Studies*, 10, 3 (June).

Bretón-Solo, Víctor, David Cortez, and Fernando García. 2014. "En Busca del Sumak Kawsay: Presentación del Dossier." Íconos: Revista de Ciencias Sociales, 48 (January).

Chuji, Mónica. 2008. "Diez conceptos básicos sobre plurinacionalidad e interculturalidad." América Latina en movimiento, September 11. <alainet.org/es/active/23366>.

Cubillo-Guevara, Ana, Antonio Hidalgo-Capitán, and José Domínguez. 2014. "El pensamiento sobre el Buen Vivir. Entre el indigenismo, el socialismo y el posdesarrollismo." *Reforma y Democracia*, 60 (October).

Cubillo-Guevara, Ana, Antonio Hidalgo-Capitán, and Santiago García-Álvarez. 2016. "El Buen Vivir como alternativa al desarrollo para América Latina." *Iberoamerican Journal of Development Studies*, 5, 2.

Cuestas-Caza, Javier. 2018. "Sumak Kawsay Is Not Buen Vivir." *Alternautas*, 5, 1 (July).

Domínguez, Rafael, Sara Caria, and Mauricio León. 2017. "Buen Vivir: Praise, Instrumentalization, and Reproductive Pathways of Good Living in Ecuador." *Latin American and Caribbean Ethnic Studies*, 12, 2 (June).

Gudynas, Eduardo. 2015. *Extractivismos: Ecología, Economía y Política de un Modo de Entender el Desarrollo y la Naturaleza*. Cochabamba: CLAES-CEDIB.

Hobsbawm, Eric. 1996. "Identity Politics and the Left." *New Left Review*, 1.

Laclau, Ernesto. 2005. *On Populist Reason*. London: Verso.

Lalander, Rickard. 2014. "Rights of Nature and the Indigenous Peoples in Bolivia and Ecuador: A Straitjacket for Progressive Development Politics?" *Iberoamerican Journal of Development Studies*, 3, 2.

___. 2017. "Ethnic Rights and the Dilemma of Extractive Development in Plurinational Bolivia." *International Journal of Human Rights*, 21, 4 (May).

Lalander, Rickard, and Javier Cuestas-Caza. 2017. "Sumak Kawsay y Buen-Vivir en Ecuador." In Ana Verdú and Norman González (eds.), *Conocimientos Ancestrales y Procesos de Desarrollo*. Loja: Universidad Particular de Loja.

Lalander, Rickard, and Magnus Lembke. 2018. "The Andean Catch-22: Ethnicity, Class and Resource Governance in Bolivia and Ecuador." *Globalizations*, 15, 5 (March).

Le Quang, Matthieu. 2017. "Interpretaciones y tensiones alrededor del Buen Vivir en Ecuador." *Papeles de relaciones ecosociales y cambio global*, 137.

Le Quang, Matthieu, and Tamia Vercoutère. 2013. *Ecosocialismo y Buen Vivir: Diálogo Entre Dos Alternativas al Capitalismo*. Quito: IAEN. <fuhem.es/media/cdv/file/biblioteca/Analisis/Buen_vivir/Ecosocialismo_y_Buen_Vivir_Le_Quang_Vercoutere.pdf>.

Löwy, Michael. 2014. "Ecosocial Struggles of Indigenous Peoples." *Capitalism Nature Socialism*, 25, 2.

Ospina, Pablo, and Rickard Lalander. 2012. "Razones de un Distanciamiento Político: El Movimiento Indígena Ecuatoriano y la Revolución Ciudadana." OSAL, 32

(November).

Sánchez-Vázquez, Luis, Esben Leifsen, and Ana Verdú-Delgado. 2017. "Minería a Gran Escala en Ecuador: Conflicto, Resistencia y Etnicidad." *Revista de Antropología Iberoamericana,* 12, 2.

Silveira, Manuela, Melissa Moreano, Nadia Romero, Diana Murillo, Gabriela Ruales, and Nataly Torres. 2017. "Geografías de Sacrificio y Geografías de Esperanza: Tensiones Territoriales en el Ecuador Plurinacional." *Journal of Latin American Geography,* 16, 1.

Vanhulst, Julien. 2015. "El laberinto de los discursos del Buen vivir: entre Sumak Kawsay y Socialismo del siglo XXI." *Polis,* 14, 40.

Villalba-Eguiluz, Unai, and Iker Etxano. 2017. "Buen Vivir vs. Development (II): The Limits of (Neo-)Extractivism." *Ecological Economics,* 138.

Walsh, Catherine. 2008. "Interculturalidad, plurinacionalidad y decolonialidad: las insurgencias político-epistémicas de refundar el Estado." *Tabula Rasa,* 9.

Section 5

Generating Cultural Interventions

16. Movement, Image, History
Walter Benjamin and Operational Politics

AK Thompson

When considering the dynamics of political contention, one is immediately struck by the paradox that people's awareness (whether conscious or not) of the immanent possibility of social transformation often coincides with a resurgence of recollections — and subsequent invocations — of the past. It was precisely this dynamic that Karl Marx observed in his "Eighteenth Brumaire" (1969: 398), where he noted how "the tradition of all the dead generations weighs like a nightmare on the brains of the living." For this reason, and at the very moment that historical actors signalled their desire and capacity to revolutionize both "themselves and things," they tended to "conjure up the spirits of the past" in order to borrow those "names, battle cries and costumes" with which they might "present the new scene of world history in this same time-honoured disguise."

By Marx's account, this dynamic was especially evident during the bourgeois revolutions of the eighteenth century, when Roman invocations served as compensation for the rising class's incapacity to square the difference between its aspirational ideals and the limited meaning that "equality" might assume within a regime founded on exploitation. In opposition to this impasse, Marx proposed that the revolutions of the nineteenth century (those proletarian insurgencies foreshadowed by the tumult of 1848) needed to break with the past's compensatory seductions so that they could embrace a confrontation that would make all turning back impossible: "*Hic Rhodus, hic salta*," he enjoined, citing a Greek fable about delivering on one's promises. "Here is Rhodes, dance here" (Marx 1969: 401).

For those who find themselves at odds with the past and its catalogue of horrors, Marx's (1969: 400) profane injunction to "let the dead bury their dead" so that we might finally advance unencumbered onto a field of open possibility can't help but be appealing. Nevertheless, even a cursory survey of the terrain on which we now struggle suggests that movements of all sorts continue to be more likely to pursue their aims by conjuring up "the spirits of the past" than they are to clamour toward the point of dead reckoning favoured by Marx. Given that this is the case, scholars and radicals on the left are immediately tasked with the challenge of documenting the historical citations that pervade the field so that we might discern the logic governing their deployment. With such knowledge comes the possibility that we might anticipate — and thus strategize to further — the outcome of our actions in this milieu. So long as we proceed without this knowledge, however, we remain beholden to the same time-honoured disguise.

Although it is too soon to tell how our current period of social instability (of resurgent fascism, ecological collapse, and financial ruin) will play out, something of its importance can be gleaned from the fact that — on both left and right — invocations of the kind observed by Marx have become more frequent and more purposefully deployed. On the right, the practice has tended to invoke mythical pasts whose waning glory might yet be recovered should the call be heeded. The acolytes are summoned to, through concerted action, "Make America Great Again" (MAGA) by collapsing the interval between past and present. But what past is being invoked by this political theology? The slogan never says, and it is for precisely this reason that its appeal has been so great. Prompted by an anxious subterranean longing, visions of America's past greatness bundle together the suburbanization, segregation, and white working-class advancement narratives of the postwar period so that they might be woven into a fabric cross-stitched with tales of antebellum gallantry and patched with Confederate flags.

By invoking these citations in pursuit of a contradictory but workable mythology, the far right has turned bricolage into a beacon with the power to summon the legions of dejected white men who never thought their own privileges would be undermined by capitalist progress.[1] Inchoate though it may be, this mythology found vivid, violent expression during the summer of 2017, when an unholy alliance of conservatives, fascists, and Internet trolls descended upon Charlottesville, Virginia, brandishing the borrowed names, battle cries, and costumes of their forebears to defend the image and honour of another mythologized figure named Robert E. Lee.

Concurrent with these citations, which are now just as likely to find expression on the street as they are to be broadcast from the highest levels of government,[2] the uncertainty of our times has also led movements on the left to invoke historical images more frequently and in more concerted ways. Responding to Trump's Muslim ban and to the increased frequency of ICE raids and deportations, activists have recalled both the resistance and the shortcomings of the resistance to Nazi ascent. Thus it was that Martin Niemöller's famous poem of elegiac warning became a defiant meme: "First they came for the Muslims and we said, 'Not this time Motherfucker.'" Following suit, others picked up the "Never Again" first popularized in the aftermath of the Nazi genocide to beat out an ominous warning. Considered from this vantage, there could only be one conclusion: "'Never Again' is Now."

By the spring of 2017, organizers for the International Women's Strike in New York City were building historical citations directly into their plans for International Women's Day. After a late-afternoon rally in Washington Square, thousands of protestors marched through downtown Manhattan on a route designed to showcase sites of historical significance. After brief stops at the Stonewall Inn, the African Burial Ground, and the spot where, in 1911, one hundred and forty-six textile workers died in the Triangle Shirtwaist Factory fire, the march concluded in Zuccotti Park. There, in the shadow of that looming public monument the occupiers had once dubbed "the orange thing," activists unfurled a banner from days gone by: "Occupy Wall Street!"

Although the connections between the Women's Strike and Occupy was never concretely conveyed to rally participants, the action's constellated invocations could not help but suggest that the Women's Strike was itself the means by which a historical balance sheet beleaguered by unfinished business might finally be reconciled. In contrast to the far right's stubborn recollections of mythic past greatness, the left opted for citations that could illuminate those internal relations that give discrete events their overarching coherence. Significantly, these citations recalled the enduring and unfulfilled dimensions of the broader struggle.

Invocations of this kind are loaded with historic responsibility. They enjoin those who *recognize* them to become arbiters of a theodicy whose last chapter remains (and may always remain) unwritten. In their temperament, they alternate between the solemn hushed tones of prophecy and revolution's boisterous refrain. So why did the Women's Strike, which numbered in the thousands in Washington Square, turn up with just a few hundred at Zuccotti before dissolving imperceptibly into the night? And why, despite the threadbare state of its borrowed standards and costumes, has the far right's appeal continued to grow?

One common story told about Charlottesville is that it marked the beginning of the end for the coalition galvanized by Trump's ascendency. Between internal rancour, legal prohibitions, and strong public condemnation following the murder of Heather Heyer, far-right efforts to organize post-Charlottesville have confronted significant obstacles. Still, it would be imprudent for left forces to discount the breakthroughs that took place on that day. Whether measured in numbers, levels of commitment, or unity in action, Charlottesville makes clear that — through its growing mastery of citation — the far right has learned to compel adherents to conceive history itself as both their field of operations and their object of struggle. And while the obstacles we've set in their path are significant, it's clear that the far-right movement's high-water mark (the mark to which all subsequent efforts will aspire) is still to be found on that pitch they call Lee Park.

Conversely, while the citations marshalled by Women's Strike organizers on March 8 were *analytically* revelatory, their effect — especially when measured comparatively — remained muted. Since the constellation went unrecognized (since it remained imperceptible to the action's participants), its invocations failed to transmit the burden of responsibility for the demands they implied. And so, while the Women's Strike helped ensure that the energy unleashed by the Women's March of January 21 was not syphoned off by Democratic Party opportunists, and while the decision to foreground the term "strike" helped to guide International Women's Day back to its radical roots, the action itself did little to transform the left's established repertoire of action. It is little wonder, then, that the 2018 Women's Strike yielded diminishing returns.

To understand these diverse outcomes, it's necessary to foreground the mechanics of citation rather than focusing solely on the form or content of a given citation's expression. When approached in this manner, it becomes clear that decisions regarding the form or content of movement invocations are subordinate to more pedestrian strategic challenges like gathering numbers and strengthening commitment. For this reason, we must not presume that any given mode is (or ought to be) the exclusive purview of left or right. And while people's allegiance to one pole of the antagonism may coincide with a predisposition toward one citation modality (and while such a predisposition may seem to be of a piece with a contender's politics and habitus), we must not shy away from the fact that expanding our repertoire to cover a wider array of circumstances might foster movement growth.

The left is therefore enjoined to consider what might be learned from (and not merely about) our adversary. Scandalous on its face, the proposition becomes more agreeable when we recall that, in pursuit of strategic advantages, right-wing factions have made diligent efforts to learn from *us*. How, then, might we respond? Since our mobilizations have relied on citations that (despite their objective correctness) have failed to prompt scalar shifts like the one witnessed in Charlottesville, how might we learn from our enemy as we clamour for traction on the field of borrowed names, battle cries, and costumes?

Whatever the answer might finally be, it's clear that outflanking right forces in the war of citation first requires that we familiarize ourselves with the mechanics of the genre. Only then can we consider how the various means by which history is invoked might be learned, sequenced, and cultivated as part of an overall movement strategy. Such a strategy pertains not solely to the appropriate *selection* of citable images and artifacts; it demands also that we consider how the marshalled invocations are to be deployed in a variety of ways, under a variety of conditions, and in pursuit of a variety of aims. When arranged in deliberate sequences and incorporated into broader mobilization frameworks, citations drawn from the past (whether to recall a utopian myth or an unresolved trauma) can help to demonstrate how people might assume responsibility for history itself. At their threshold, they have the power to deposit us before the "*hic rhodus, hic salta*" moment toward which Marx looked with anticipation. It is toward this point that we too must turn.

Walter Benjamin

A familiar reference point across the social sciences and humanities, Walter Benjamin has thus far received little attention from social movement scholars. Given the explosion in movement-based citation since Trump's election, however, we are enjoined to determine his relevance to the field. Through citation, and through the mobilization of what he called "wish images" and "dialectical images," Benjamin thought that movements could generate historical relays that would entangle moments of present-tense reckoning with their promise-laden but unrealized antecedents. Thus it was that, for Robespierre, "ancient Rome was a past charged with the time of the now which he blasted out of the continuum of history" (Benjamin 1968: 261). In Benjamin's view, this capacity could be cultivated; however, while all such citations are indexed to the possibility of disrupting the continuum of history, they do not all yield the same effect. And though they share an important bond, wish images and dialectical images must clearly be distinguished.[3]

In "Paris, Capital of the Nineteenth Century," Benjamin made clear that wish images enabled people to anticipate the future by recalling traces of a mythical past whose promise has yet to be fulfilled.

> In the dream in which, before the eyes of each epoch, that which is to follow appears in images, that latter appears wedded to elements from prehistory, that is, of a classless society. Intimations of this, deposited in the unconscious of the collective, mingle with the new to produce the utopia that has left its traces in thousands of configurations of life, from permanent buildings to fleeting fashions. (1978a: 148)

Analytically, such images can be used to clarify the desires that compel people to persevere. Politically, they can be mobilized to stimulate action in pursuit of those aims. However, as Susan Buck-Morss (1992: 148) maintains, "the real possibility of a classless society in the 'epoch to follow' the present one revitalizes past images as expressions of the ancient wish for a social utopia in dream form. But a dream image is not yet a dialectical image, and desire is not yet knowledge." In order to determine how we might move from one state to the other, the attributes of the dialectical image must therefore be clarified.

Through its constellation of matter and memory, Benjamin imagined that a dialectical image could force people to consider what might be required to act upon history as such. In one early formulation, he clarified:

> It's not that what is past casts light on the present, or what is present its light on what is past; rather, image is that wherein what has been comes together in a flash with the now to form a constellation. In other words, image is dialectics at a standstill. For while the relation of the present to the past is a purely temporal, continuous one, the relation of what-has-been to the now is dialectical: is not progression but image, suddenly emergent. (Benjamin 2003: 462)

In contrast to the wish image, which tended to refract its profane promise through the distortions of the dream state, the dialectical image was inseparable from the recognition of the revolutionary possibility inherent in "the now." Commenting on the distinct but interrelated character of these two image forms, Buck-Morss (1992: 146) proposed that, with the dialectical image, wish images were "negated, surpassed, and at the same time dialectically redeemed." In other words, the dialectical image provides a means of "completing" the wish image's dream of liberation by exposing it to the shock of recognition — by making both the *promise* and the *means* by which it might be achieved visible all at once.

Along with his distinction between wish images and dialectical ones, Benjamin's analysis suggests that both image types manifest differently depending on the degree to which consciousness marks their emergence. When considered from the standpoint of *recognition*, the dialectical image appears as an immediate and absolute presence (and it is for this reason that Benjamin so frequently invokes "shock" as an analytic category). When considered from the standpoint of its *production*, however, the shock of recognition begins to seem like a by-product of the highly mediated work of constellation. Attending to this duality, Buck-Morss (1992: 220) observed that "as an immediate, quasi-mystical apprehension, the dialectical image was intuitive. As a philosophical 'construction,' it was not."

Although Benjamin never formalized his conceptualization of image types to precisely this degree, exegesis suggests that, just as wish images and dialectical images denote antithetical poles on an axis plotting a decision's concreteness and intensity, so too are they divided *internally* by the degree to which the prompted recognition erupts into consciousness.

Operational Politics

In the following diagram, we can see how the field of dreams is constituted through the interaction of wish images and the unconscious. In the field of propaganda, wish images are either made conscious or consciously deployed. In this way, they become susceptible to both practical, instrumental mobilizations as well as to manipulation. In the field of awakening, dialectical images exist on the verge of becoming conscious but have not yet done so. They remain in the unconscious, where they might yet be discovered through what Buck-Morss called "quasi-mystical apprehension." In the field where consciousness and the dialectical image converge to prompt production, we encounter both the "conscious production" of the image itself and those forms of political action that take history to be the object of a redemptive labour process.

Connecting these four fields and operating as a kind of mediator between them is what Benjamin called *the trick*. As explained in his essay on surrealism, he viewed this trick as one of substituting historical accounts of the past with political ones (Benjamin 1978b: 182). By learning to proceed in this way, left movements increase the likelihood that they might move constituencies from one field to another in pursuit of their aims. Although the far right is of necessity predisposed to operating on

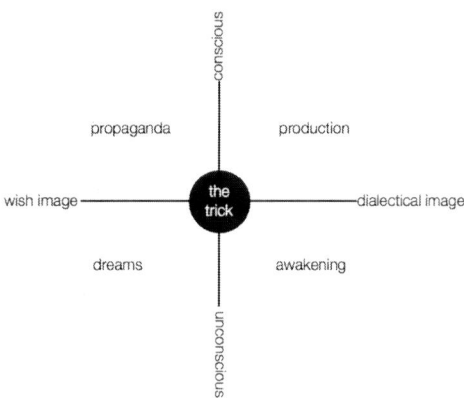

the *wish* side of the plane, the left must learn to orient toward these fields in a more deliberate way. At its logical conclusion, revolution demands that people (regardless of where they might begin) be moved to the plane's top right quadrant, the point where the distinction between politics and production collapses.

Engaging with Benjamin in this way allows for a clear operationalization of his insights. Nevertheless, this same engagement brings with it a series of strategic dilemmas with no easy or obvious resolution. In the short term (and as Charlottesville makes plain), it seems easier to mobilize myth than it is to produce moments of reckoning like the one hoped for by the Women's Strike. How, then, should we relate to the dynamics of citation as we work to improve our chances in the struggle against fascism?

One strategy might involve striving more consciously to produce dialectical images. While the particular constellation assembled by the Women's Strike may not have risen to the level of conscious recognition, we may reason, this does not mean that others will not. Indeed, through a more deliberate selection and activation of citable history, it might yet prove feasible to generate the cessation of happening for which Benjamin had longed. However, by emphasizing the production of dialectical images without also considering the conditions that enable recognition to emerge from the field of *awakening*, this strategy commits the adherent to unending experimentation with few rules guiding the process of assemblage.

In light of this challenge, left radicals may feel compelled to enter the field of *dreams* to stimulate those desires underlying (but rarely acknowledged within) the struggle for liberation. But this strategy, too, is marked by dilemmas. In response to the far right's MAGA, for instance, radicals have tended to point to the realities of genocide, colonialism, slavery, and unending exploitation to remind the world: "America was never great." By foregrounding the historical need for redemption, this slogan presages dialectical reckoning; however, because it does little to stimulate those intrinsic aspirations that might serve as incentives for movement participation, it has not enjoyed a broad resonance beyond the radical milieu. Once again, we double down on *production*, which is where emancipatory action is most likely to arise. But because this field tends to be activated by people's movement across the plane of citation (and especially across the axis of *consciousness*), it's not likely that this strategy will yield its desired result.

The problem becomes clear when we contrast "America was never great" to the sensibility encoded in "This Land is Your Land," that cherished American folk anthem penned by Woody Guthrie in 1940. Guthrie's song recounts a love for America and its people discovered through rambling — that vagabond path familiar to his contemporaries through the collective experience of the Great Depression. Because the scene is interrupted by private property and privation, the songsmith's desire for harmony leads inexorably toward a contest of sovereignties. Referring to our diagram, Guthrie's strategy involves activating the wishes lying dormant within the field of *dreams* so that they might be pushed toward the conflict lying in wait within the field of *awakening*.

Guthrie's resolution might be accused of suppressing the struggle that turned "this land" into "America" and thus of ignoring the limits that the colonized might wish to place on even a democratic settler sovereignty "made for you and me." For this reason, activists may choose instead to hijack the myths of the right by decoupling the desire that animated the initial attachment from its posited object resolution. In this scenario, a desire like "security" (which is now customarily associated with the right) is acknowledged as a valid first premise so that the question might be posed: given that the greatest threat to the American people may well be the hatred fostered by border imperialism, what must be done to achieve true security? This strategy requires that the initiate learn to move people from the field of *propaganda* back to the field of *dreams* before trying to push them toward *awakening*.

As these various rehearsals make plain, the challenges that arise when devising a movement-based citation strategy are considerable. For one, the field is already populated, and the procedures demanded by existing invocations are distinct from those required when advancing citations of one's own. Moreover, since the unconscious can never be known except through its symptomatic expression, devising strategic premises for work within the field of *dreams* or of *awakening* requires that (in the interest of mastering the trick) we commit to a steady regimen of inductive experimentation — which is exhausting, but it's precisely this work that the far right is now carrying out on the *wish* side of the plane. If we are to defeat them, we must keep dreams from finding their resolution in the right's mythic propaganda by pushing them instead toward *awakening*. Only from there might they ascend to the field of *production*.

Conclusion

By systematizing Benjamin's observations regarding time, image, and movement, I have shown how various citation modalities might be distinguished and classified. This is analytically significant; however, the true value of the schema presented here is strategic. By learning to operate within (and in accordance with the discrete logics underlying) the fields of *propaganda, dreams, awakening*, and *production*, left movements can improve their chances in the fight against fascist myth.

For understandable reasons, left movements have oriented toward the field of *production* while fascists have operated primarily in that of *propaganda*. Of these two positions, the latter is closer to *dreams*, and fascists have thus far proven to be more effective than we have at operating in this field. Like Charlottesville's Lee Park, it is contested territory — and left movements must learn to reclaim it. By drawing on Benjamin to strengthen our understanding of the uses to which movements can put historical citation while pursuing their aims, I hope to have contributed to this process.

Notes

1. Bricolage is the forming of something from an array of materials, objects, images, and concepts that are available at hand. It can refer, for example, to the assemblage of symbols and concepts (e.g., nation, race, land) that can be mobilized by the right.
2. Trump has advanced the slogan and policy of "America First" with little regret that the phrase was first popularized by the Ku Klux Klan. More recently, Melania Trump visited a Texas detention centre holding migrant children separated from their parents wearing a jacket bearing the scrawled slogan "I really don't care do u?" in a none-too-oblique reference to Mussolini's "Ne Me Frego."
3. Wish images can be thoughts and/or physical/virtual manifestations in things like photos or the writing of desires on the part of individuals, groups, or societies. Dialectical images refer in the most general terms to images (conceptual, virtual, or physical) that are flashes from the past that typically have been lost or marginalized. A photo of urban ruins from decades ago is one example, as is a fleeting reference in a written passage to the violent repression of a strike or walkout.

References

Benjamin, Walter. 1968. "Theses on the Philosophy of History." In *Illuminations*. New York: Schocken Books. <blog.wbkolleg.unibe.ch/wp-content/uploads/Benjamin_Illuminations_Philosophy-of-History.pdf>.

___. 1978a. "Paris, Capital of the Nineteenth Century." In *Reflections*. New York: Schocken Books.
___. 1978b. "Surrealism." In *Reflections*. New York: Schocken Books.
___. 2003. *The Arcades Project*. Cambridge: Belknap/Harvard.
Buck-Morss, Susan. 1992. *The Dialectics of Seeing: Walter Benjamin and the Arcades Project*. Cambridge: MIT Press.
Marx, Karl. 1969. "The Eighteenth Brumaire of Louis Bonaparte." In *Karl Marx and Frederick Engels: Selected Works, Volume I*. Moscow: Progress Publishers.

17. Disintegration of the Neoliberal Order and the Challenges for the Radical Left

Terry Maley

Here I will explore some issues on the radical left that deal with the ideological and institutional crises/disintegration of the neoliberal global order from the 1970s to today. I want to invoke Herbert Marcuse's idea of the counterrevolution of the global capitalist elites, as well as discussions of how liberal democracies are becoming increasingly undemocratic, and argue that we can build on Martijn Konings's important recent intervention regarding the sustainability and legitimacy of neoliberalism. These discussions, I contend, will help us to augment the traditional Marxian understanding of capitalist crisis.

Konings poses a key question: What accounts for the continuing viability of neoliberalism despite ongoing global protests against it by social movements? He looks at the relationship between *affect/emotion* and risk in the reproduction of the legitimacy of neoliberalism among broad segments of the population.[1] Like the chapters by A.T. Kingsmith and William S. Jaques, Konings's analysis addresses the complicated issue of the affective binds or ties that hold together or "manage" a crisis-prone neoliberal hegemony. Augmenting Konings's discussion with Herbert Marcuse and others may help to clarify the complexity and difficulty of political change for the radical left now, in the Trumpist era of neoliberal disintegration.

In looking at how these arguments augment each other, I wish to gather together intellectual and political resources on the radical left that have animated critiques of neoliberalism for more than forty years. A common theme in the "dialogue" between these views is that capitalist crises are not aberrations from otherwise healthy liberal democracies, nor are they isolated "events." Rather, they are part of a "new normal" of global precarity and volatility, as Max Haiven argues in his chapter, that has not yet become completely totalizing but that has to be actively managed by the state.

Historically, capitalism has always had crises. But the periodic disintegration produced by neoliberal crises has allowed corporate and state elites to further undermine the political potential and organizational resources of an increasingly precarious working class that is deeply but unevenly integrated into global capitalism. In this regard, Konings's and Marcuse's arguments complement each other. They also both augment, or add to, the traditional Marxian analysis of capitalist crises, implying there is something affectively new in the near-permanent neoliberal forms of crisis management.

There has been concern on the radical left about why neither the traditional working class nor global social movements, after two decades of protest, have been able to bring about more significant change. Konings (2018: 50) notes that for the left, "explanations for why neoliberalism is still at present operational have tended to focus on the ability of financial elites to capture public discourses and institutions." Even with trenchant critiques of growing inequality, austerity, and the global concentration of wealth, it has been difficult to dislodge the affective legitimacy of neoliberalism. Despite the fact that many forms of protest and organizing have been highly visible, tech savvy, and often innovative, the left seems paralyzed and in need of new modes of social and institutional transformation. Thompson and Jaques's chapters in particular point to new fields of potential affect and action, involving aesthetic interventions beyond the dichotomy of reason versus affect.

The Complexities of State Capture

Forms of state capture, as Konings (2018: 48) argues, "conceive of the legitimating spirit of neoliberalism as an external ideological moment, portraying populists' loyalty to neoliberal discourses as a kind of cognitive impairment or moral failure." There is a long history of liberals and social democrats seeing the working class as immature and unfit to govern (Maley 2011; Wainwright 2017). The implication of this "cognitive impairment/moral failure" view is that any thinking person could not possibly have voted for a populist demagogue like Trump, whose politics run so directly against their own (i.e., working-class) interests. Lurking behind this view is the old Marxian/Lukacsian idea of false consciousness that has fallen out of favour on the left in an era of global protest movements.

There are still many examples of "state capture" (and tactics) that have blocked change from the left for decades. In fact, neoliberal parties everywhere (both of the liberal and social democratic varieties) still routinely use them.[2] They involve the manipulation of administrative knowledge/power and parliamentary procedures to thwart progressive legislative change. Under Trump's assault on liberal democracy, or the even more authoritarian consolidation of neoliberal power in Russia, China, Turkey, and Brazil, the state-capture thesis does not seem so far-fetched. Technically complex institutions, once "captured" or occupied by parties through the democratic electoral system, can then be used in highly anti-democratic ways. The tactics of Trump and US Republicans may seem extreme, but they are not unusual.

Referring to the political mood that followed the 2007–08 financial crash, Konings (2018: 50) rhetorically questions "precisely how elites could continue to access such tremendous material, institutional and symbolic resources even in a context where discontent with key neoliberal institutions was at an all-time high and the political air was thick with contempt and distrust towards bankers." This contradictory mood is part of the "new normal" of precarity today. Konings's answer combines two things that are intertwined culturally under neoliberalism. One is affect, or the ambivalent emotional connection people have to neoliberal values and institutions — to the self-reliant "legitimating spirit of neoliberalism," despite its all too apparent defects. The other is the cultural hegemony of risk. Both are related to the affective "logic of neoliberalism."

As the relative security of the welfare state has been stripped away from the former industrial working class, the ideology of capitalist risk-taking has become normalized. The insecurity of precarious populations that take the brunt of capitalist risk-taking has become globally pervasive under neoliberalism. This experience of profound economic insecurity has generated widespread fear and precarity among large sections of the population.

Toronto Star columnist Rick Salutin (2018) notes that Trump loyalists "feel so disdained and patronized that when someone shows up who they believe really cares, an earthquake could not shake them, so great is their need." This affective mix of fear, alienation, and desperation is volatile, as Haiven also argues in his chapter on affective revenge. It can reinforce emotional attachments to symbolic sources of (real or imagined) security and can also lead to rebellions against perceived causes of that volatility. Sheldon Wolin (2008: 36) has captured the contradictory effects of this neoliberal dynamic: "The democratization of advanced industrial societies has come down to this: the labor, wealth, and psyches of the citizenry are simultaneously defended and exploited … protected and extracted, rewarded and commanded." Henry Giroux (2014, 2018) notes that neoliberalism's uncertainty and fear foster a narrow range of aggressive emotions that devalue more public-minded emotions such as cooperation, sharing, and kindness. Marcuse (1964) emphasized that these destructive forms of domination could only be replaced by a "new sensibility" if capitalism was transcended.

After World War II, the destructive affective consequences of market volatility were contained by the welfare state. Konings identifies this with Karl Polanyi's "double movement," in which market crises were rebalanced by state social policy. In Polanyi's (1944) view, markets were historically embedded in society. When capitalist crises knocked this out of whack, social pressure and government programs returned a kind of balance to the relationship between markets and society. Konings notes that under neoliberalism, this "re-embedding" or new balance has not emerged. Instead, as Wolin has noted, the state has become "auto-legitimating," and autonomous from society. The neoliberal state has largely succeeded in insulating itself — and financial markets — from popular democratic control.

The state's capacity to re-embed markets in society has, by serial acts of self-inflicted deregulation, been seriously diminished. Perpetual risks and crises, at the intersection of the global economy, the state, and the working lives of most people, have been normalized. Konings argues that what the left had previously thought were "states of exception," deviations from liberal-democratic norms, are no longer exceptional but part of the logic of neoliberalism. The normalization of crises and "states of exception" have become part of what Wolin has called "managed democracy."

Illiberal Democracy under Neoliberalism

Neoliberalism has a kind of "dialectic" in which the state manages market insecurity/risk alongside an affective/cultural reaction/need for an authoritarian identification with ruling elites by destabilizing populations. I will spell this out further through a discussion of Marcuse's *One-Dimensional Man* (ODM), which outlined the "administered society" of "state monopoly capitalism" in post–World War II America. This world was defined by standardized mass production (Fordism) and mass consumerism. It was thus one-dimensional because of the uniformity of full-time blue- and white-collar (mostly white male) jobs and consumer goods. To wit, Marcuse's critique of one-dimensionality exposed the deep affective and cultural identification of the working class with capitalist consumerism in the welfare-state era. As he said in ODM, "the people, previously [historically] the ferment of social change has 'moved up' to become the ferment of social cohesion [i.e., reaction]" (Marcuse 1964, cited in Maley 2017: 256).

Yet Marcuse (1964: 256) also made the following well-known comment on the revolutionary potential of the working class: "Underneath the conservative popular base is the substratum of the outcasts and outsiders, the exploited and persecuted of other races and other colours, the unemployed and unemployable." The "substratum of the outcasts and outsiders" has grown dramatically under neoliberalism and now includes what Giroux calls "disposable" populations. Marcuse's remarks foreshadow the warnings of Giroux, Cornell West, Wendy Brown, David Harvey, and others who have written eloquently about the ways neoliberalism is producing growing numbers of surplus, mostly racialized populations that the global plutocracy is happy to exploit but is no longer willing to include in the neoliberal version of the affluent, but highly unequal, society.

A precarious, increasingly non-unionized working class under a host of pressures can be pulled in multiple, contradictory directions — more progressive after World War II, more recently authoritarian, even proto-fascist. For Marcuse, there is no revolutionary subject in the abstract, outside of the contradictions of neoliberalism's volatile political economy of affect. Marcuse's work, like the chapters in this section, is in many ways attuned to the dialectic between the potential of the people, the demos, as an agent of social change, and the vulnerability of the same demos to becoming an agent of reaction.

In the early 1970s, Marcuse presciently saw the future of illiberal democracy under neoliberalism — a toxic mix of aggression, nationalism, racism, militarism, and rampant, escapist consumerism that are all different affective aspects of an ambivalent, sometimes fearful identification with corporate, technological, state, and military power. Marcuse saw that under these conditions, if the fundamental changes in consciousness that the "New Left" encouraged could not be sustained, the demos could become reactionary. Here Marcuse's analysis augments Wolin's and Konings's. Wolin (2008: xii) asked, "What causes a democracy to change into some non- or antidemocratic system, and what kind of system is democracy likely to change into?"

For Giroux (2018), "neoliberalism is the new face of fascism" and Trumpism is enabling a new politics of cruelty. It is not only a structure of organized aggression, but also the elevation of hardness and cruelty as an organizing principle of everyday life. Citizens will tolerate public cruelty and a more openly authoritarian politics if they are made to feel safe again by populist leaders who vent their frustrations on the excluded and marginalized.

Witness the Trumpist dictate of forcibly separating toddlers and children from their mothers at the US-Mexican border. The marginal, whether from outside or within, are punished, disciplined, and brutalized. The outcasts and outsiders are now, under neoliberal fascism, disposable. The pretense that the current system is still democratic is being challenged. It is under immense pressure from corporate forces not only outside of the state, but from within.

Against this backdrop, we need to retrieve aspects of radical left thinking provided by Marcuse and others. In 1972, Marcuse summarized this complex terrain of struggle and the need for a strategic shift in emphasis from revolution to revolt as "motivated by the notion of a crisis of capitalism different from the traditional Marxist concept" of recurring economic crises. He "suggested it in terms of a structural disintegration while the economy, in its institutions, still operates: a moral disintegration, in the daily practice, at work and outside of work" (Marcuse 1972: 173).[3]

Marcuse did not think that revolution would inevitably follow from economic crises. The disintegration of capitalist democracies would not bring about radical change on its own. It requires a fundamental change in both consciousness and affect — both inseparable parts of a new sensibility — as well as organization. This "structural/moral disintegration," a defining characteristic of neoliberalism, is precisely what has produced both a counterrevolutionary "proto-fascist syndrome" and the global protests against it.

Structural and Moral Disintegration

Structural disintegration is not only moral disintegration. It also the process whereby the institutions of the liberal-democratic state are being hollowed out from above by elected leaders. This concern has now migrated from the radical left to the mainstream liberal media. Economist Paul Krugman (2018) has noted how this form of disintegration — the dysfunction of liberal-democratic political institutions and values — is fundamentally entangled with a crisis-prone neoliberal economy. In Turkey, the neoliberal economic system continues to function while the country experiences a huge crisis of legitimacy due to the authoritarian "capture" and corruption of state institutions by President Erdoğan, who has conducted massive purges of key state institutions (the military, the civil service, the judiciary, and universities). The hollowing out/disintegration of the state and the consolidation of power in Erdoğan's hands has occurred at breathtaking speed. Now the economy (and society) function in a more authoritarian form, with fewer labour rights, severely reduced academic and journalistic freedom, and a massive shift of wealth to Erdoğan's cronies. Krugman argues that something similar is happening in the US under Trump.

In his New Left writings, Marcuse thought that there were still openings in a system that seemed to be disintegrating already then, in which social movements — the women's movement, the student movement, national liberation movements in the Global South at the time — could join with the broader working class to create non-repressive, non-commodified new sensibilities. In 1967, Marcuse argued that "in established societies there are still gaps and ... interstices [that] are still open, and one of the most important tasks is to make use of them to the full" to create "the basic organization of libertarian socialism" through an "organized spontaneity" (Kellner 2004: 27) that includes employed workers, blue and white collar, intelligentsia, and women. Francis Dupuis-Déri (2017) has made a parallel argument about today's movements, accounting for key historical differences. In some ways, Marcuse's support of the movements in his New Left writings prefigured today's movements that have rebelled against neoliberalism.

These are fluid, diverse terrains of struggle not always unified under one party, ideology, or a single kind of organization. The World Social Forums, landless peasants, then Occupy, Idle No More, the Indignados, now Black Lives Matter and #MeToo. These are the diverse forms of what Wolin has called fugitive democracy, struggles that are affectively complex, involving multiple forms of organizing that are building new emancipatory, affective/cultural sensibilities and political capacities.[4]

Hilary Wainwright (2017) makes an important point when she notes that these new forms do not have to be organized under one unified/universal theory/idea/party or form of the state. She notes that movements such as UK Uncut (and possibly Momentum now) are "purposefully autonomous from political parties [and provide] an example of the decisive material impact of a new kind of multi-centred, molecular campaign, bringing together all kinds of social actors" (Wainwright 2017: 60). These movements have been "coordinated horizontally and [with] rotated responsibilities, developing ... a diffuse leadership through which capacities were developed and spread."

In the Indignados movement in Spain, as Wainwright (2017: 60) notes, people participated in "decision-making by thousands, many of whom have never occupied anything."[5] These are *new forms of knowledge and affective solidarity* that reject the top-down technocratic knowledge still thought necessary by left parties seeking to capture state power. Under neoliberalism, elected and unelected officials in right-wing administrations are now deploying this kind of technocratic, specialized knowledge openly against the demos.

Yet some leading left commentators, such as Leo Panitch, Greg Albo, and Sam Gindin (2017), suggest that we have, with the Sanders and Corbyn insurgencies into established parties, moved from protest to politics. The implication is that there needs to be a party to organize a new hegemony through a different kind of state. Protest movements agitating for change outside of the state are not enough. Wainwright's more recent discussion of the Corbyn insurgency into the UK Labour Party and its relation to Momentum, the movement organized outside of the party to support Corbyn, suggests two things.

First, pressure from movements that are autonomous from the state and electoral politics is still critical for significant change to occur — even though the gulf between protest movements and those running the neoliberal state is often fundamental. Second, moving the mainstream liberal or social democratic parties further to the left is still painfully difficult and faces significant resistance from within, which the Corbyn and Sanders insurgencies have encountered.

The global movements outside of the state are rightly critical of the technocratic systems of knowledge and power upon which the neoliberal state, parties, and global capital rely. But Panitch, Albo, Gindin, and Wainwright all make a critical point: movements have to find multiple ways of engaging with — and sometimes strategically against — the state. This is a key dilemma for an augmented left. Can the modern state, which both the far left and far right have subjected to withering criticism, still be a means of radical social transformation into what Kingsmith and Haiven characterize as a sense of injustice or anger that is focused and empowering? And what kind of affective transformation do people need to go through for that to happen? The mayor of Barcelona, Ada Calou, and her new municipal party, En Comú (In Common), are perhaps the best recent example of how a social justice movement (anti-eviction, in this case) can retain features of radical, transformative politics while still holding institutional power.

Conclusions

The En Comú experiment in democratic municipal governance demonstrates two things that previous examples of more direct democratic participation, such as the World Social Forum and participatory budgeting exercises, have shown. First, the state is not monolithic; there are openings within and between different levels of the state. The state can be partially "steered," to some extent, toward more progressive ends. Second, the En

Comú example again shows that more radical, far-reaching change takes place most effectively when a movement's goals, policy ideas, and principles are supported by officials (elected or bureaucratic) within the state. It is this synergy, at the intersection of the movements and the state, that can nurture the new sensibilities and the affective resilience necessary to move beyond neoliberalism.

Another thing is necessary for moving past the logic of neoliberalism. That logic, as discussed by Konings, Marcuse, Wolin, and Giroux, has produced a "one-dimensional" narrowing of affect in the direction of an authoritarian identification with capitalism and neoliberal elites. That identification is attractive to those who are vulnerable because it simplifies the realities of neoliberal globalization, reducing complex histories, identities and struggles to one-dimensionality.

At the same time that Marcuse wrote *One-Dimensional Man*, the forgotten French critical theorist Joseph Gabel wrote about how racist and other political ideologies such as McCarthyism reflected this phenomenon, reducing entire categories of people to the same one-dimensional plane along an ahistorical present, eternally outside of the possibly for different pasts or futures. Gabel called this de-dialectical thinking, a process that "spatializes" or flattens the complexity and diversity/difference of the historical experiences of others, freezing time and affect in a simplified, either/or present. This involves devaluing/reducing whole groups of historically complex, non-identical, and diverse social beings to simple either/or, good/bad categories — just as Trump did when he called Mexicans rapists and drug dealers.

Gabel, in what would be controversial today, called this a form of false consciousness. For Gabel (1997: 17), "the spatio-temporal structure of false consciousness is characterized by the preponderance of static, spatial, anti-dialectical experience." As a result, false consciousness is not simply being mistaken about one's class interests.[6] It is the political-economic and affective cultural order of neoliberal capitalism. It shapes our consciousness, our needs and affective lives. Rather than focus on the moral impairment or cognitive failure discussed by Konings, Gabel would urge us to think dialectically again, valuing and struggling to be open to the diversity and complexity of our own and others' experiences. Within this struggle lie possibilities for creating a new "intercultural common-wealth," in Charles Reitz's (2015) wonderful phrase, free from neoliberal market-based competition and aggression, yet within, as Marx and Marcuse suggest, a larger social whole.

Notes

1. I am using *affect* to signify emotional attachment and mobilization (see Stavro 2018).
2. Of course, there is a long history in the US that pre-dates Trump. Republicans' voter suppression tactics and gerrymandering are infamous. The right-to-work movement has had similarly damaging effects (Marvit 2018). Marcuse's *Counterrevolution and Revolt* (1972) prefigured today's critiques of the ongoing revolt from above by plutocratic elites. As he said at the time: "The defense of the capitalist system requires the organization of counterrevolution at home and abroad. [It is] altogether preventative. Here there is no recent revolution to be undone, and there is none in the offing" (Marcuse 1972: 1–2).
3. The discussions of anxiety in this section deal with the affective consequences of what I see, building on Marcuse's notion, as neoliberal forms of disintegration.
4. For examples of emancipatory, affective/cultural sensibilities and new capacities, see Patricia McDermott's "Gender and Consumption" and Richard Day's "Beyond the Impasse," both in Maley (ed.) (2017).
5. The Indignados movement (which means "the indignant") began in Spain in 2011. It inspired Occupy Wall Street and other anti-austerity organizing in the EU, growing out of previous movements in Spain like ViaVivenda (which protested for affordable housing), Precarious en movimiento (a network of groups protesting precarity in the economy and socially), and Youth Without a Future (which began in the universities in 2011). The Indignados organized virtually, online, bringing thousands into the streets and neighbourhood squares across Spain in local assemblies from 2011 to 2015 (it has also been called the "Take the Square" movement).
6. The way Konings describes the "cognitive impairment" view is closer to how some Marxists and critical theorists (e.g., Herbert Marcuse) after George Lukacs used the term *false consciousness*. These thinkers argued that forms of domination in capitalist societies contain contradictions (between the 1 percent and the working class, between people's true needs and consumerism). Within these contradictions supposedly lay the potential for liberation from capitalism. But capitalist ideologies of individualism and consumerism make these contradictions and the potential for liberation hard to perceive. If workers do not see capitalism's contradictions — and so do not organize to revolt against them — they have false consciousness.

References

Dupuis-Déri, Francis. 2017. "Radical Opposition to Neoliberal Globalization." In Terry Maley (ed.), *One Dimensional Man 50 Years On: The Struggle Continues*. Black Point: Fernwood Publishing.

Gabel, Joseph. 1997. *Ideology and the Corruption of Thought*. New York: Routledge.

Giroux, Henry. 2014. *Neoliberalism's War on Higher Education*. Chicago: Haymarket Books.

___. 2018. "Neoliberal Fascism and the Echoes of History." *The Bullet: Socialist Project*, August 20.

Kellner, Douglas. 2004. "Introduction: Radical Politics, Marcuse and the New Left." In *The New Left and the 1960s: Collected Papers of Herbert Marcuse, Vol. 3*. New York: Routledge.

Konings, Martijn. 2018. "From Hayek to Trump: The Logic of Neoliberal Democracy." In Leo Panitch and Gregory Albo (eds.), *Rethinking Democracy: The Socialist Register*. London: Merlin Press.

Krugman, Paul. 2018. "Turmoil for Turkey's Trump." *New York Times*, May 24.

Maley, Terry. 2011. *Democracy and the Political in Max Weber's Thought*. Toronto: University of Toronto Press.

___. (ed.). 2017. *One-Dimensional Man 50 Years On: The Struggle Continues*. Black Point: Fernwood Publishing.

Marcuse, Herbert. 1964. *One-Dimensional Man: Studies in the Ideology of Advanced Industrial Society*. New York: Beacon Press.

___. 1972. *Counterrevolution and Revolt*. New York: Beacon Press.

Marvit, Moshe. 2018. "For 60 Years This Powerful Conservative Group Has Worked to Crush Labour." *The Nation*, July 8.

Panitch, Leo, and Sam Gindin. 2017. "Class, Party and the Challenge of State Transformation." In Leo Panitch and Gregory Albo (eds.), *Rethinking Revolution: The Socialist Register*. London: Merlin Press.

Polanyi, Karl. 1944. *The Great Transformation*. New York: Farrar & Rinehart.

Reitz, Charles. (ed.). 2015. *Crisis and Commonwealth: Marx, Marcuse and McLaren*. Lanham: Lexington Books.

Salutin, Rick. 2018. "How to Make it Through the Stresses of Trumptime." *Toronto Star*, April 13.

Stavro, Elaine. 2018. *Emancipatory Thinking: Simone de Beauvoir and Contemporary Political Thought*. Montreal: McGill-Queen's University Press.

Wainwright, Hilary. 2017. "Radicalizing the Movement-Party Relation: From Ralph Miliband to Jeremy Corbyn and Beyond." In Leo Panitch and Gregory Albo (eds.), *Rethinking Revolution: The Socialist Register*. London: Merlin Press.

Wolin, Sheldon. 2008. *Democracy Incorporated: Managed Democracy and the Spectre of Inverted Totalitarianism*. Princeton: Princeton University Press.

18. Late-Stage Capitalism, Anxiety, and Tactical Art Terrorism

William S. Jaques

> The incessant clash of the movement of art against established boundaries ... its propensity to renew its materials of expression and the ontological texture of the percepts and affects it promotes brings about if not a direct contamination of the other domains [of life] then at least a highlighting and a re-evaluation of the creative dimensions that traverse all of them. (Guattari 1995: 106)

Anxiety is a central strand of the contemporary esprit de corps and can have a paralyzing effect on left projects, though it is also a potential site of mobilization (Institute for Precarious Consciousness 2014). While there is much that can and should be said about anxiety in its own right, it is used here to gesture toward an existential state related to the contradiction between one's dissatisfaction with the present material conditions of late-stage capitalism and the uncertainty that looms in any attempts to dramatically alter those conditions.[1] While consciousness raising has and will continue to be a useful aspect of left tactics, its effectiveness seems to have become muted to some degree. Perhaps this is because the viscerality of anxiety, an affection systematically generated by living with capitalism's contradictions, is more potent than affections derived from rational understanding and cognitive awareness of those contradictions.

From Engels (1968 [1893]) and Marx (1994), through Gramsci (2008) to Sarachild (1978), the Black Lives Matter movement (Rickford 2015) and #MeToo, to name only a few instances where consciousness raising has played (and continues to play) a role, a crucial component of left projects is drawing attention to and challenging the injustices and contradictions of capitalism while providing the intellectual tools needed to overcome internalized forms of oppression.[2] Radical action is, by definition, an action that risks the security of one's future material conditions since its aim is to dramatically alter the conditions that would reproduce the existing order, which includes the conditions for action itself. Successful radical or critical actions negate the conditions for their existence, or contribute to their negation. Existentially then, such actions generate anxiety, which can have a cooling effect on left mobilization such that it tends to stop short of radical action. Left movements, deradicalized through anxiety, are easily appropriated into the global capitalist market where they spawn niche markets such as the highly profitable critical academic conference racket, which in turn supports the highly exploitative tourism industry. I take this to be a prime example of what Terry Maley, in his chapter, refers to as the "affective binds" that "hold together a crisis-prone neoliberal hegemony." Art, especially unsanctioned art, works in the opposite direction. It forces an open confrontation with the anxiety produced by the contradictions of the current social order and is thus, by its nature, radical and transformative.

To complement intellectually oriented forms of consciousness raising, I suggest that the use of aesthetic forms of embodied consciousness raising aimed at actualizing more robustly visceral affections is a valuable tactic for projects of augmentation aimed at widespread mobilization for social transformations within late-stage capitalist regions. In practice, this means engaging in art terrorism and contributing to the creation of insurgent art. The aim of the art terrorist is to engage in non-institutionalized acts of subversive public artistic expression. The aesthetic experience generated through insurgent art results in a felt confrontation with the contradictions of the existing order. While such practices are not entirely new, augmented left projects should consider them a central tactic.[3]

Art Terrorism and Affective Liberation

While the term "art" eludes simple definition (Carroll 2000) I loosely take it to involve a purposive production of culturally dependent aesthetic experience tied to social contexts. Art *is* a Deleuzean social affection between subjectivities mediated by artifact, in the broadest sense of that term. Art is affection, a series of shifting intensities stirred through the encounter, which draws forth immanent capacities of the body to be unavoidably felt, lived through, or suffered by embodied consciousness.[4] Unlike a pamphlet, lecture, protest, or the like, the immediacy of aesthetic experience renders the affections produced through the encounter unavoidable. Robust, purposive, aesthetic experience infects embodied consciousness.

The term "terrorism" is equally ambiguous and perhaps more problematic since it is often deployed politically and pejoratively through a discourse of delegitimization, if not "dehumanization," using whatever arbitrary language is convenient toward that end (Saul 2010). Generally speaking, terrorism involves politically motivated acts of violence intended to incite fear in a population often characterized as innocent. Similar to the way A.T. Kingsmith's chapter considers "generalized reactive affects" induced by hegemonic forms of power, Harmon (2011: 37) notes that dominant culture(s) tend to have a somewhat schematic aesthetic "architecture" that produces affections conducive to the reproduction of the existing order. The art terrorist aims to disrupt the status quo reproduction of this order by exploiting the patterns and codes of the schema to produce different affections that lead to unconventional, potentially more transformative actions. In this sense, art terrorism is a form of what Kingsmith refers to as "situationist *détournement*," which recuperates and repurposes what in AK Thompson's chapter are discussed as social schemas and mythologies for social transformation. Art terrorism is politically motivated by a discontent with oppressive elements of the material conditions of late-stage capitalism and its generation of anxiety. Exposure to insurgent art is often not voluntary because the artifacts are conspicuously public, which adds to their effectiveness and allows them to affect and potentially mobilize broad and diverse segments of the population. By producing an immediate unexpected visceral confrontation with late-stage capitalism's conditions in the form of lived aesthetic experience, successful insurgent art commits an existential "violence" against an affective condition that Max Haiven's chapter characterizes as "revenge capitalism." As such acts are terroristic and existentially violent, they are nearly un-recuperable within the capitalist market. When recuperation does take place, new modes of artistic expression and creation tend to emerge to supplant older practices.

A good example of art terrorism might be the activities of the "Space

Hijackers," an open group of self-proclaimed "anarchitects" operating in the UK between 1999 and 2014. Their website, <spacehijackers.org>, documents insurgent art and provides information on how it can be created elsewhere. Among other things, they organized midnight cricket matches in urban centres, hosted dance parties on public transit, and reportedly arrived at the 2009 London G20 protest in a fully armoured military vehicle loudly playing "Ride of the Valkyries" to the bemusement of the vehicle's occupants. The police reportedly did not share their enthusiasm, perhaps because their armoured vehicles weren't equipped with tape decks. Artistic production related to graffiti also often produces insurgent art, such as the work of Darren Cullen (2013), documented on his website (spellingmistakescostlives.com). Some of his projects include replacing street and transit advertisements with creative, hand-painted, critical works of art designed to mimic ads, building militarized police "toys" complete with packaging and price tag, and running an "ad" campaign for "payday" loans for kids (an advance on their allowances at "just 5000% interest").

Another example of insurgent art is the practice of conducting lengthy and absurd communications with large corporations to be shared through social media, as when artist Babak Ganjei shared his attempt to sell his painting "Business Proposition," a large and "completely lifelike" painting of his actual credit card with its real details to the "art department" of the credit card company (babakganjeiworks.com). In the end, they passed on the purchase and advised him to destroy the painting. Encounters with these types of artifacts produce a felt awareness of capitalism's contradictions without the need for extensive arguments or explanation. The artifacts follow patterns of the dominant aesthetic architecture with seemingly innocuous alterations to the content being delivered, replacing the intended coded affection with a more critical one. The resulting aesthetic experience is familiar in both its pattern and the critical "meaning" behind its content, since the content only aims to make explicit the contradictions the subject already experiences under capitalism.

A typical advertisement aims to generate affections that help reproduce the existing order by masking any contradictions behind the synthetic desire to consume created by their content. Cullen's "ads" emulate their general format but invert the meaning by explicitly drawing attention to the contradictions as part of the aesthetic experience or affections he aims to create. Another result of insurgent art's capacity for subversive or radical affection is that it seems relatively resistant to the repressive apparatuses of capitalism. Following established aesthetic patterns makes it difficult to condemn the artifacts without condemning the corresponding artifacts of capitalism. While insurgent art pushes against boundaries, "legal" violations are typically so minute that prosecution seems absurd and risks turning the courts into a more visible stage on which to create insurgent art.

As a tactic for an augmenting left, art terrorism complements cognitively centred forms of consciousness raising and should be deployed as often as those tactics. Its immediacy and the radical affections it produces in lived aesthetic experience can mobilize transformations that are beyond the reach of skewed counterarguments or crowdsourced justifications for inaction or counteraction. The remainder of this chapter explores the theory underpinning art terrorism as a left tactic and further explains its utility in mobilizing under the conditions of late-stage capitalism.

Cognitive Bias: "Information" and (in)Action

In many ways, the phenomenological tradition, as well as various incarnations of postmodern thought, collapse the false dualities erected by certain dominant strands of philosophy, including the separation of mind-body and the separation of body-world. While left theorizing generally tends to be materialist, it is not always clear that the implications of this claim in terms of abandoning dualisms have been taken seriously. The ontology presumed in this chapter is a version of material or physical monism through which we must understand the mind to be coextensive with body (it is embodied) and the body to be coextensive with the world around it (as enmeshed or embedded in a *lebenswelt* or life-world).[5]

Collapsing the mind-body and body-world dualisms is a crucial step in reaching beyond what Mallin (2009: 108) terms "one of the most difficult 'Western metaphysical prejudices' to overcome." The prejudice is both philosophical and lived through a sort of logocentrism where language, symbols, and the generally "cognitive" aspects of conscious being are taken as the only mode of genuine knowledge production and thus the only proper basis for action that is not confused. Put simply, the assumption is that thought and cognition are more reliable than feeling, emotion, or, more generally, the multiplicitous affections in a given encounter. The bias suggested by Mallin entails a tendency to treat cognition as separate from and superior to other aspects of bodily consciousness, as though it is somehow isolated from the multiplicitous affections and varying intensities involved in a given encounter.

According to Bergson and Pogson (2001: 3), while it is somewhat natural for consciousness to make a distinction between "external" objects, or the things in the world we are capable of experiencing, and our "internal" experience or representations of them, any distinction between the dualisms of mind-body/body-world is merely a matter of convenience. This "natural attitude," as Husserl (2010: 15) terms it, sets up a sort of epistemological-ontological solipsism that cannot be resolved because the gap between object and experience can never be closed short of actually becoming the object experienced. Thus, the natural attitude of consciousness necessitates a philosophical commitment to logocentrism or the belief that language, symbol, and representation — the proper tools of cognition and thought — are the only valid means through which knowledge can be gleaned from our experience of the world. Essentially, our beliefs about the world, or our "consciousness," might be false, but cognition can remedy this. I might, for instance, fail to understand the exploitative nature of the society of which I am a part and my complacency within it. Cognition-oriented consciousness raising aims to fix this incongruity between my understanding of reality and reality itself by providing more accurate information.

The prescription from the left is to produce pamphlets, create reading groups, organize and exchange information, attend conferences, write papers, and other tasks so that transformative action might one day occur when enough people rationally understand the contradictions of capitalism. The presumption here is that anyone who adequately understands the systematic injustices of a capitalist society, anyone who elevates the contradictions of the order from *experienced* to *cognitively known*, would take the actions necessary to alter it.

While this might be the ideal mode of operation, it is far from actual. It is not clear that cognitive understanding is enough to produce social transformations, an issue that is compounded by the paralyzing effect of anxiety production related to the double bind between a desire for radical change and the uncertainty that would entail. The revelation of widespread privacy invasion, for example, by both state and corporate actors, revealed by individuals like Edward Snowden and Chelsea Manning, as well as undeniable tax evasion by the wealthiest individuals from advanced capitalist nations around the globe, as detailed in the Panama Papers, and the marked lack of public action or institutional reforms related to these revelations are perfect examples of the disconnect between cognitive information and transformative action.[6]

Regions of Consciousness: Visceral Fields of Affect and Action

Rejecting the aforementioned dichotomies opens up a different way to understand consciousness such that there are different modalities through which the embodied embedded mind can be said to "understand." Mallin (2009: 108) suggests that there are interconnected "regions of consciousness," which act as points of contact between a body and its life-world and correspond to different modes of knowing. There are at least four regions: the emotive, the motor-practical, the perceptual, and the cognitive, though the distinctions are not all that important here since the regions are coextensive (Merleau-Ponty 1962). What is important is that cognition is not the only form of consciousness, rationality, or mode of "knowing." In fact, it is often the case that our cognitive representations are depreciated versions of things we "know" intimately more through other regions of consciousness.

Speaking, for example, involves cognition, but the act of making particular noises is perhaps more a matter of motor-practical consciousness/rationality than it is of representational thought. Even the most astute poet struggles to place love within the bounds of language, yet it is "known" by lovers every day. "Thoughts," as Nietzsche (1974: 203) suggests, "are the shadows of feelings — always darker, emptier, simpler." The point is that other modes of "knowing" exist, they are powerful, and we are bereaved if we continue to undervalue them. Extending consciousness-raising tactics beyond cognitive information production into a practice of producing subversive aesthetic experiences increases the potential for left mobilization because the latter engages embodied consciousness in all of its "regions." We live and feel the contradictions of capitalism every day. Art terrorism generates immediate visceral confrontations with those contradictions.

The terms *affect* and *affection*, while deeply related to "emotional experience," should be understood more robustly as Deleuze and Guattari describe it through their work on Spinoza. Affection refers to a certain viscerality connected to events experienced through the regions of consciousness with varying degrees of intensity. When I read the word "love," the affects it draws forth related to my cognition are less intense than the affects it draws from my emotional consciousness, because the afflictions produced in terms of words are not nearly as intense as the emotions I experience. This process is largely obscured by the bias toward cognitive rationality, which itself is just a certain set of affects. Deleuze (1991: 93) explains the link between affect, which is the latent "capacity of a thing/being to be affected and to affect something," and affections, which are the actual (visceral) states stirred up through an encounter where affects draw each other forth to enable particular actions.

Affect and affection are coextensive since they always lead to each other, though it would be a mistake to liken an affection to a mere effect. Rather, an affection is more like an awakening of capacities, a drawing fourth of a certain existential experience, a mood, a set of dispositions, through the regions of consciousness. In this sense, traditional consciousness raising is the production of affection, but it is unnecessarily limited to one region of consciousness: the cognitive. Affections provide the basis for or context through which a conscious subject may act in various ways. The term *affliction* might be a better analog because affections are something we must suffer for any action to be possible and insofar as they are noticeable to subjectivity, they are also a disturbance of the experiential states that precede them or a variation of intensities across the regions of bodily consciousness (Deleuze 1991).

Affections are the existential contexts that enable action. Affects exist within a given body and, once called forth though an encounter with other affects, produce affections that provide intensive states needed for action. As noted, there are at least four modes in which subjectivity may have affections, each of them bodily and coextensive with the others. As I read a given passage, the passage affects my body cognitively as the mind draws forth representations, emotionally as the words stir sentiments, motor-practically as my eyes run across the page, and perceptually as I filter out the various sensations around me and draw myself into the page and its world (Merleau-Ponty 1962). As regions of my consciousness are affected by what I am doing with my *lebenswelt*, affections occur as varying intensities in my body, creating a field of action. Reading an article about mass tax evasion by the extremely wealthy and the lack of funds for public education draws forth affections and opens my being to potential actions.

The bias toward cognition suggests that action occurs at the end of a causal chain, beginning with a perception, mediated by cognition, and resulting in an action that is more or less correct, depending on the rigour put in at the cognitive phase and its basis in a supposedly transcendent reality. Phenomenologically, though, embodied subjectivity is such that interaction with an object or event is both a reaching out of the immanent affects in the body — the regions of consciousness — and a reaching out of the immanent affects of the object/event, which opens up of fields of potential actions, actions that were always imminently there but are rendered more viable once stirred by the encounter (Jaques 2013). The potential actions arise as a result of subjectivity's communion with particular aspects of its *lebenswelt*.

Affections are activated, suffered, as a communion between affect and affectation, where the result is an emergent field of action, an activation of the latent possibilities of the body. What matters in this is not that there can be a disjunction between the world and our experience, a falsity of consciousness, but that we are experiencing (and this makes actions possible through an affliction) a suffering of a new power to do something right now (Deleuze 1991). Art engages varied affects and, more immediately, generates affections through a robust aesthetic experience beyond what is possible through encounters centred around affect related primarily to cognition. Art, generally, and insurgent art, in particular, are thus more likely to mobilize action.

As embodied subjectivity suffers the affections of encounters, a field of potential action opens between the two as affects are called forth across the regions of consciousness, rendering particular actions more viable. The emergence of particular actions is not the result of cognitive calculations within the subject, but the processual strain of the encounter itself, described by Kingsmith as the ongoing tension between active and reactive forces. This process is at the base of all action, whether between a human and an object/event, a human and a social structure, two humans, many humans and history, and so on. Robustly aesthetic experiences that engage affects beyond cognition, though not excluding it, enrich the general potential for varied action. Left projects aiming to generate social transformations should use art tactically, alongside more traditional forms of consciousness raising, to dramatically increase the potential for radical action. The tactic of art terrorism and the production of insurgent art, as noted, produce subversive and robust aesthetic experiences that involve a felt confrontation with the anxiety-producing contradictions of late-stage capitalism. For this reason, an augmenting left should engage in these activities as a central component of mobilization.

Notes

1. Late capitalism, or late-stage capitalism, is a term coined by continental European socialists in the late 1930s that has come to refer to modern capitalism from World War II onward. Social media website Reddit describes it as "the horrible things the hypocrisies and absurdities of capitalism forces people to do to survive."
2. It should be noted that the BLM and #MeToo movements employ a variety of tactics. As Rickford points out of BLM, the use of "confrontation politics" is about much more than raising awareness. That said, both movements do involve aims of consciousness raising and importantly so.
3. I understand it is a bit cumbersome to outline the theoretical framework of this chapter last, but I take the tactic and action to be more primary. The claims made here are grounded in post-positivist theory, existential philosophy, and phenomenological methodology.
4. Massumi (2007) seems to take a hard stance against conflating affect/affection with personal feeling. I take this to be related to Deleuze's problematic of active/passive affection, but here I trace Deleuze's notion of intensity (1991) to its roots in Bergson, where it is deeply connected with phenomenological experience.
5. These arguments are treated extensively in Husserl (2006), Heidegger (2013), and Merleau-Ponty (1962), among others. There is a more contemporary articulation of this in cognitive science and the philosophy of mind in the form of a neo-emergentism based in dynamic systems theory (Thompson 2007) or "embodied embedded cognition" (Van Dijk et al. 2008), although their use of the terms "cognition," "mind," and "consciousness" are a bit misleading. It should also be noted that this type of materialism does not necessitate reductionism or determinism. See Thompson (2007), for example.
6. The Panama Papers are an unprecedented leak of 11.5 million documents that detail financial and attorney-client information from the database of Panamanian law firm and corporate service provider Mossack Fonseca. The documents, some dating back to the 1970s, were leaked in 2015 by an anonymous source.

References

Bergson, Henri, and F.L. Pogson. 2001. *Time and Free Will: An Essay on the Immediate Data of Consciousness*. Mineola: Dover Publications.

Carroll, Noël. 2000. *Theories of Art Today*. Madison: University of Wisconsin Press.

Cullen, Darren. 2013. "Pocket Money Loans." Atom Gallery London. <spellingmistakescostlives.com/pocketmoneyloans>.
Deleuze, Gilles. 1991. *Bergsonism*, trans. Hugh Tomlinson and Barbara Habberjam. New York: Zone Books.
Engels, Friedrich. 1968 [1893]. "Engels to Franz Mehring." *Marx-Engels Correspondence*, ed. Sally Ryan, trans. Donna Torr. <marxists.org>.
Gramsci, Antonio.2008. *Selections from the Prison Notebooks*, eds. Quintin Hoare and Geoffrey Nowell-Smith. New York: International Publishers.
Guattari, Félix. 1995. *Chaosmosis: An Ethico-Aesthetic Paradigm*. Sydney: Power Publications.
Harmon, Raymond S. 2011. *Bomb: A Manifesto of Art Terrorism*. <issuu.com/subliminal/docs/bombmanifesto>.
Heidegger, Martin. 2013. *Being and Time*, trans. John Macquarrie and Edward Robinson. Hoboken: Wiley-Blackwell.
Husserl, Edmund. 2006. *The Crisis of European Sciences and Transcendental Phenomenology: An Introduction to Phenomenological Philosophy*, trans. David Carr. Evanston: Northwestern University Press.
___. 2010. *The Idea of Phenomenology*, trans. Lee Hardy. New York: Kluwer Academic.
Institute for Precarious Consciousness. 2014. "We Are All Very Anxious." *Plan C*, April 4. <weareplanc.org/blog/we-are-all-very-anxious/>.
Jaques, William S. 2013. "Fractal Ontology and Anarchic Selfhood." MA thesis, McMaster University. <hdl.handle.net/11375/12917>.
Mallin, Samuel B. 2009. *Body on My Mind: Body Hermeneutic Method*. Toronto: University of Toronto Press.
Marx, Karl. 1994. *Selected Writings*, ed. Lawrence H. Simon. Indianapolis: Hackett Publishing Company.
Massumi, Brian. 2007. "Notes on the Translation." *A Thousand Plateaus: Capitalism and Schizophrenia*. Minneapolis: University of Minnesota Press.
Merleau-Ponty, Maurice. 1962. *Phenomenology of Perception*. New York: Routledge.
Nietzsche, Friedrich Wilhelm. 1974. *The Gay Science: with a Prelude in Rhymes and an Appendix of Songs*, trans. Walter Kaufmann. New York: Random House.
Rickford, Russell. 2015. "Black Lives Matter: Toward a Modern Practice of Mass Struggle." *New Labor Forum*, 25, 1.
Sarachild, Kathie, 1978. "Consciousness-Raising: A Radical Weapon." *Redstockings Magazine*. New York: Random House.
Saul, Ben. 2010. *Defining Terrorism in International Law*. Oxford: Oxford University Press.
Thompson, Evan. 2007. *Mind in Life: Biology, Phenomenology, and the Sciences of Mind*. Cambridge: Belknap Press.
Van Dijk, Jelle Van, Roel Kerkofs, Iris van Rooij, and Pim Haslager. 2008. "Special Section: Can There Be Such a Thing as Embodied Embedded Cognitive Neuroscience?" *Theory & Psychology*, 18, 3.

19. *Détourne* Down for What?
Culture Jamming in the Age of General Anxiety

A.T. Kingsmith

During the 2016 US presidential election, culture jamming was definitively culture jammed. Memes, sub-advertisements, hacking, conspiracy theories, pranks, and info dumps consistently scandalized the media and galvanized support for the alternative "outsider" candidate, who also happened to be a billionaire reality-television host (Mueller 2018). What binds these different fields together is the ability to build an *affective economy* that appeals to people and activates crowds (Karppi et al. 2016). We can see it happening — the material infrastructure of affect management — in the sentiments, emotions, and feelings that have proven no less instrumental in maintaining power than "the economy."[1] And yet what actually happens in the process is difficult to describe, as we currently lack the proper frameworks for interpreting how subjects can be manipulated through their capacity for unawareness. In a society where the affective conditions of neoliberalism prefigure even our most local and partial experiences, we see a collapsing of the real and imagined distinctions people impose between the processes of resisting authority and the emotional logics of late capitalism.

Emboldened by racial, cultural, and economic anxieties wrought by three decades of extensive neoliberal reform, right-wing populists affectively manipulated anti-establishment sentiments (exemplified today by discourses of "fake news" and "alternative facts") to achieve stunning electoral victories in the face of fragmented and increasingly insular radical left groups. To probe such a disconnect further, this chapter briefly traces out the genealogy of *détournement* — a precursor to culture jamming meaning "hijacking" or "derailing" — as a leftist tactic for rerouting the Fordist social factory, before mapping our present condition of generalized anxiety, where the absence of cohesion, agency, or alternatives to neoliberalism has created a situation of helplessness. This inaction reproduces a cyclical mythos of apathetic powerlessness, taking a negative toll on mental health that Walter Benjamin (1974 [1931]) first described as "the persistent condition of Left melancholy": an attachment to loss that supersedes any desire to be unburdened by it. In response, I analyze the recuperation of *détournement* in the "self-jamming society" as symptomatic of the larger condition of *reflexive paralysis* on the radical left. Finally, I call for the activation of a "communal voice," a shared expression of trust and feeling — "we are all very anxious" — that cuts across the anxiety-inducing axioms of neoliberal exploitation.

Détournement as Active Force

This chapter draws upon a Marxian-Deleuzo-Guattarian framework for *materializing affect*, an approach in which radical affects of active-becoming are contrasted with those of reactive-blockage and which theorizes that each phase of capitalism has a *generalized reactive affect* that is particularly induced by its dominant forms of power (IPC 2014). In the Fordist period, the generalized reactive affect was *monotony*; in the neoliberal period, it has become *anxiety*. Importantly, each generalized reactive affect persists as long as effective expressions of feeling and communal voice have not been formulated. By blaming the oppressed for their oppression, each phase personalizes the reactive affect, creating a "public secret," which everyone experiences yet nobody acknowledges in a discursive landscape characterized by social isolation and increasingly invasive systems of distraction.[2]

When affect — defined by Spinoza (via Deleuze 1988) and discussed in more detail by William S. Jaques in his chapter as emotive, non-conscious, pre-personal, transmittable experiences of intensity — is an active force, it can enable groups to cultivate dissident positions that shed light on alternatives to the current conditions. When it is a *reactive* force, in contrast, affect has its origins in statism and capitalism. "It aims to make social space neat and orderly [by] creating and recreating governable subjects that are conducive to top-down quantification and control [while simultaneously] providing the work-discipline and speed which capitalism demands" (IPC 2014: 272). Reactive force should be theorized in continuity with alienation and decomposition because ultimately, through being disempowered and segmented, reactionaries are active forces turned inward: "Processes of alienation convert active into reactive force, attacking the field of abundance and creating a situation of scarcity" that is continually reproduced (IPC 2014: 272). In reactive systems, the active forces of social organizing are disjointed so as to prevent their flourishing — creating an order actively denying life, while force-feeding the body to a near saturation point.

In retaliation to growing concern with the mediation of affective relations through consumer goods, the Situationist International (SI) developed *détournement* as an indispensable means of counteracting the "society of the spectacle" — a simulated reality which, according to Guy Debord (1967), generates the desire to consume by positioning workers as consumerist cogs within the exploitative machinations of capitalism. By the late 1960s, the Fordist model of workplace management had, in the Global North, expanded out from the physical factory to blanket the whole of society with monotonous work that created the experience of a world with no outside. For the SI, this marked a reactive shift from expression through directly lived experiences to individuated expression by proxy through the exchange or consumption of commodities: a shift that inflicted significant and far-reaching damage by obscuring the extent to which the relations of production mediate and direct our affective conditions (Plant 1992).

As mechanized wide-scale production techniques spread across advanced industrialized economies, the entrenchment of monotony became the *generalized reactive affect*. In response to this empire of signs — where life in industrialized areas, driven by the forces of Fordism, became wearisome, sterile, gloomy, conditioning, linear, and productivity-driven — *détournement* offered a new kind of political tactic that activated the affective conditions of domination to turn practices in the Fordist system and its media culture against itself. Rather than merely adding to the stock of worthless copies that surround us, practices of *détournement* worked to reroute the endless pressures of commodification by activating political agency through the act of appropriation. In other words, the fundamental aim of *détournement* was not to appropriate the image, but to appropriate the power of appropriation (Wark 2009).

By insisting that "we do not want a world in which the guarantee that we will not die of starvation is bought by accepting the risk of dying of boredom," *détourners* attempted to communalize the public secret of boredom (Vaneigem 1967: 18). Deploying radio jamming, phone phreaking, and other subversive tactics against mass media in order to sow confusion within the dominant culture, *détourning* imbued ordinary life objects, texts, and geographies with ideological and artistic qualities that mutated their semantic function. A billboard advertisement becomes an anti-capitalist installation. News broadcasts become inaudible noise performances. Importantly, such strategies never claimed to be "authentic" or to create something fresh from the start (Knabb 2006). The SI took what was routine and gave it new context. Such distortions activated the bored, apathetic audiences of Fordism and invoked a shared energy in them: "By creating new situations, such interventions were intended to be a catalyst for social change filtered through a reorientation of normal life" (Goldsmith 2011: 36).

While denouncing previous left tactics such as forming new Leninist parties and staging A-to-B marches, and calling public meetings "boring" or simply recuperative, the SI offered a new way to disrupt the passive fetishization of commodities by negating the ideological conditions of artistic production — in which all artworks are ultimately commodities — while also playing on the affective expectations of viewers and bystanders (IPC 2014). By cutting and recombining the ideological apparatuses of consumer society in shocking and surprising ways, *détournement* was not intended to be a new form of conditioning, but a playful "reversal of perspective that replaces knowledge by praxis, hope by freedom, and mediation by the will to immediacy" (Vaneigem 1967: 19).

As the function of Fordist conditioning was to assign and adjust the hierarchies of the social factory, *détournement* entailed a kind of anti-conditioning that rerouted the literary and artistic heritage of humanity for the purposes of radical politics. It sought to make the shames of consumer fetishism — all the racist, sexist, classist, and ableist forms of capitalist exploitation — more shameful by exposing them to the ruling elites and, more importantly, to the publics ruled by them. This reversal of perspective, a communalizing of the public secret, is closely tied to the sense of empowerment that underpins waves of resistance strategies and countercultural exodus from dominant forms of boring work and rigid social roles still practised by activist groups (Artflux; Orange Alternative; Guerrilla Girls) and movements (May 1968; Autonomia in the 1970s; anti-globalization in 1990s; Occupy Wall Street in the early twenty-tens).

The Age of General Anxiety

In 1993, Mark Dery projected that for as long as the receiver of a message experiences the freedom to "feel" in a different way, *détournement* maintains an appropriative power to divert the monotony of passive reception. As the basic principle of *détournement* resides in the transgression of the original phrase, object, and feeling, however, "if the *détournement* doesn't surpass the initial remark, it comes to a sudden stop, it aborts" (Vaneigem 2015: 205).

In the nearly three decades since Dery's diagnostic, which wove together an assortment of *détournements* into an oppositional aesthetic for the new millennium, the affective distinction between appropriation and recuperation has become increasingly strained. Naomi Klein (1999) details how corporations like Nike repeatedly approach *Adbusters* with lucrative contracts in order to develop "ironic" promotional campaigns, highlighting the gradual recuperation of "alternative" medias, which have become increasingly limited by the satirical reproduction of the cultural norms in which they are produced and consumed (Waltz 2005). Such trends have proliferated through the appropriation of the DIY ethic by a commercialized "maker movement" led by Apple, Instagram, and Pinterest, which produce an experience of empowerment without substance by allowing users to tinker, but only within certain pre-circumscribed limits (Davies 2017).

Such examples are emblematic of a more general neoliberal shift from the Fordist social factory to what Maurizio Lazzarato (2009) terms the "enterprise society" — a shift underpinned by individualization, insecuritization, depoliticization, and simulated scarcities that have become totalizing. The SI asserts that in active creativity everyone possesses the ultimate weapon. But this weapon, as Vaneigem (1967: 20) warns, must be used wittingly: "where creativity is mobilized against the grain, in the service of lies and oppression, it turns into a sad farce, and is duly consecrated as art." In a recent study of the "advertising psychology spectacle,"

Pamela Odih (2013: 355) points to the ways in which current strategies of neuromarketing and advertising have perfected techniques of affect management to redirect *détourned* affects back "into the sign-currencies of Western capitalist commodity culture." The ease through which interventions by today's advertising "creatives" have dissolved the tenacious distinction between commercial advertising and the subversions of the artistic avant-garde raises many fundamental questions about the efficacy of culture jamming in initiating a reversal of perspective today.

While the appropriation of *détournement* has always run the risk of giving new life to the very forces they endeavour to hijack, the practice of commandeering the monotonous in scandalous and outrageous ways has become increasingly saturated by a neoliberal condition of generalized anxiety. The resultant affective economy is such that the productions of anti-capitalism are not an antithesis to capitalism. Instead, as highlighted in Terry Maley's chapter, affects are used to reinforce capital. In the same way that Fordism's overhaul of the workplace initiated an ensuing transformation of social consciousness via the rise of mass consumption and scientific management, neoliberalism has brought about fundamental changes that are inherently destructive to social bonds, trust, and the conditions for communal voice.

Neuromarketing now provides a wider range of niche products for increasingly individualized distractions. Companies have also adopted flattened management models, inciting employees to not only self-manage, but to invest their souls in their work. By enclosing and securing the freedom to appropriate within such flattened hierarchies and niche markets, capitalism has recomposed with an altered affective structure. As "Bifo" Berardi (2009) points out, this recomposition is directly linked to a network of global outsourcing, lean production, and financialization. Indeed, there is a material isomorphism between generalized anxiety about the future and an economy with an explosion of speculative capital that lacks any prospect of redemption in the "real" economy (IPC 2014). As a result of the transformation from the social factory to the enterprise society, generalized anxiety has eclipsed perpetual monotony as the dominant public secret.

Research by Beat Weber (2004) suggests that most workers are unstable — mentally, physically, financially — yet reluctant to admit it due to social taboos. Recent data collected by the Public Religion Research Institute

(Cox, Lienesch, and Jones 2017) corroborates Weber's hypotheses, finding that a "culture of anxiety" was by far the most common reason given by first-time Republican voters who helped to secure Trump's electoral victory. Moreover, intensification of the surveillance state increasingly takes the form of *pre-emptive control techniques* that stop social actions before they start or before they can achieve anything (IPC 2014).

Today the presence of anxiety, depression, and stress are often recognized, but only as *personal* challenges, "explained away as neurological problems, faulty cognitive schemas, or a lack of coping strategies" (IPC 2014: 277). Indeed, the public discourse suggests that we need *more* stress and anxiety, so as to keep us "safe" or "competitive." To this end, the proliferation of casual and semi-self-employed work is justified by innumerable varieties of *management* discourse — time management, anger management, parental management, and self-branding — all of which offer anxious workers an illusion of control in return for ever-greater conformity to the affective economy of neoliberalism (Moore 2017).

A Self-Jamming System

Rather than being lauded as a catalyst for reorienting everyday life, the SI-inspired techniques of jamming have come under fire for their role in bringing us to this point. In response to the general anxieties of neoliberalism, voters clung to an unorthodox candidate who not only acknowledged fundamental problems (declining public infrastructure, lack of secure work, a failing health care system, increasing inequality, etc.) but also promised to elevate them, infamously, by Making America Great Again (MAGA).

In the run-up to Trump's win, MAGA media hoaxing — "culture jamming in its purest form" according to Dery (2010 [1993]) — played the news cycle with pernicious "alternative facts" that nudged voters into the hands of a dangerous incompetent (Hall, Goldstein, and Ingram 2016). As Gavin Mueller (2018) observes, Trump himself *détourned* the establishment media's criticism of reactionary propaganda by making "fake news" a rallying cry against CNN and the *New York Times*. Tactics of culture jamming, like graffiti artist Shepard Fairy's (2008) "Barack Obama Hope," which were relatively recently viewed as having helped elect the

US's first Black president, are increasingly coming under fire for their role in stoking the flames of right-wing populism.

Not surprisingly, attempts to address the generalized reactive affect of anxiety through the electoral system have resulted in further unease. Matt Aibel (2018) points to the rise of what is now called "Trump Affective Disorder" because mental health services in the US have observed increasing reports of patients claiming Trump-related stress, trauma, and anxiety.

In a situation characterized by the deep disappointment in a supposedly anti-establishment president whose twenty-four cabinet appointees possess more wealth than the GDPs of eighty-seven countries combined, culture jamming today seems to offer the radical left little more than the power of a fleeting sneer — what Mueller (2018) calls a "radicalism bereft of seriousness."

This jamming of culture jamming is symptomatic of a larger reactive blockage of the radical left. On the one hand, many strategies are focused on mitigating the worst effects of capitalism. For instance, a universal basic income could relieve short-term anxieties around income, but right-wing thinkers also champion it as a way to replace social welfare with an imagined "Tocquevillian civil society" governed by the neoliberal capacity for self-management (Murray 2006). On the other, social movements today do not have the proper mechanisms in place for combating anxiety. Calls for deliberate exposure to high-anxiety situations — physical confrontations with the police, open marches in the streets — are indicative of the reactionary disposition of contemporary tactics toward anxiety. A traditional tactic, what activists call the "do-ology," is that of the vague injunction: "Just stop being afraid!" Yet the question of overcoming the social and political manifestations of anxiety is rarely as simple as personally and consciously rejecting it.

Mark Fisher (2009) points to the extent to which politicians, media, and voters rushed to support massive bailouts during 2008 financial crisis as demonstrative of the inability of the left, and of enterprise society more generally, to sustain conversations about tactics and strategies that directly address our general and personalized feelings of frustration, anxiety, and fear. The imposition of such self-censorship has hardened, manifesting as a "reflexive paralysis" where we agree on the flawed nature of capitalism but lack the means of affecting change.

As Oliver Jutel (2017) observes, when faced with such prevailing tendencies, much of the self-identified left has been quick to retreat from any kind of broad, far-reaching struggle that could be attractive to the politically curious. Needed now are not just better tactics for alleviating the personalized responses to increasing precarity within expansive regimes of measurement, surveillance, and self-care, but long-term strategies for combatting general anxiety. This is crucial for the emotional transformation of fear into a sense of injustice, a type of anger that is less resentful and more focused, and a move toward a reversal of perspective (IPC 2014). As emphasized by AK Thompson in this volume, such a transformation requires learning to operate within the discrete logics underlying different assemblages of dialectical images, dreams, and production in ways more effective than the constant far-right appeal to MAGA mythology.

Communalizing the Public Secret

In reflecting on the present conditions, Dery (2010 [1993]) asks whether culture jamming has become a "socially sanctioned release valve — a tactical outlet for class resentments and pent-up dissent over social injustices and economic inequities that might have found more profoundly political expression if they hadn't been harmlessly exorcized via *rituals* of resistance." As jammings are saturated in a paralyzing situation of permanent contradiction, the very tactic of attacking and distancing oneself from the sign systems of capital seems to create a fantasy of transgression that merely softens our complicity within the overarching system. Instead of decrying *détournement* for lacking a revolutionary strategy it never claimed, it is more pertinent to ask: where do tactics for jamming still prove useful in the activation of communal voices to compose new ways of relating our shared feelings of anxiety?

Moving forward, an augmented left should not get caught in paralyzing debates over whether *détournement* and its outgrowths are no longer "useful" — or, for that matter, ever were — for a reversal of perspective. As part of a larger repertoire of tactics for fighting the affective economy of monotony (strikes, wage struggles, street protests, and occupations), radical left iterations of culture jamming continue to draw attention to the ways that the logics of power violate populations everywhere according to dominant socio-material logics controlled by white, wealthy, minoritarian groups.[3] In a context where the structural conditions of oppression are increasingly normalized and individualized, the hijacking of signs is vital in connecting divisions across different intersections of shared oppression by emphasizing the importance of a communal exorcism of the public secret of general anxiety.

Our general yet also personalized struggles against anxiety must offer an alternative to processes that begin and end with the development of critical capacities, as well as to approaches that funnel critical development into traditional organizations; this will require a "reconfiguration of horizontal connections which provide a kind of groundedness for life, warding off both meaninglessness and isolation" (IPC 2014: 290). Ultimately, this process requires learning to take time off from the obligation to perform, to value our responsibilities to self and other, becoming unburdened of loss by learning to reconstruct elements of fragmented lives into active patterns of joy, love, and movement-connected anger. The affective "safety net" or respite function of groups is here particularly appropriate in reactivating people's active force.

In the face of a deep crisis of political legitimacy for long-established liberal institutions, Max Haiven's chapter reiterates how anxiety and related emotions such as depression, resentment, anger, heartbreak, excessive stress, and so on can provide the clear focus needed for augmenting the left. As an ethical and political obligation to compose relations for struggle, the left must focus on that which truly unites people: the situations in which they find themselves, not abstract ideas determined in advance. By recognizing the reality and the systemic nature of our experiences through a shared anger that affirms that our pain is really pain, that what we see and feel is real, and that our problems are not only personal, the shared experience of anxiety is a mechanism through which to confront this juncture. The point here is not simply to recount our experiences but to transform and restructure them through the activation of communal voice. To this end, I contend that personal but also generalized experiences of anxiety can act as a lightning rod for communalizing the public secret of anxiety, in order to shift people's perceptions of the enterprise society from a localized game to the globalized reality of intensifying oppression.

Notes

1. The term "economy" on its own seems to refer to the financial economy, even if this is ill-defined — I consider the term to be broader than that. In the original Greek, "eco" means household, habitat, or milieu, and "nomos" has to do with

the law/rule/principle determining this domain. Economy is not strictly tied to money; many speak of affective economies in terms of quantitative methods and analytical precision — for example, Mikołajewska-Zając's (2016) work on "Couchsurfing as an affective enterprise."
2. A public or open secret is a concept or experience that is "officially" (de jure) secret or restricted in knowledge, but in practice (de facto) it may be widely known. In other words, it is something that is widely known to be true, but which few are willing to categorically acknowledge in public.
3. "Minoritarian" is a neologism developed by Deleuze for describing a political structure in which a minority segment of a population has majority control of that entity's decision-making processes. For instance, a minoritarian state is one in which legislative power is held or controlled by a small, elite segment of the populous.

References

Aibel, Matt. 2018. "The Personal Is Political Is Psychoanalytic: Politics in the Consulting Room." *Psychoanalytic Perspectives,* 15, 1.
Benjamin, Walter. 1974 [1931]. "Left-Wing Melancholy* (On Erich Kästner's new book of poems)." *Die Gesellschaft,* 8, 1.
'Bifo' Berardi, Franco, and Eric Empson. 2009. *Precarious Rhapsody.* New York: Minor Compositions.
Cox, Daniel, Rachel Lienesch, and Robert P. Jones. 2017. "Beyond Economics: Fears of Cultural Displacement Pushed the White Working Class to Trump." Washington: Public Religion Research Institute. <prri.org/research/white-working-class-attitudes- economy-trade-immigration-election-donald-trump/>.
Davies, Sarah R. 2017. *Hackerspaces: Making the Maker Movement.* New York: John Wiley & Sons.
Debord, Guy. 1967. *The Society of the Spectacle.* New York: Bureau of Public Secrets.
Deleuze, Gilles. 1988. *Spinoza: Practical Philosophy.* San Francisco: City Lights.
Dery, Mark. 2010 [1993]. *Culture Jamming: Hacking, Slashing, and Sniping in the Empire of Signs.* <markdery.com/?page_id=154>.
Fairy, Shepard. 2008. "Hope." Obey Giant. <obeygiant.com/obama/#more-541>.
Fisher, Mark. 2009. *Capitalist Realism: Is There No Alternative?* London: Zero Books.
Goldsmith, Kenneth. 2011. *Uncreative Writing: Managing Language in the Digital Age.* New York: Columbia University Press.
Hall, Kira, Donna Goldstein, and Matthew Ingram. 2016. "The Hands of Donald Trump: Entertainment, Gesture, Spectacle." *Journal of Ethnographic Theory,* 6, 2.
IPC (Institute for Precarious Consciousness). 2014. "Anxiety, Affective Struggle, and Precarity Consciousness-Raising." *Interface,* 6, 2.
Jutel, Olivier. 2017. "The Alt-Right and the Death of Counterculture." *Overland,* 229, 2.
Karppi, Tero, Lotta Kähkönen, Mona Mannevuo, Mari Pajala, and Tanja Sihvonen. 2016. "Affective capitalism: Investments and investigations." *Ephemera: Theory and Politics in Organization,* 16, 4.
Klein, Naomi. 1999. *No Logo: Taking Aim at the Brand Bullies.* Toronto: Vintage

Canada.

Knabb, Ken. 2006. *Situationist International Anthology*. New York: Bureau of Public Secrets.

Lazzarato, Maurizio. 2009. "Neoliberalism in Action: Inequality, Insecurity, and the Reconstitution of the Social." *Theory, Culture & Society*, 26, 6.

Mikołajewska-Zając, Karolina. 2016. "Sharing as Labour and as Gift: Couchsurfing as an Affective Enterprise." *Ephemera*, 16, 4.

Moore, Phoebe V. 2017. *The Quantified Self in Precarity: Work, Technology and What Counts*. London: Routledge.

Mueller Gavin. 2018. "No Alternative: How Culture Jamming Was Culture-Jammed." *Real Life Magazine*, January 22. <reallifemag.com/no-alternative/>.

Murray, Charles. 2006. *In Our Hands: A Plan to Replace the Welfare State*. Washington: AEI Press.

Odih, Pamela. 2013. "Détournement á la Mode Situationist Praxis: History and Present of Cultural Political Resistance to the Psychology of Advertising Spectacle." *Journal for Cultural Research*, 17, 4.

Plant, Sadie. 1992. *The Most Radical Gesture: The Situationist International in a Postmodern Age*. London: Routledge.

Vaneigem, Raoul. 1967. *The Revolution of Everyday Life*. New York: Rebel Press.

___. 2015. *Self-Portraits and Caricatures of the Situationists International*. London: Colossal Books.

Waltz, Mitzi. 2005. *Alternative and Activist Media*. Edinburgh: Edinburgh University Press.

Wark, Mc Kenzie. 2009. "Détournement: An Abusers Guide." *Angelaki: Journal of the Theoretical Humanities*, 14, 1.

Weber, Beat. 2004. *Everyday Crisis in the Empire*. <republicart.net/disc/precariat/weber01_en.htm>.

20. Thirteen Theses Toward a Materialist Theory of Revenge Capitalism
Max Haiven

I. Revenge Capital

Beginning perhaps with Francis Bacon's (1625) treatise on the subject, colonial "Western" political philosophy has, by and large, dedicated itself to castigating and defaming the vengeance of the exploited. It has largely served to justify the perpetual revenge of the powerful upon the oppressed, the endless normalized cruelties of enclosure, colonialism, exploitation, and the control of people and populations (Federici 2005; Newsinger 2006). Whereas Christian doctrine stresses turning the other cheek and surrendering vengeance to God's will on Judgment Day, dominant European political thinkers, including Thomas Hobbes (1985) and Adam Smith (1759), have legitimated the state as the monopolist of vengeance. This monopoly is supposed to ensure the "rule of law" based on the unassailable virtue of private property. But the history of state violence, from the witch trials to imperialism to slavery to settler colonialism, indicates that modern forms of sovereign power can be seen as one-way revenge systems.

My argument is that today's capitalism is the evolution of this tendency. I intend to sketch this argument on three levels. First, like all systems of domination, the hegemonic institutions of capitalism frame the actions of its opponents as meaningless, nihilistic revenge precisely because the economies of justice these opponents insist upon are unintelligible in the moral algebra of the system. Second, revenge should not be understood as simply a transhistorical individual human passion (and certainly not only as a personal emotion), but rather as something manifested by and through the reproduction of systems-in-crisis. I want to argue that today's particularly crisis-ridden, highly financialized, carceral, and neocolonial mode of global capitalism can be fruitfully interpreted as a system of revenge. In this way, I am echoing some of the insights emphasized across this section by Terry Maley, William S. Jacques, and A.T. Kingsmith, who all posit that political affects are in fact deeply structural. Third, I suggest many of the political and cultural pathologies of our moment, including the recent global rise of far-right and neo-fascist tendencies, can be seen as produced by and reproductive of the underlying system of vengeance.

Alongside AK Thompson, who argues that an augmenting left must dare to learn from the dispiriting success of reactionary responses to our current crisis, I want to close by suggesting that we are ill-served by the normative aversion to revenge of our times; perhaps it is time to reclaim some sort of bottom-up form of "avenging"? Here I agree with Jaques's insistence that "the use of aesthetic forms of embodied consciousness raising aimed at actualizing more robustly visceral affections is a valuable tactic for projects of augmentation aimed at widespread mobilization for social transformations within late-stage capitalist regions."

II. Vengeful Accumulation

The transformation of capitalism into a revenge system has roots in the slave trade and colonial adventure, the literal origins of many of its key institutions and technologies, including joint stock corporations, insurance regimes, promissory notes, and fiat currencies (Baucom 2005; Robinson 2000). Already we can observe how, at what are presumed to be the "margins" of capitalism, "free trade" and the transformation of people and the planet into commodities fundamentally rely on the exercise of excessive surplus cruelty and abuse. This excess was not accidental; it represented a kind of unwarranted, unearned vengeance on subjugated populations, aiming not only to extract value and labour, but to break down non-capitalist social and economic structures through extreme violence. Vengeance is reflected in capitalism's beginning and its end, and it flows through, and deepens, the channels of white supremacy, cis/heteropatriarchy, settler colonialism, and other systems of oppression.

III. Torture as Economic Policy

Marx almost never mentioned revenge in his work, except to signal that history itself will bring about the vindication of the proletariat. He and Engels (1874) argued that individual acts of vengeance, which they associate with working-class militants like Auguste Blanqui, were not only foolhardy, but threatened to set the proletarian struggle back because they were not strategic. At the same time, Marx (1849) was keen to show that "legitimate" forms of capitalist exploitation and population management, like England's horrific poorhouses, represented the vengeance of parasitic capital against its own source of wealth: the proletariat. In crises, capitalism turns to a kind of frantic systemic sadism, such as the gory reprisals against the Paris Communards of 1871 (Marx 1871). Another example is the army of retribution whipped up by the British to avenge the 1857 "Sepoy Mutiny" in India, which saw the British destroy and loot huge territories, killing some ten million people (Newsinger 2006). For Marx (1857), the alleged sexual revenge-crimes of the Sepoys that justified expedition were in fact a reflection of Britain's own vengeful colonial occupation of India, where "torture formed an organic institution of financial policy."

IV. Collective Revenge Fantasies

Revenge has regularly been a key theme in the struggles of the oppressed and exploited. This vengeance is not the irrational, bestial hatred of the mob, but a method for countering the vengeance that capitalism and colonialism wreak on communities. In working-class songs and speeches throughout the history of capitalism, workers have exhorted themselves to a collective recognition of how their own energies and inherent value have been stripped by the inherent irrational vengefulness of the capitalist system itself (Kornbluh 2011). Singing or rallying together in the name of expropriating the expropriators is a ritual for defining and reclaiming a sense of collective value and power. While there is certainly a risk that vengefulness might be reduced to the kind of "one-dimensional" affective politics stressed by Maley, I believe even more is at stake. We would do better to frame vengefulness in Kingsmith's terms, as a kind of public secret "which everyone experiences yet nobody acknowledges."

V. Revenge and Reaction

The recent rise in revenge politics on the far right in the US, the UK, and elsewhere must be understood as integral to broader currents in *revenge capitalism*, not as an anomaly. The "new normal" of neoliberal precariousness, indebtedness, and mass surveillance and incarceration represents the vengeance of the ruling class against those who fought in or were the beneficiaries of the radical struggles that resulted in the unhappy postwar compromise. The unequal existential, economic, and social collapse wrought by revenge capitalism on our bodies and communities has prompted revanchist dreams of "returning" to some fabled bygone era of hierarchical dignity and ethnonational integrity. This revanchism is possessed by a kind of tragic and apocalyptic romanticism that projects the relatively privileged subject as the victim of his own tolerance, patience, and largess.[1] The result of this "betrayal" is that hegemonic cis-hetero, white masculinity has its "back against the wall," closed in on from all sides, conspired against, the victim of a revenge plot now brought to terrible fruition. The only option left is an apocalyptic nightmare to reset the scene, to return things to their rightful order.

VI. Witch Hunt

As much as this revanchist dream is about whiteness, it is also about masculinity, and the victories of far-right, reactionary, and white-supremacist forces, though their ranks include many women. The precursors to the figure of aggrieved, betrayed, and "cuckolded" masculinity included a decade of techno-patriarchal doxing, the rise of men's rights cults, and the explosion of "revenge porn" (Nagle 2017). The all-too-common argument that men who "speak out" against the norms and conventions of "political correctness" are subject to vindictive "witch hunts" makes for a pornographic display of wounded white masculinity. Indeed, the complaint that he is the target of a "witch hunt" is among Trump's favourite deflections.

But the appropriation of this term also disguises the ways that today's press gangs of online revanchist masculinity are themselves the echo of history's real witch trials, which were integral to the birth of capitalism and colonialism and the destruction of the cultures and economies of the commons (Federici 2005). In these trials, the social agony of the birth of capitalism and its destruction of social life was marshalled by reactionary religious forces and redirected against women (and some men) accused of witchcraft. Witchcraft was associated with, among other things, surplus female vengefulness, and the witch trials were orchestrated as public spectacles by the state to "prove" that social misery and discord were the result of occult conspiracies masterminded by women taking vengeance against the natural Christian order.

Today's far-right accusations of "witch hunts" targeting outspoken or powerful men rely on and reproduce the same logics, to the same general effect: women and gender non-binary people (and some men) are targeted both as irrational, vengeful spirits who will destroy civilization and as diabolical conspirators striving to take over that order and leave men bereft. Revenge porn, the abuse of intimate images to threaten, humiliate, or blackmail women online, is only one manifestation of this trend.

VII. Avenged Ancestors

Walter Benjamin (1969) was interested in revenge, too. In "Theses on the Concept of History," written as he fled the Nazis, Benjamin meditated not on the betrayal of socialism by the German working class, but the opposite: the betrayal of the working class by the social democrats. In tethering their notion of emancipation to gradual, technologically driven nationalist progress, the social democrats had severed what Benjamin saw as the "sinews" of the proletariat's greatest strengths: "hatred and spirit of sacrifice." This strength was generated not only by the utopian dreams of "liberated grandchildren," but also by the proletariat claiming their collective role as "avengers that complete the task of liberation in the name of generations of the downtrodden" (Benjamin 1969: 260). Benjamin's Marxist analysis led him to believe that capitalism had produced a historically unique proletariat that could finally throw off the shackles of oppression and exploitation and build a truly egalitarian, communist world.

We may or may not hold fast to Benjamin's faith that the proletariat are destined to liberate not only themselves but the oppressed of history itself. In any case, we would do well to dwell on the ghosts of vengeance he invokes and on his condemnation of social democracy. Then and now, social democrats have sought to banish "hatred and the spirit of sacrifice" from politics, insisting that participation in conventional institutions is sufficient to liberate ourselves and our futures. This is due to the strongly technocratic and elitist orientation of many social democrats, who, as Maley notes in his chapter, presume people are unable to overcome nihilistic violence. Today's social democrats have fatally misjudged the cultural politics of resentment and anger brewing underneath modern technological progress, "spirits of the past" that Thompson's chapter contends could be mobilized as "wish images" toward a common good. In this way, they fail to organize the "downtrodden" as avenging angels who can collect on debts owed for the generations of systemic trauma and vengeance that have built the current order.

VIII. Revanchist Cities

Readers might be tempted to see revenge as merely a contingent affect or emotive by-product of capitalist domination, a kind of regrettable cultural side effect of everyday economic torture. My curiosity, however, is drawn to revenge as a useful description of a structural tendency emerging from capitalism's crises and contradictions.

Late Marxist geographer Neil Smith (1996) recuperated the language of revanchism to help describe the financialized structural transformation of American urban space in the 1980s. Smith catalogues the ways in which property developers, far-right politicians, agents of speculative capital, media, and law enforcement orchestrated a "whitelash" campaign constituting an "all-out attack on the social policy structure that emanated from the New Deal and immediate post-war era." "Revenge" Smith continues (1996: 42–43), "against minorities, the working class, women, environmental legislation, gays and lesbians, immigrants became the increasingly common denominator of public discourse." This enabled a massive wave of urban enclosures, allowing wealthy, overwhelmingly white capitalists to reclaim areas of inner cities once abandoned by postwar urban planning and white flight.

Smith provides a framework for understanding the structural and systemic forces at work in gentrification beyond the knee-jerk moralism of hipster-bashing. Capitalist urban revanchism, then and now, relies both on the rekindling of a reactionary wealthy white-supremacist loathing of those racialized, poor subjects seen to be "ruining" the city with crime and squalor and also on the broader financialized tendencies within capitalism as a whole. In this process, it recalls and renovates earlier moments when capitalism has called up the spirits of white vengeance to restore order (Wang 2018).

IX. Prison: Revenge Factory

The prison-industrial complex in the US — that unprecedented "golden gulag," as Ruth Wilson Gilmore (2007) dubs it, where lives (disproportionately Black, Latinx, and Indigenous lives) are transmuted into vessels for both speculative capital and an almost inexplicable kind of socialized, retributive vengeance — is a key site of this noxious combination of white-supremacist revanchism and "revenge capitalism" (Wang 2018). Loïc Wacquant (2014) sees "hyper-incarceration" as the extension and expansion of Smith's logic of revanchism. Here, extreme financialized neoliberalism reacts to the crises of accumulation and of care (that in themselves have fomented) through the proliferation of prisons, the production of prisoners, and the expansion of the prison's austere, vengeful, and brutalizing logic throughout what remains of state institutions and into the fabric of social life. Financialized neoliberalism, like the forms of colonialism and capitalist exploitation that gave rise to it, not only uses new forms of social vengeance to punish those who rebel or refuse or simply get in the way of its already vengeful operations; it also renders whole populations "surplus," no longer worthy even of exploitation, and must discover methods and institutions of containment, control, and liquidation (Gilmore 2007; Wang 2018).

It's not only that the common narrative of the prisoner is of a bestial character who must pay a "debt to society" for the infraction of having taken vengeance into their own hands by breaking the laws of the state. It is also that, fittingly, the society within the prison, as it is projected in the media, utilizes torture as "an organic institution of financial policy" (Marx 1857). Thus, the prison operates through an economy of revenge: a lawless state of nature where the ability to avoid premature death is dependent entirely on one's ability to threaten vengeance against others who might enact abuse. Regardless of the complex reality of prisoner solidarity (Berger 2014; Davis 2005), the prison is transformed into a monument to the unspoken capitalist revenge economy that exists no less on the "outside" as it does on the "inside."

X. Cultural Illogic

Fredric Jameson (1984) famously called postmodernism the "cultural logic of late capitalism," signalling that, today, the realms of "culture" and "economics" can no longer be separated. Borrowing this framing, I am tempted to call revenge the "cultural illogic of belated capitalism."

The structural phenomena I associate with revenge capitalism seem to have accelerated the system's inherent propensity for crises beyond any measure of sustainability: ecological, sociological, or economic. We are in a moment of unpredictable extremism now, where even the world's most powerful capitalists are scared, frustrated, and lost as to what to do about the demons they have unleashed. Of course, capitalism's illogics have always operated beyond the control of any single capitalist or conspiracy of capitalists, being driven precisely and inexorably toward crisis by the competition of capitalists within and between different sectors or nation-states (Harvey 2006). But today, under what I have termed a "belated capitalism," that competition, and the crises it generates, seems to have accelerated into a kind of suicidal structural absurdity. In such circumstances, as Rosa Luxemburg (2003) taught us, capital often opts to place itself in escrow, calling up the spectres of fascism and authoritarianism or, horrifically, inviting total war and accelerated imperialism with increasingly destructive power and fury.

XI. The Means and Ends of History

This all follows the so-called end of history, in which, we were told, the global rule of free markets would bring about unprecedented peace and tranquility, allowing different people and cultures to sublimate their otherwise destructive rivalries and vendettas into the neutral arena of the competitive market (Fukuyama 1993). The sovereign market was supposed to be the final evolution of Leviathan, the great suppressor of revenge. (Trust the sovereign to provide justice, or else.)

Identifying financialized, neoliberal capitalism instead as a revenge system places it in a genealogy of colonial modes of power that enact vengeance on those whom they oppress and exploit while claiming to bring the benevolent rule of law, to save the oppressed and exploited from their own vengeful nature.

Frantz Fanon's (1963) work identifies ways that colonialism gaslights its victims, hiding its own vengeful nature while instilling in the colonized subject an idea that they need to be rescued from their own irrational, subhuman, untimely prehistory of endless vengeance. Thus, for Fanon and others, anti-colonial thought relies in part on a kind of revenge against the colonists' thought-world, a refusal of "recognition" within their oppressive and exploitative order (Coulthard 2014).

Of course, anti-colonial action was inevitably interpreted and framed as the irrational revenge of ungrateful "savages." White fears of the possible revenge of enslaved or formerly enslaved Africans, Asians, and Indigenous Peoples, as well as other exploited and marginalized non-white workers, have defined the colonial imagination and continue to animate white-supremacist worldviews today.

Fanon (1963: 139), however, is clear that "racialism and hatred, a 'legitimate desire for revenge,' cannot sustain a war of liberation" and that "hatred alone cannot draw up a program." Anti-colonial thought and action rests on and reveals the legitimacy of the revenge of the oppressed precisely by identifying the inherent vengeful illogic of the colonial regime. However, a simple form of vengeance cannot overcome it.

XII. Profits of Forgiveness

The insufficiency of revenge for creating deep, meaningful, and revolutionary change has, however, recently become a dreary, sanctimonious, and saccharine theme among liberals. Today, the horrifically reanimated corpses of three radical leaders have been summoned to justify a stifling culture of bleached reconcilophelia. Mahatma Gandhi, Nelson Mandela, and Martin Luther King Jr. were all complex and savvy political actors whose choice to employ non-violence and advocate forgiveness was arguably less moralistic than strategic in their circumstances (Gelderloos 2007). But today the complexities and contradictions of their particular decisions and words have been lost to an individualizing fetishization of their personalities to the extent they can justify the moral cowardice and inaction of would-be moderates. What is lost is that, in all three cases, forgiveness was tied to a broader notion of avenging the crimes and cruelties of the colonial or oppressive regime through its abolition. Forgiveness was not proposed for its own sake, but rather as a means to catalyze a strategic, revolutionary kind of patience or to set the stage for what was supposed to be a new post-colonial order.

XIII. Dig Two Graves

In *The Devil Finds Work*, James Baldwin (2011), in a meditation on race, film, and revenge in America, makes the important point that "revenge is a human dream" that can sustain all sorts of subjects and systems in its suspension, much the same way that Hamlet is a dreamlike narrative of suspended vengeance. When the dream comes true, as it does at the end of that famous play, the world is turned upside down and we are forever changed. As Baldwin (2011: 44–45) puts it, once vengeance is executed, "you have no way of conveying to the corpse why you made him one. You have the corpse and are thereafter at the mercy of a fact which missed the truth, which means that the corpse has you."

The fantasy moment of Hollywood melodrama, when the righteous avenger reveals their motivations before pulling the trigger, never really arrives for most of us, in spite of our individual and collective revenge fantasies. Moreover, what is never pictured is what comes *after* the satiated avenger rides away into the sunset. The all-consuming revenge fantasy can only be sustained, and can only sustain the obsessive fantasist, in the suspension of its own execution. Those who swear an oath to vengeance sign away their life and soul to be suspended in vengeance. They become the walking dead, dedicated to an act of death that is also an act of self-annihilation. To actually take vengeance is to abolish that all-consuming part of yourself that the oath created.

For this reason, the Confucian adage that "if you set out for revenge, first dig two graves" is indeed apt. But what if the broader system of vengeance has already dug those graves and the victims and would-be avengers of this primary systemic vengeance simply seek to fill them and end the cycle? Marx proposes an answer: Capital is itself an undead beast, a vampire sucking on our own productive energies. Capital is reanimated dead labour, the encrypted form of the living labour, the cooperative potential of the proletariat, which now takes command of and feeds off its original progenitors. Capital's grave stands agape, but so too does "ours," its gravediggers, for we, too, are made into the walking dead by it.

What, then, does it mean to avenge oneself and one's proverbial ancestors against such a system of revenge? The negation of the negation not only means the abolition of capitalism and its aligned systems of racial and gendered power and violence; it also means the abolition of the avenging, revolutionary subject as well.

XIV. Conclusion

The takeaways for left augmentation are not readily intuitive. I am not so much suggesting that we cultivate vengeful narratives and sentiment as much as acknowledge that they are already at work throughout and across the political landscape. If I were to boil things down to a single concentrated frustration it would be the near constant demand from many that organizing must be "positive," "constructive," "propose solutions," and avoid appearing "angry" for fear of alienating possible adherents. I would suggest, contrariwise, that (along with other authors in this section and across this volume) the movements that can be successful in the years to come will be those that dare to work on the terrain of depression, hopelessness, resentment, anxiety, anger, and heartbreak. They might cultivate a common platform to avenge what has been done not only to our lives, our bodies, our humanity, and the planet, but also to link this to the eerie call to, in Benjamin's (1974: 2) terms, acknowledge the debt we owe to past generations — whose struggles and oppression we inherit, a debt that "cannot be settled cheaply."

Note
1. Revanchism is the political manifestation of the will to reverse territorial losses incurred by a country, often following a war or social movement. It draws its strength from patriotic and retributionist ways of thinking that are often motivated by economic or geopolitical factors. As a term, *revanchism* originated in 1870s France, in the aftermath of the Franco-Prussian War, among nationalists who wanted to avenge the French defeat and reclaim the lost territories of Alsace-Lorraine.

References
Bacon, Francis. 1625. "On Revenge." *CommonLit*. <commonlit.org/texts/on-revenge>.
Baldwin, James. 2011. *The Devil Finds Work: An Essay*. New York: Vintage International.
Baucom, Ian. 2005. *Specters of the Atlantic: Finance Capital, Slavery, and Philosophy of History*. Durham: Duke University Press.
Benjamin, Walter. 1969. "Theses on the Philosophy of History." In Hannah Arendt (ed.), *Illuminations*. New York: Schocken.

___. 1974. "On the Concept of History." <sfu.ca/~andrewf/books/Concept_History_Benjamin.pdf>

Berger, Dan. 2014. *Captive Nation: Black Prison Organizing in the Civil Rights Era*. Chapel Hill: University of North Carolina Press.

Coulthard, Glen. 2014. *Red Skin, White Masks: Rejecting the Colonial Politics of Recognition*. Minneapolis: University of Minnesota Press.

Davis, Angela. 2005. *Abolition Democracy: Beyond Empire, Prisons and Torture*. New York: Seven Stories.

Engels, Friedrich. 1874. "The Program of the Blanquist Fugitives from the Paris Commune." *Der Volksstaat*, June 26. <marxists.org/archive/marx/works/1874/06/26.htm>.

Fanon, Franz. 1963. *The Wretched of the Earth*. New York: Grove.

Federici, Silvia. 2005. *Caliban and the Witch: Women, Capitalism and Primitive Accumulation*. New York: Autonomedia.

Fukuyama, Francis. 1993. *The End of History and the Last Man*. New York: Perennial.

Gelderloos, Peter. 2007. *How Nonviolence Protects the State*. Cambridge: South End Press.

Gilmore, Ruth Wilson. 2007. *Golden Gulag: Prisons, Surplus, Crisis, and Opposition in Globalizing California*. Berkeley: University of California Press.

Harvey, David. 2006. *The Limits to Capital*, 2nd edition. New York: Verso.

Hobbes, Thomas. 1985. *Leviathan*. London: Penguin.

Jameson, Fredric. 1984. "Postmodernism, or the Cultural Logic of Late Capitalism." *New Left Review*, 146.

Kornbluh, Joyce L. (ed.). 2011. *Rebel Voices: An IWW Anthology*. Oakland: PM Press.

Luxemburg, Rosa. 2003. *The Accumulation of Capital*, trans. Agnes Schwarzschild. London: Routledge.

Marx, Karl. 1849. "A Bourgeois Document." *Neue Rheinische Zeitung*, January 4. <marxists.org/archive/marx/works/1849/01/04.htm>.

___. 1857. "The Indian Revolt." *New York Tribune*, September 16. <marxists.org/archive/marx/works/1857/09/16.htm>.

___. 1871. *The Civil War in France*. The Marx/Engels Internet Archive. <marxists.org/archive/marx/works/1871/civil-war-france/index.htm>.

Nagle, Angela. 2017. *Kill All Normies: The Online Culture Wars from Tumblr and 4chan to the Alt-Right and Trump*. London: Zero Books.

Newsinger, John. 2006. *The Blood Never Dried: A People's History of the British Empire*. London: Bookmarks.

Robinson, Cedric J. 2000. *Black Marxism: The Making of the Black Radical Tradition*, 2nd edition. Chapel Hill: University of North Carolina Press.

Smith, Adam. 1759. "The Theory of Moral Sentiments." *Marxists.Org*. <marxists.org/reference/archive/smith-adam/works/moral/index.htm>.

Smith, Neil. 1996. *The New Urban Frontier: Gentrification and the Revanchist City*. London: Routledge.

Wacquant, Loïc. 2014. "Class, Race and Hyperincarceration in Revanchist America." *Socialism and Democracy*, 28, 3.

Wang, Jackie. 2018. *Carceral Capitalism*. Los Angeles: Semiotext(e).

Afterword

Augmenting the Left or Rethinking Progressive Politics?

Ronaldo Munck

Having read through the preceding rich and complex set of chapters, I realize I cannot do justice to them in a short afterword or even attempt to summarize the lessons learned. Instead, I will go for a riposte of sorts that, to a degree, challenges some of the authors' reasoning but always from a shared commitment to radical transformation. I also want to propose a fundamental rethinking of progressive politics but from a somewhat different perspective. The task set here, of "augmenting the left," is about a fundamental rethinking of a new starting point of left mobilization and organization in terms of class consciousness, race and class, affect, and many other forms that offer ways to confront the radical right. I want to add to this some further reflection on root-and-branch rethinking about what we mean by the left (and radical left) and its adequacy for the tasks of transformation in the twenty-first century.

I will start from my own recent revisiting of Karl Marx (Munck 2016), which is very different from the rather dogmatic (Althusserian) Marxism of the 1970s that I first learned. For me, despite all the diversity and dynamism Marxism still possesses (or is regaining), it has very clear limitations as a guide to action in the twenty-first century if understood in a closed or orthodox manner. We do not really have a proper conception of capitalism and capitalist crisis that is adequate for our complex, globalized world. We need to build a much better understanding of social reproduction — sometimes outside the market — and not just focus on the world of commodity production. As the prior chapters by Fernandes, Ravensbergen, and Cuestas-Caza, Lalander, and Lembke underscore, we also need to bridge the gap between Marxism and our understanding of the global warming crisis — an epistemic gap that is limiting both sides of the debate on alternative futures. Basically, we need a thorough, self-critical rethinking of Marxism. To render it fit for today, we would need to carry out a more serious integration with the advances of feminism, ecology, and decolonizing perspectives.

For me, the main "rectification" of Marxism I have been engaged with is the need to decolonize progressive thinking to remove the Euro- (or North Atlantic–) centrism that has characterized it since its inception, Eastern/Third Worldist Marxisms notwithstanding. Late in life, Karl Marx did realize the limitations of his evolutionary paradigm and recognized that in the periphery (specifically Russia), socialism might actually "skip a stage," so to speak. Marx (and particularly Engels) also felt directly the interpellation of Irish revolutionary nationalism (led by the Fenians) of the mid-nineteenth century and coined the phrase "A nation that enslaves another cannot itself be free," which has since fallen into disuse.

Jordan House's chapter calls to mind a well-known aphorism that a left that does not have class at its core can only be a liberal pressure group. I might well understand why someone would want to press this argument as a way of not allowing the left to be subsumed within a tame liberalism. However, we cannot just assert the primacy of class and ignore all the gains made since Laclau and Mouffe's original critique of "class essentialism" in the 1980s. The idea of a universal social subject — the proletariat — marching toward an inexorable destiny is no longer plausible or particularly helpful in practice. We are now much more attuned to the idea that capitalism is decentred and fragmented and that the process of class formation is diverse, uneven, and, above all, complex (see the contributions in Latham et al. 2019). We understand — just by looking at the alter-globalization movements, for example — that there is a plurality of contemporary struggles and that progressive politics is contingent and not predetermined. A fundamentalist concern with a "retreat from class" will not help us understand or respond to the pressing challenges of neoliberal capitalism, imperialism, sexism, and racism.

Marxist debates on class transformation on a global scale have long since moved beyond Althusser-type taxonomies of class structures, which were always very North-centric as well. The chapter by Cuestas-Caza, Lalander, and Lembke opens the debate even further with an analysis of the Andean political philosophy of *Buen-Vivir/Sumak Kawsay*, which has the potential to subvert any temptation to return to monochromatic class categories. This approach radically questions previous Eurocentric analyses of Latin America — not only has it (re)introduced ethnicity and colonialism into the debate around progressive transformation, but it has also brought back an important utopian element that integrates pre-conquest political imaginaries and an Indigenous cosmology in addressing climate change and extractivism. At the risk of being accused of being a liberal, I would recall the 1960s slogan "let a thousand flowers bloom" as a principle for augmenting/reinventing the left.

What we could consider next is where this working class and its project of social transformation might be heading today. Put another way, where does this leave us in terms of articulating the notion that *another world is possible* from a transformative labour perspective? The first point to make is that globalization has fundamentally altered the terrain of labour struggles. As this volume recognizes, the organizational forms, political thinking, and even cultural references of the 1950s are simply inadequate for our present situation, not least because they all assume the nation-state to be a self-sufficient framework for action. The workers of the world today exist in a global context, not just an inter-national one. Capitalism reformed itself as globalization precisely to meet the challenges posed by labour in the 1970s and 1980s. What is most noticeable today is how discrete labour struggles so rapidly become global. As Hardt and Negri argue in *Empire*, "each struggle, though firmly rooted in local conditions, *leaps immediately to the global level* and attacks the imperial constitution in its generality" (Hardt and Negri 2000: 56, emphasis added). These new struggles that are always already global can be economic, political, social, or cultural — in brief, they are biopolitical — and they articulate a new conception of life beyond commodification and show, in practice, that another world is possible.

In political terms, there is a pressing need to move "beyond the fragments," a term previously deployed by feminists seeking to create a new political methodology in the 1970s (Rowbotham, Segal, and Wainwright 1979). Against the political sectarianism of that era, it created a vision of citizens forming horizontal connections across civil society, across politics and economics. Since then, the "old" politics of class and the "new" politics of identity have become more polarized. For the latter, the whole language of class is an anachronism. For the orthodox proponents of class, only the working class can create the dynamic for social transformation to a new order based on socialism. We could, however, with the likes of Hardt and Negri, argue that the new social movements are but different aspects of the struggle against capitalism, still part of labour's DNA, whether it wants it or not. The new struggles and new subjectivities are thus not to be seen as somehow antagonistic to, or a negation of, working-class struggles. In fact, what globalization has created is a huge blossoming of new contradictions and struggles, all pointing toward the need for a society not based on exploitation and oppression.

A strategy for social transformation will depend on the ongoing debates across the labour movement and other struggles, but we can put forward the provisional framework of a new "global social movement unionism," defined by Kim Moody twenty years ago as "a perspective that can maximize working-class power by drawing together the different sectors within the class ... a perspective that embraces the diversity of the working class in order to overcome its fragmentation" (Moody 1997: 290). A simple model would posit economic unionism as one focused on labour in the market, a political unionism centred on labour and the state, and a social unionism that conceived of labour as offering a social alternative to the global order. The social movement unionism of the 1970s and the "community unionism" of the 2000s were distinguishable by their complex understanding of workers as not restricted to the workplace but as part of communities. This tendency within global unionism is unevenly developed and is subject to massive setbacks, as much when it wins (leading to co-optation) as when it loses. The divisions within the working class seem to accentuate with crisis but we still need to go "beyond the fragments" to learn from the era when labour took shape as a social movement that Marx not only commented on but also participated in.

This "social" or social movement unionism takes labour not as an economic unit or political actor solely but, rather, in its full social complexity and as part of communal, household, gender, and cultural relations. This approach prospered during democratic challenges to authoritarian regimes in the South but it is now seeing a revival of sorts in parts of the North that have been devastated by neoliberalism. As Topak's chapter implies, we might bridge the migration/development and migration/democracy theoretical and practical divides in articulating a new form of migrant-oriented social unionism. This approach would restore human agency in what are sometimes rather technical debates on migrant remittances and migrant political networks. Generally speaking, trade unions have been slow to embrace a more social-movement approach to labour organizing. The continued relevance of trade unions for a multi-ethnic, multi-status workforce is clearly in question. Yet there has been a concerted drive by many in the trade union movement to organize migrant workers in particular. Immigrant-driven campaigns to organize, unionize, and agitate for better conditions have become more widespread.

Often a campaign that began in one particular ethnic community has expanded to embrace an array of migrant workers. In many cases, it was not standard trade unions doing the organizing but, rather, a range of hybrid community organizations, workers' centres, faith-based groups, and nationality-based organizations. The dominant organizational form has been, more often than not, based on these varied networks, with their members working within but also without the organized labour movement. It is too early to determine whether the renaissance over the last decade or so has changed the impression that trade unions in the North existed to serve a basically white male clientele, but certainly there is a counter-tendency emerging. At a global level, we are seeing more innovative trade union and labour movement thinking in which migration comes to the fore as both a challenge and an opportunity for labour. Of course, this dilemma can take shape in a totally negative way (think Trump's wall or Eastern Europe), in contrast to the positive outcomes we have witnessed in Southern Europe, where trade unions have been very decisive in opening their ranks to migrant workers, including "illegal" ones.

There was a time, not so long ago, when the ringing call of the *Communist Manifesto* — "workers of the world unite; you have nothing to lose but your chains" — sounded faintly anachronistic to many. This was a period in the 1950s in the Global North, when some workers had "never had it so good," according to the politicians. The problem was an excess of consumerism, not one of putting bread on the table. Yet now, after four decades of pro-market and anti-labour policies, workers everywhere are struggling to make ends meet. For the majority — those in the Global South — affluence was never a problem and many continued to be affected by a brutality not really captured by Marx's term "extra-economic coercion." Today, as workers — be they settled or migrants, rural or urban — face an economic order that has had no clear strategy since the 2008 financial crisis, they need increasingly to seek alliances across geographic regions and gender, age, race, and ethnic divides. Not only do they stand to lose their chains, but they will also be part of constructing another, more humane world. The labour movement had emerged in the mid-nineteenth century in what was a pre-national form — that is to say, it was international in its concerns and perspectives. State formation and national consolidation would later force labour into its national (even nationalist) format. But around 1850, we can discern a globalized labour condition that has a resonance with the globalization wave of the 1990s, hence the notion that we might go "back to the future." It would be Marx himself, as theorist and activist immersed in his era, that would be a guide for that journey and not the simplistic Marxism developed since.

I would finally like to reiterate and agree with the central claim made in this volume's Introduction, namely that:

> The left is in a unique position today to *take advantage* of the great diversity of approaches and issues, which have been the hallmark of its otherwise bemoaned fragmentation. More precisely, the worldwide trend of popular disaffection presents a major opportunity for the left, *if* it is willing to take fragmentation, intra-left conflict, and a history of refusals and defeats as a starting point for next steps in the struggle against capitalism and the far right, rather than as the basis for more conflict or defeatism.

References

Hardt, Michael, and Antonio Negri. 2000. *Empire*. Cambridge: MIT Press.
Latham, Robert, Karen Murray, Julian von Bargen, and A.T. Kingsmith (eds.). 2019. *The Radical Left and Social Transformation Strategies of Augmentation and Reorganization*. London: Routledge.
Moody, Kim. 1997. *Workers in a Lean World*. London: Verso.
Munck, Ronaldo. 2016. *Marx 2020: After the Crisis*. London: Zed Books.
Rowbotham, Sheila, Lynne Segal, and Hilary Wainwright. 1979. *Beyond the Fragments: Feminism and the Making of Socialism*. London: Merlin.

Index

activism, 70
    accessibility of, 57–59, 101–3, 193
    of contending masses, 19–21, 24, 32, 71, 110–11, 193
    critique within, 33–35, 100–3, 109–16, 125–27, 223–26
    environmental, 33, 86–95, 146–48, 155, 158–69
    hunger striking, *see* Migrant Hunger Strikers
    identity-based, *see* identity-based movements
    issue-based, 19–21, 32, 86–87, 101–3, 114–17, 130–32
    Muslim-focused, 81, 99–100, 102
    self-selection, 28, 33–36
    solidarity, 74–77, 82–83, 143, 186; *see also* solidarity
    student, 36–37, 48, 82, 91, 98, 202
    summit-hopping, 34–35, 151
    sustained, 16, 23, 33–36, 101–3, 126–31, 147, 226, 239–40
    working-class, *see* working class
    zero-waste, 99–101
adaptation, left-wing, 3, 129–34, 146, 163, 173, 222
Afghanistan, 79
affect, 12, 50, 206n1, 208, 227, 232–33
    versus affectation, 216–17
    liberation and, 203–5, 206n3, 209–14, 243
    neoliberalism and, 196–202, 205, 209, 219, 223–25, 236
    reactive, 33, 220–21, 226
African-Americans, 51
    voting choices, 52–55, 57, 59
    see also Black people
agitation, *see* provocation
agribusiness growth, 159, 161, 166, 176–77
Alabama, elections in, 54–55, 59
alt-right movement, 98
    tactics, 102–4
    see also far right
American Civil Liberties Union (ACLU), 138–39
anarchism, 1, 32, 113, 122
    anti-organizational, 30–31, 109–10, 115
    solidarity, 82
Anthropocene,
    crisis of the, 11, 147–49
    left politics and the, 153–55
    see also Holocene mentality
anti-capitalism,
    attitudes toward, 16–20
    climate change and, 146–48, 161, 163
    development of, 10, 16, 109–12, 129
    messaging, 19, 110, 222
anti-capitalist struggle, 130–32, 138, 164, 198
    arc of, 19–21, 24–26
    critiques of, 13, 30–35, 103, 108–12, 129–33, 224
    inclusion in, *see* inclusivity, movement; radical left, recruitment
    Indigenous and, 88, 161–64
    potential of, 19–21, 105, 115, 248
    reformism, 6, 8, 19, 23, 28, 102, 143
    tactics, 33, 113, 117–26, 147–50, 171, 188–94, 204, 208–14, 220–27; *see also* art; culture jamming
    working-class, 17, 21–25, 29, 35–36, 89–91, 109–10, 154, 246
anti-colonial movements, 70–71, 91–94, 171–72, 177, 239–40
    support for, 3, 87–88
    see also decolonization
anti-globalization movements, 16, 33, 82, 109, 223, 244–45
    critiques of, 34, 130
anxiety, 16, 213, 219–20, 223–28
    overcoming, 9, 105, 208–10, 217, 241, 248
apolitical stance, 42, 78–79
art,
    provocations, 33, 208–9, 216–17
    terrorism, 12, 209–12, 214
Asian people, 57–58, 239

Association of Indigenous Peoples (APIB), 167
austerity, 98
  countering, 23, 92, 95, 113, 197, 206n5
  effects of, 80, 82
authoritarianism, 31, 147, 198, 205, 238, 246
  nationalist, 2, 75
  populism and, 62–72, 118, 200–2
automation, 8, 29, 150–52
auto workers, 21, 30, 56, 111; *see also* United Auto Workers (UAW)
Arab Spring, 1–2, 68
Argentina, 20
assumptions, 21, 24, 130, 212, 245
  right-wing, 65
  shifting left-wing, 2, 12, 29, 31, 34, 148, 245

Bacon, Francis, 231
Bakunin, Mikhail, 31
Baldwin, James, 240
banking, community, 20, 25
Bastani, Aaron, 151–52
Benjamin, Walter, 11, 189–94, 220, 235, 241
Berardi, "Bifo," 224
Bergson, Henri, 213
Black Lives Matter, 10, 87, 92, 124–25, 203, 208
Black people, 6, 226, 237
  radicalization, 21, 26n7
  workers, 21–23, 142
  see also African-Americans
Blair, Tony, 123, 125
Blanqui, Auguste, 233
Bolivia, 11, 158, 162–63, 169–74, 179n1
Bolsonaro, Jair, 159
borders, 56
  crossing, 80–82, 193
  policing of, 76, 79, 116n1, 201
  see also immigration; migrants; migration
Bouie, Jamelle, 58
bourgeoisie, 68, 104
  consumption, 64, 67, 100
  democracy, 108, 121, 136, 184
  see also petty bourgeoisie

boycott, divestment, and sanctions (BDS) campaign, 143
boycott, right to, 135, 139, 141–43
Brazil, 2, 11, 149–50, 158–67, 198
Brazilian Communist Party (PCB) 161
bridge-building, 3–4, 8, 10, 23–25, 113–14, 244, 246
Brown, Wendy, 63
Buchanan, James, 141–43
Buck-Morss, Susan, 189–91
Buen-Vivir, 11, 153, 158, 162, 169–73, 245
  bifurcation of, 174–79
business class, 1, 76, 136, 223
  interests of, 25, 26n1, 52, 57, 138–42, 197, 201
  pro-, 1, 5, 22, 139, 160
  struggles against, 50–51, 81–82, 166, 211, 214

climate change, 4, 7, 77, 111, 146–52, 158–63, 166, 245
campaigns, 31, 136, 152, 223, 236
  art-based, 211; *see also* art
  election, 51, 53–54, 56–59, 115, 122, 124–26, 142, 151
  meaningful, 28, 36–37, 247
  single-issue, 19, 34–35, 101, 143
Canada, 88, 135, 144
  characterization of, 93, 56, 139–40
  labour movement in, 29–30, 87, 98
Canadian Communist League/Workers' Communist Party, 109
Canadian Labour Defense League (CLDL), 139–40
capitalism, 40, 94, 100, 233
  apprehension under, 4, 12, 18–19, 22–23, 190–91, 208–10, 220
  contradictions of, 162, 198–201, 206n6, 208–14, 236, 246
  core-periphery divide, 76–77, 147–49, 153, 244
  crisis of, 2, 24–26, 50, 63, 89, 196–202, 243–44; *see also* global financial crisis
  destructiveness of, 17, 66–67, 80–82, 147–48, 222–26
  fossil fuel, 147, 153–54
  hegemony of, 6, 23, 26n1, 65, 71–72,

88–89, 120–22, 231–32
  hierarchies under, 71, 75–83, 103–5, 154, 206, 224
  instability of, 16, 63–64, 71, 185, 224
  late-stage, 208–10, 217n1, 219, 232
  liberal, *see* liberal capitalism
  migration under, 76–79
  post-, 148, 151
  reforming, *see* anti-capitalist struggle, reformism
  revenge, 234–38
  self-reinforcement, 2, 11–12, 94, 120–22, 155, 206n2
  struggle against, *see* anti-capitalist struggle
  progressive, 6, 11, 174–76
  see also anti-capitalism
capitalist production, 29, 41, 78, 89–92, 104, 120, 147, 221
  challenging, 11, 44–48, 88, 100, 115–16, 146, 192–94
capitalists, 138–39, 143
  interests of, 41–45, 89–90, 160, 205, 238
Capital Volume II, 91
caste identification, 64, 70–72
centrist liberalism, 10, 71, 114, 159
  narratives of, 5–6, 12
Charlottesville, VA, 185–87, 192, 194
China, 58, 66, 68, 198
Chomsky, Noam, 52
civil liberties, 10, 129, 135–43
civil rights struggles, 30, 54, 136, 141–43
citizenization (Ecuador), 174–77, 179n5
citizenship, 54, 170–74
  gradations in, 64, 67, 83, 142
Citizens' Revolution (Ecuador), 170, 174–77
class, 28, 64, 149
  composition, 87–94; *see also* social reproduction
  conflict, 5–6, 32, 51, 89–90, 120–21, 176, 227, 248
  consciousness, 3, 18–25, 32–35, 38–46, 78, 189–91, 210–16, 243–44; *see also* consciousness raising; false consciousness, workers'
  contending masses versus, 17–18,

24–25, 35–36
  decomposition, 29, 41–44, 89–90, 92
  importance of, 17–18, 28–29, 42–44, 101–3, 244
  Indigenous struggles, 86–88, 91–94
  interests, 22–25, 41–46, 87, 119–24, 138–43, 161–62, 198, 205
  intersectional connections, 51, 59, 76, 103, 178, 222, 244–48
  objective condition of, 78
  organizing, 28–29, 35–37, 75–82, 89, 114–16
  party versus, 111, 119–21, 124–25, 128–33, 203–4
  racialized, 51–55, 59, 88, 95, 200
  recomposition, 29, 87, 90–95, 224
  research on, 38–43
  stratification, 3, 29, 42–43, 65–67, 138–40, 174
  struggle, 25, 32–33, 44–46, 64, 75, 87–95, 111–15, 246
  see also capitalists; middle class; precariat; working class
Clinton, Hillary, 51–55, 57
Cold War, post-, 62–63
  geopolitics, 65–66
collective action, 31, 36, 136, 140–42
collective rights, 10, 135–36, 139–41, 143, 170–71, 176, 179n3
colonialism, 10, 177, 231–33, 238–40
  see also anti-colonial movements
colour line, political, 50, 55
  voter behaviour, 52–54
communism, 104, 121, 140, 161, 235
  automated luxury, 8, 151
Communist Manifesto, The, 44, 247
Communist Party, 20–21, 23, 109, 119, 123, 139
Communist Party of Canada, 116n2, 139–40
Communist Party of Great Britain (CBGB), 117–26, 128, 130
  British Road to Socialism, 119, 122
  "New Times," 118, 120, 122–23
Communist University of London (CUL), 117–18, 122–23
conflict, 32, 102, 193
  class, *see* class, conflict
  global, 31, 176–77

factional, 13, 149, 248
  responding to movement, 8, 62–63, 82–83, 128–33, 174, 189–92, 232, 244
conditional hospitality, 79–80, 83
consciousness raising, 2, 17, 23–24, 201, 208–17, 217n2
  workers', 32–34, 38–48
conservativism, 135, 141–42
  libertarian, 143
  narratives of, 5, 64, 67–69, 143
  revenge and, 5, 185–86
consumerism, 66, 99, 200–1, 206n6, 221–22, 247
contending masses,
  anti-capitalist struggle, 19–25, 30, 36, 140
  identification of, 17–18
  reality of, 17, 24
Contribution to the Critique of Political Economy, 150
cooperatives, worker, 20, 23, 151
Corbyn, Jeremy, 104–5, 125, 151, 154, 203–4
corporate interests, 141; *see also* business class
counterrevolution, 135, 196, 202, 206n2
criminalization, 74, 78–80, 83, 113
  discursive, 75–77
  see also migration, criminalization-humanitarian nexus
crisis, 50, 68, 232, 243, 246
  capitalism's, *see* capitalism, crisis of
  environmental, *see* ecological crisis
  financial, 2, 20, 62–63, 93, 152, 226, 248; *see also* global financial crisis
  housing, 131
  migration, *see* migration, crisis
  opioid, 131–32
  political, 2–3, 23, 160, 196, 202, 209, 228
culturalism, 62, 64–67, 71–72
  chauvinism, 63–64, 67, 72
culture jamming, 12, 33, 219–22, 224–27;
  see also détournement

Dalla Costa, Mariarosa, 91
Debord, Guy, 221
decolonization, 94, 178, 244

defeatism, 16, 33, 142
  overcoming, 13, 20, 23–25, 133, 193, 248
degrowth economics, 11, 100, 147–48, 150, 153–54, 162
Deleuze, Gilles, 209, 215, 217n4, 229n3
demands, movement, 1–5, 35, 81, 114–15, 139, 150, 158–67, 192–93
  attainable, 8, 93–94, 104, 142, 172
  lack of concrete, 16, 34, 121, 126, 187–88, 241
Democratic Party (US), 5, 12, 52, 56, 59, 152, 187
democracy, 31, 105, 121, 126, 141–43, 174
  crisis of, 63, 65, 72, 128, 131, 196–203, 246
  neoliberalism, 62–64, 71, 200–2
  social, *see* social democratic politics
  societal, 31, 111, 115, 117, 136–37, 199, 204
Democracy in Chains, 141–42
Derrida, Jacques, 79, 83
Dery, Mark, 223, 225, 227
détournement, 210, 219–25
Detroit, MI, 21–24, 30
Devil Finds Work, The, 240
dialectics, 165, 200
  images, 11, 189–92, 194n3, 227
  theory of, 43, 45–48, 201, 205
Dias, Jerry, 56
dictatorships, 2, 80–81
Dirlik, Arif, 65–66
disaffection, 16, 206n3, 213, 219–20
  overcoming, 5–7, 9, 11–13, 105, 208–10, 248
  see also anxiety
discourse, 59, 120, 197, 225, 236
  capitalist political, 19, 53, 150, 172–73, 210, 219
  dichotomy in, 104, 163, 176–77
  movement, 28, 78, 82, 101, 104, 115
  nationalist, 62, 69, 72, 76–77
dos Santos, Fabio Luis Barbosa, 160
Du Bois, W.E.B., 9, 50, 58–59

ecological crisis, 2–4, 17, 98–100, 170–76
  capitalism and, 67, 94, 104, 153, 160–62, 175–78, 238

discourse on, 33, 69, 71, 158–67, 236
revolution and, 6–7, 11, 31–32,
  114–15, 146–51, 154–55, 163–65
ecological responsibility, 4, 8, 39, 86–88,
  151, 155n1
ecomodernism, 11, 147–50, 152, 155n1,
  162
economics, 8, 16, 23, 26n1, 29, 44, 126,
  138–40, 228n1, 238, 241
  affective, 219–25, 227
  austerity and, 80, 82, 98
  capitalist, 5–6, 18–20, 57–58, 62–72,
    147–50, 154, 158–60, 198–202; *see
    also* capitalism
  degrowth, *see* degrowth economics
  ecological, 98–100, 147, 151–53,
    169–70, 175
  inequality, 1, 12, 51–52, 92, 135–36,
    142–43, 227; *see also* inequality
  reorganization of, 35, 40, 59, 111,
    121, 129–33, 163–64, 231–34,
    245–48
  see also global economic crisis;
    political economy
eco-socialism, 11, 101, 115, 147–54,
  159–67
  Andean intercultural, 169–78
Ecuador, 11, 149, 162, 169–79
education,
  access to, 28–31, 63, 102–5, 216
  radical, 17, 19–20, 24–25, 108,
    111–16
  worker, 23, 32–33, 121–23
Egypt, 1
Ehrenreich, Barbara, 19
"Eighteenth Brumaire," 184
elites, 66, 68, 70, 104, 197–200, 205–6
  interests of, 2, 33, 79, 142, 222
  revolt against, 2, 50–53, 59, 196
emissions, carbon, 8, 146–47, 159
Empire, 245
En Comú (Barcelona, Spain), 204–5
Engels, Friedrich, 12, 208, 233, 244
environmental crisis, *see* ecological crisis
environmental justice, 86–87, 152–53,
  155n1
Erdoğan, Recep Tayyip, 9, 62, 202
ethnic identification, 5, 64, 67–72,
  171–78, 179n3, 179n7, 245–48

ethnonationalism, 64, 98, 234
  undermining, 3
Europe, 1–2, 16, 26, 90, 127, 130
  migration, 63–64, 74–81, 140, 247
extractivism, 150, 158–59, 167, 172,
  179n2, 245
  neo-, 160, 163, 170, 174–77

false consciousness, workers', 3, 24, 198,
  205, 206n6, 213
Fanon, Franz, 239
farmers, struggles of, 42, 71, 91
far right, 13, 191–92, 204, 227, 248
  recent gains, 51, 53, 98, 159, 185–87,
    193, 232–36
fascism, 53, 70, 200–2, 238
  anti-, 30, 192, 194
  contemporary, 62, 65, 92, 185–86,
    232
Federici, Silvia, 91
feminism,
  analysis, 87, 90–92, 153, 166, 244–45
  struggles, 30, 95, 110, 119–20, 167
Fisher, Mark, 226
Ford, Doug, 98
Fordism, 90, 120, 200, 220–24
Foster, John Bellamy, 164–65
free-speech "crisis," 135, 137, 141,
  143–44; *see also* civil liberties

Gabel, Joseph, 205
gender, 54, 63, 118–20, 136, 202, 236
  activism, 50, 103, 111, 130, 174,
    186–87, 192
  intersectional connections, 51, 59,
    103, 87–88, 178, 222, 244–48
  relations, 9–10, 31, 39, 76, 91–92,
    103, 234–35, 241
  voting behaviour, 55, 59
geopolitical-economic context,
  importance of, 8, 62–67, 70–72,
    241
"gig" economy, 29; *see also* precariat;
  precarious workers
Gindin, Sam, 111
Giroux, Henry, 199–201, 205
global financial crisis, 71, 152, 160, 226,
  248
  reactions to, 1, 20, 63

Global Inequality: A New Approach for the Age of Globalization, 56
globalization, 65, 228, 243, 248
    alter-, 244–46
    neoliberal, 6, 29, 64–67, 82, 201, 205
    political, 66
    see also anti-globalization movements
Global North, 158, 160, 221, 247
    activism in, 10, 16, 100, 246–47
    populism, 62–66
Global South, 158
    activism in, 164–68, 202, 246
    dispossession in, 76–77, 164, 247
    populism, 62–72
Good Muslim, Bad Muslim, 65
Gramsci, Antonio, 16, 19–20, 50, 121, 125, 208
Grassy Narrows, ON, 87
Greater Toronto Workers' Assembly (GTWA), 112–14
Greece, 20, 80–83
Green New Deal, 152–53, 162
Gudynas, Eduardo, 163
Guthrie, Woody, 193

Hall, Stuart, 120, 123, 125
Hardt, Michael, 245–46
Harper, Stephen, 98
health care, 104, 225
    struggle for, 17, 21, 30
    universal, 39, 105
Henwood, Doug, 33–34
Hill, Marc Lamont, 53
Hinduness, 64, 67
    nationalism, 69–72
historical materialism, 35, 150, 164
history, 31, 50, 53, 76–77, 206n2
    approaches to, 11, 147–48, 170–71, 191–94, 231–32, 248
    left-wing movement, 6–7, 24, 120, 135–38, 197–200, 203
    lessons from, 2, 7–8, 18–20, 81, 88, 117, 177, 184–90, 238–39
    narratives, 6, 62–65, 68–70, 142–43, 153–54, 205
    working-class, 21–22, 44, 89–91, 233–35
Hobbes, Thomas, 231
Hobsbawm, Eric, 119

Holmes Jr., Oliver Wendell, 137–38
Holocene mentality, 11, 146, 148, 150, 155; *see also* Anthropocene
housing, struggle for, 7, 17, 29–30, 104, 115, 131, 206n5
    racism in, 21–22, 24–25
    see also squatting
human rights, 143
    discourse on, 76, 78–79, 104
Husserl, Edmund, 213

identity-based movements, 74, 245
    appeal of, 3, 10, 63–65, 87–89, 94–95
    cultural chauvinism and, 64–70, 72, 197
    failure of, 9, 74, 77–78, 99–104, 170–73, 205
    moving beyond, 28, 80–83, 121, 178
ideology, 213
    Indigenous, *see* Indigenous ideologies
    leftist, 6, 8, 45, 101, 108, 112, 203
    popular, 4, 19, 75–76, 170–71, 177, 205
    right-wing, 3, 59, 67–72, 196–97, 206n6
    transformation, 2, 31, 48, 154, 222
Idle No More, 10, 87, 92, 203,
imagination, leftist, 148–49, 172
    expansion of, 1, 154–55, 219, 245
    goals, 16, 28–30, 132
    popular appeal, 2–7, 9, 226
immigrants, 77, 81, 120, 130, 247
    hatred of, 5, 19, 50, 56–57, 63, 80, 236
    surveillance of, 79, 139–40
imperialism, 72, 77, 79, 153, 193, 231, 238
    anti-, 62, 113, 147, 149, 244–45
in-betweenness, 9, 16–18, 21, 23–26, 129
incarceration, 17, 234
    mass, 29, 237
    racialized, 55, 237
inclusivity, movement, 3, 10, 17–19, 24–26, 116n3, 159–61
    critiques of, 28–31, 102–3, 125–26
    strategies, 81–83, 101–5, 178–79
India, 2, 4, 233
    authoritarian populism, 9, 62, 64–72
    Bharatiya Janata Party (BJP), 67, 70–71

Hindutva, 69–72
  neoliberalism, 70–71
Indigenous ideologies, 153, 169–70, 172, 245
  co-optation of, 11, 158, 162, 173–79
Indigenous Peoples, 11, 237, 239
  government discourse versus, 159–62, 169, 172–79, 245
  rights of, 86–87, 171, 176
  settler solidarity, 86–87, 93–94, 115, 169
  sovereignty, 94, 231; *see also* self-determination, Indigenous
  struggles, 70, 86–88, 91–94, 149, 155n1, 166–67
Indignados, 203, 206n5
inequality, 6, 29
  global, 51, 65–66, 149
  income, 2, 51, 93, 143
  media coverage, 1, 19
  rising, 18, 31, 130, 197, 225
  struggle against, 4, 101, 136, 147
  see also redistribution
inflation, 19
infrastructure, political, 4, 115, 139, 153, 201, 219, 229
  left-wing, 36–37, 83, 144, 151–52, 173, 232
  new, 10, 87, 128–34, , 155, 203
insecurity, 223
  economic, 18, 198–99, 200
  food, 131
  housing, 17, 131
intellectuals, leftist, 2, 209
  activism of, 19–21, 24–25, 179n1
  critique of, 34, 70, 102, 118–19, 124
  discourse, 8, 120–21, 196–97
intersectional politics, 51, 55, 59, 76, 88, 103, 178, 222, 244–48
Innu people, 86, 93
Inuit people, 86, 93
Inventing the Future, 150–51
Islamophobia, 50, 70–71, 100
IWW (Industrial Workers of the World), 111

Jameson, Fredric, 238
jobs, 63, 71, 200
  carbon-intensive, 11, 163
  green, 152, 161
  secure, 17, 24, 39–45, 56, 82
Jones, Doug, 54–55

Klein, Naomi, 7, 147, 223
Koch brothers, 142–43
Konings, Martijn, 196–99, 201, 205, 206n6
Kosoy, Nicolas, 100
Krugman, Paul, 202

labour, 105, 132
  capitalist, 4–5, 32, 138, 152–54, 164, 232, 240
  rights of, 141–43, 202
  social reproductive, 29, 87–91
  struggles, 29–30, 109–12, 119, 124–25, 139–40, 245–48
  unions, *see* unions
  waged, 29, 89, 120, 151
Labour Party (Britain), 118–20, 122–25, 127, 151, 154, 204
  New, 123
Labrador Land Protectors, 86, 93–95
land-grabbing, 77, 176
Latin American Eco-socialist Alliance (Brazil), 167
Latinx people, 51, 53, 57, 237
learning opportunities, 38–43, 88, 92–95, 130, 188, 191–94, 227–28
  accessible, 28, 33, 101–5
left, the, 25–26, 80, 125–27
  activists of, 103, 111
  climate change and, 146–52, 159–67
  critiques of, 3–12, 98–105, 109–16, 170
  focus of, 28–37, 50–51, 55–59, 126–27, 169–75, 228, 243–48
  government versus, 61–62, 118–25, 159–67, 174, 204
  international solidarity, 75, 78, 80–82
  narratives, *see* narratives, left-wing
  perspectives of, 23, 75–78, 87–88, 130–36, 177, 197–99
  tactics, 33, 38–43, 112–14, 131–33, 143–44, 185–94, 213, 226
  see also radical left
Leninism, 16, 25, 31, 222
liberal capitalism, 62, 66, 94, 114, 205,

226, 238, 244
  failure of, 6, 92
liberalism, 70, 177, 244
  centrism, *see* centrist liberalism
  discourse of, 6, 63, 100, 104, 116, 124, 199–200
  global, 2, 26n1
  goals of, 7, 9, 198
  failure of, 1, 6, 62, 128, 141–43, 196–97, 228, 239
  leftist, 75, 78–79, 99, 101–2, 109, 118
  political parties, 5, 23, 135–37, 204
Liberal Party (Canada), 5
Libya, 2, 77, 79
lifestyle activism, 6, 99–101
  failure of, 9, 100–1
Löwy, Michael, 163–64
"Lula" Da Silva, Luiz Inácio, 159–60
Luxemburg, Rosa, 238

MacLean, Nancy, 141–42
MAGA, 4, 185, 192, 225, 227
"Make America great again," *see* MAGA
Mamdani, Mamood, 65
Manning, Chelsea, 214
Maoism, 108–9
Marcuse, Herbert, 196–97, 199–203, 205–6
Marxism, 100, 104, 220, 233
  anti-capitalism, 25, 89, 91, 150, 154, 197–98, 201, 235
  autonomist, 87–92, 95
  narratives, 6, 105, 117–19, 128, 147, 163–65, 243–48
  organizing, 17, 32, 87–88, 108–10, 120–26, 208
  post-, 25
  theory, 8, 18, 38, 41–48, 91–92, 120–21, 184–85, 206n6, 240; *see also* dialectics
Marxism Today, 117–18, 120–26
McAlevey, Jane, 29, 35
McNally, David, 109
media, 35, 100, 117, 202, 225–26
  activist, 21, 30, 105, 221–25
  mainstream, 1, 19, 42, 56–57, 141, 150, 219–22, 236–37
Merkel, Angela, 79
methylmercury contamination (Muskrat Falls), 86, 93
#MeToo movement, 203, 208, 217n2
Mexico, 56–58, 201, 205
middle class, 5, 26n1
  concerns of, 17, 23, 142
  definition of, 40, 56
  rising, 64, 66–67, 70
  see also bourgeoisie
Middle East, 68–69
Migrant Hunger Strikers, 75, 78, 80–81, 83
migrants, 194n2
  characterization of, 10, 76–83
  criminalization of, 74–78
  death of, 76, 79
  as global proletariat, 74–83, 88, 246–47
  undocumented, 5, 247
  victimization of, 74–75, 77–79, 83
migration, 246
  causes of, 77, 80–81
  criminalization-humanitarianism nexus, 19, 53, 74–80, 83
  crisis, 74–76, 81
  culturalization of, 77
  global, 74–76, 80–81, 247
  see also immigration
Milanovic, Branko, 56
militant research, 92–95
military interventions, 65, 68, 77, 79; *see also* state, the
misogyny,
  movement-based, 50–51
  Trump's election and, 9, 54–57, 59
mobilization, 33, 87, 108, 163, 175, 243
  new strategies for, 148–49, 166–67, 188–93, 208–17
  in organizing, 28, 31, 34–36, 101, 117–18, 232, 236
  right-wing, 63–72, 188–93, 194n1
  working-class, 16, 20, 41–43, 78–82, 111
  workplace, 38–48, 110–16
Modi, Narendra, 9, 52, 71
Mondragon cooperative, 23
Moore, Roy, 54–55
Morales, Evo, 172
Morrison, Toni, 58
movement building, leftist, 1–3, 18–21,

45, 59, 87, 141, 155n1
anti-globalization, *see* anti-globalization movements
autonomous, 87, 89, 95, 175, 203–4, 223; *see also* Marxism, autonomist
continual improvement, 38, 78, 108–13, 118, 177–78, 188–94, 226–28
environmental, 87, 115, 152–53, 155n1, 159–66
global, 64, 74–83, 90, 163, 196–98, 204, 244–48
grassroots, 34, 100–1, 158–59, 165–66, 203–4
history, *see* history, left-wing movement
identity-based, *see* identity-based movements
intersectional, 3–4, 51, 87–91, 115, 154, 169, 202, 246–48
mass, 8, 28–36, 74–77, 81–82, 114–16, 128–31, 152, 159
mobilizing and, 10, 34–36, 74–77, 94–95, 141–42, 173–75
obstacles to, 11–12, 23–24, 28–33, 135–36, 160, 185–86, 209
state co-optation of, 11, 123, 160–61, 169–78, 203–5, 246
Muskrat Falls hydro dam, 86–87, 92–95
Muslimness,
activism, 99–100, 102, 186
criminalization, 50, 56, 75–80
demonization of, 70–71, 100
Sunni-, 64, 67–68
see also Islamophobia
Muslim countries, 81
immigration ban, 50, 186
mutation, process of, 129–34, 222

NAFTA (North American Free Trade Agreement), 56, 58, 114
Nalcor (Newfoundland and Labrador Crown corporation), 86, 93
narratives, 137
developing, 3, 5–8
left-wing, 2–4, 19, 149, 175, 240–41, 253
othering, *see* othering
popular, 3, 6, 21, 82, 132, 185, 237

right-wing, 4–5, 126
weakness, 4, 146–55
nationalism, 26n7, 173, 241n4, 244
aggrieved, 4, 63
authoritarian, *see* authoritarianism, nationalist
cultural, 64, 67, 69–72
ethno-, *see* ethnonationalism
migration versus, 75, 77, 79–80, 83
mythologization, 4–7, 185–86, 188–89, 192–94, 227
right-wing, 6, 58, 171
surge of, 2, 125, 127, 201
working-class divisions, 75, 235, 248
National Council of Canadian Muslims, 100
Nazism, neo-, 83, 98, 186
NDP (New Democratic Party), 110, 112, 114–15
Negri, Antonio, 245–46
Nietzsche, Friedrich, 214
neoliberalism, 6, 238
anti-, 72, 110–14, 169, 178, 200–6, 244
ascendance of, 18, 62, 65–66, 77, 126–27
globalization, 6, 29, 64–67, 82, 201, 205
hegemony of, 11–12, 122, 196–201, 219–20, 220–26
implications of, 31, 66–67, 72, 94–95, 198–206, 234, 246
nationalism, 57, 69–70, 72
right-wing, 52, 62–63, 92, 104, 114, 201
New Democratic Party, *see* NDP
Newfoundland and Labrador, 86, 93–94
New Left, 19, 201–3
Nickel and Dimed: On (Not) Getting by in America, 19
Nixon, Richard, 142–43
non-sectarianism, 32, 109–10
North America, 1–2, 10, 16, 26n1, 127, 141

Obama, Barack, 53, 225
Ocasio-Cortez, Alexandria, 98–99, 104–5, 152
Occupy movement, 6, 90, 151, 186, 203,

206n5, 223
lessons from, 1–3
One-Dimensional Man, 200, 205, 233
Ontario Coalition Against Poverty (OCAP), 110
organizations, leftist, 99–100 136, 186–87, 203
   building, 28–35, 101–4, 108–11, 228
   collective, 113, 115, 139, 158, 166–67
   education versus, 17–18, 23, 28, 32–34, 102–4, 111–13
   importance of, 21, 28–33, 36–37, 45, 131, 167
organizing, 135
   anti-capitalist, 3, 17–19, 25–26, 40, 117–26, 147–50, 188–94, 202–3
   class-based, 3, 17, 28–29, 35–48, 75–82, 89–95, 103–4, 114–16
   critiques of, 32–37, 101–3, 108–16, 123–24, 128–29, 163, 236, 241
   disagreement over, 1, 28, 30–31, 172–77
   global, 80–83, 105, 197, 206n2, 206n5
   identity-based, 100–2
   inclusiveness of, *see* inclusivity, movement
   instances of leftist, 6–7, 20–26, 28–30, 36–37, 72, 86–87, 130–34, 139
   labour, *see* labour, struggles; unions
   provocation in, *see* provocation
   society, 20, 34–36, 98–99, 146–54, 164–67, 203–4
   strategies, 10, 101–5, 109–16, 141–43, 148–49, 166–67, 188–93, 208–17
Orientalism, 76, 78
othering, 58, 65, 70, 228
   narratives, 76, 78–80, 83
overdose crisis, *see* crisis, opioid

Paris Commune, 25, 121, 189, 233
Parkdale, organizing in, 36–37, 131, 133
particularism versus universalism, 170–74, 176–78
parties, political, 20, 24, 129, 154
   alternatives to, 87, 129–33, 203
   bigotry in, 21, 51–54, 67–71, 83
   creation of, 43, 111, 114, 116n3
   divisions among, 23, 67–71, 100, 118–21, 166
   flaws of, 7, 10, 23, 100, 108–9, 117–24, 149–50, 158–59, 187
   propaganda, 19, 77, 118, 122–25, 143, 160–61
   utility of, 5, 108, 115–16, 130–32, 142, 151–54, 203–4
partisanship, 1, 138–39
Peterson, Jordan, 98
petty bourgeoisie, 17
Philippines, the, 2
Phillips, Kevin, 142–43
Piketty, Thomas, 26n3
"Pink Tide" governments (Latin America), 149, 159–61, 165
pipelines, struggles against, 87, 125
pluri-nationality, 170, 175–76, 179n3
Polanyi, Karl, 199
police, 58, 76, 116, 140, 211, 226
   violence, 29, 36, 113
political economy, 8, 12, 62–65, 103, 150, 201
   moving beyond, 23, 72, 87, 92, 118–20, 126
political subjectivization, 81–83
populism, 19, 103–4, 117, 126–27
   authoritarian, 62–72, 118, 200–2
   neoliberalism and, 62–64, 197–98
   reductionism, 51–52, 56, 58, 198
   revolt, 50–51
   right-wing, 9, 59, 98, 114, 121–22, 130, 219, 226
   rising power, 62–72
Portugal, 20
post-politics, 66, 74–80
post-work economy, 8, 152
poverty, 80, 109, 113, 137, 147, 160, 173
   blame for, 6, 77
   campaigns about, 19, 80, 83, 131
   fuel, 94
   racialized, 51–52, 236–37
precariat, 17
precarious workers, 63, 66, 80, 98, 111–13, 197–200, 227, 234
prison, *see* incarceration
privilege, 113, 120, 234
   ethnic, 9, 64, 67
   white, 9, 58, 185
professional class, 5, 35, 40
proletariat, 16–18, 29, 121–22, 184, 233,

235, 244
conscious, 20–21, 24–26, 119, 240
global, 74–77, 80–83
propaganda, 7, 11–12, 33, 45, 191–94, 225
protests, 16, 50–51, 80–83, 93, 112–13, 186, 202–4, 211, 227
critiques of, 24, 34–35, 109, 131–33, 151, 197–98
provocation, 28, 30–31, 139, 204, 247
critiques of, 32–34
right-wing, 141

Pruijt, Hans, 20

Québec Solidaire, 114, 116n3
Quebec student movement, 36, 202
queer struggles, 6, 30

race, 67, 243
intersectional connections, 51, 76, 87–88, 92, 103, 248
relations, 10, 39, 54
views on, 12, 52, 59, 130, 240
racism, 19, 67, 80, 125, 201, 244
nationalist authoritarianism, 5, 63, 71
right-wing politics and, 9, 51–59, 98, 232, 234, 236–37, 239
struggles against, 24, 26n7, 30, 88, 103, 115, 166, 179n7
radical left, 131,
critique of the, 165, 219–20, 226
discourse of, 103–5, 146–50, 161, 196–97, 201–2
liberal left versus, 101–2, 243
recruitment, 98–99, 102–4, 227
rallies, 34, 186
election, 56
see also protest
Rancière, Jacques, 63, 77–78, 81
Reactionary Mind, The, 141
reactionary movements, 2, 136, 143
mindset of, 5, 12, 54, 59, 221, 225–26, 234–36
undermining, 3, 31, 232
Reagan, Ronald, 16
Rebuilding the Left (RTL), 109–12
recession, 19
redistribution, 150

progressive income, 6, 147
wealth, 1, 29, 45, 63, 65, 137
reformism, 6, 143, 174 219
anti-capitalist, 19, 151
futility of, 1, 8, 23, 102
refugees,
discourse on, 10, 64
movements, 76–79
religious identification, 39, 72, 99–100, 174
discrimination based on, 64–68, 70, 235
Republican Party, 52, 54, 59, 142–43, 206n2
Trump's takeover, 51, 52, 198, 225
resistance, 124, 177, 186
developing, 9, 95, 113, 128–29, 219
new, 4, 91, 222
sources of, 2–3, 91–93, 138, 174, 204
tactics, 24, 80–83, 86–88, 165–67, 211–12, 227
revanchism, 71
capitalist, 12, 210, 232, 234, 236–38
logic of, 5, 199, 231, 233–40, 241n1
revenge, *see* revanchism
revolution, 16, 21–22, 108, 130, 184, 239–41, 244
Citizens' (Ecuador), 170, 174–77
counter-, *see* counterrevolution
ecological, 11, 147–48, 153–54, 174–77
Egyptian, 1
idea of, 2, 6–8, 33–35, 99, 128, 187, 190, 200–2
transnational, 2, 24, 29, 150
strategies for, 19–20, 25, 30, 105, 122, 126, 192, 227
rights, 115, 129, 234
civil, 30, 54, 59, 136–38, 141–43
collective, *see* collective rights
human, *see* human rights
Indigenous, *see* Indigenous Peoples, rights of
individual, 10, 140–43
of nature, 162, 166–67, 169–71, 175–76
workers', 57, 139–43, 202
right wing, 31, 67–69
appeal of the, 3–4, 59, 105, 116,

125–27, 200
hate speech, 10, 135, 144, 185–86
narrative, 4–5, 7, 75–78, 121, 141, 185, 193–94, 226
politics, 63–64, 98, 114, 125, 135–44, 160, 165–66, 203
populism, *see* populism, right-wing
racism, 92, 98, 141–42
tactics of, 12, 105, 126–27, 135, 188
see also far right
Robin, Corey, 141
Rocker, Rudolph, 32, 36
Rousseff, Dilma, 159–60
"rule of law," enforcement of, 141, 231, 238
Russia, 25, 108, 138, 140, 198, 244

Said, Edward, 76
Salutin, Rick, 56, 199
Sanders, Bernie, 51, 203–4
mobilization strategies, 98, 103–4, 126
scapegoating, ethnic, 5, 64, 80
sectarianism, 30–32, 64, 67–69, 108–9, 119, 130, 146, 245
secularization (in Turkey), 68–70
security, job, *see* jobs, secure
self-determination, Indigenous, 88, 115, 179n3
self-jamming system, 220, 225–27
settlers, 193, 231–32
Indigenous solidarity, 86–87, 93–94
sexism, 19, 103, 112, 115, 222, 244
Should We Eat Meat?, 100
Situationist International (SI), 210, 221–23, 225
Smith, Adam, 231
Smith, Neil, 236
Snowden, Edward, 214
Social Democratic Party, 23
social democratic politics, 98, 114–15, 118, 126, 151, 236
green, 150–52, 204
working class and, 109, 116, 198, 235
socialism, 8, 23, 65, 126, 140, 217
movement toward, 19, 99–101, 105, 108–9, 117–18
visions of, 8, 29, 35–36, 114, 128–29, 147–55, 160–64

Socialism and Freedom Party (PSOL; Brazil), 161, 165, 167
socialist left, 2, 12
eco-, *see* eco-socialism
focus areas, 8, 36, 160–67, 244, 246
narratives, 6, 19–20, 118–21, 126–27, 163, 172, 178
organizations, 21, 30, 101–15, 125
participation of, 29–32, 100–1, 166
tactics, 25, 101–5, 109–16, 121–22, 165–67
weaknesses of, 7, 77, 109–16, 120, 150, 178
Socialist Project (Toronto), 101, 110–12, 114–15
Socialist Workers Party, 21
social media use, 101, 124, 135, 144, 211; *see also* Twitter, use of
solidarity, 2, 10, 237
Indigenous-settler, 86–87, 93–94, 115
international, 74–76, 78–83, 164
intersectional, 4, 51, 59, 95
strategies, 12, 30–31, 203
Spencer, Richard, 98
Srnicek, Nick, 150–51
squatting, 20
Standing, Guy, 17
Standing Rock reservation, 125
state, the, 24–25, 75, 248
behaviour of, 4–5, 93, 231, 235
capitalist, 7, 87–88, 138–40, 160, 177, 197, 208, 238
capture, 24, 128, 132, 154, 197–98, 202–5, 214
climate change, 151–54, 158, 160, 163–66
Indigenous Peoples and, 159–62, 169, 171–79, 245
left strategy and, 3, 7, 87, 111, 114–15, 128–31, 179n3, 203
minoritarian, 227, 229n3
neoliberalism, 63–65, 80–81, 197–200, 246
right-wing politics in, 67–70, 92, 141–43, 201
technocratic, 1, 74, 162, 173, 203–4, 236
violence, *see* violence, state 2, 116, 225, 237

welfare, 26n1, 173, 175, 198–200, 226
working-class organizing and, 29, 31, 108, 121, 245–46
see also austerity; borders
strikes, 135, 143, 227
  hunger, 75, 80–83, 93
  labour, 16, 36, 122, 124, 139–41
  rent, 34, 36, 133
  wildcat, 21–22
  see also Women's March
Sumak Kawsay, *see* Buen-Vivir
Sunni-Muslimness, *see* Muslimness, Sunni-
surveillance, societal, 76, 79, 90, 225, 227, 234
syndicalism, 110–11
Syria, 2, 69, 77

taxation, 54, 142
  evasion of, 214, 216
  unfair, 5
technology, 120, 126, 201
  left vision of 8, 11, 146–48, 150–53, 155n1, 225
  neoliberalism, 29, 77, 79, 90, 197
tenant organizing, 36–37, 133
terrorism, 33, 122, 210–12
  art, *see* art, terrorism
  discourse on, 71, 74–76, 193
Thatcher, Margaret, 16, 117–19, 122, 124–27
Toronto, ON, organizing, 36–37, 101, 109–13, 128, 130–33, 140
Toronto Harm Reduction Alliance (THRA), 131–32
Toronto Overdose Prevention Society (TOPS), 132
trade, 34
  agreements, *see* NAFTA
  free, 56, 232
  protectionism, 56–58
  unions, *see* unions
transformation, societal, 2, 16, 50, 66–67, 83, 109, 117, 121, 184, 187
  of capitalism, 18–19, 24, 46–48, 143, 224, 232, 236–37
  ecological, 8–9, 88, 114, 146–48, 154, 164, 173
  leftist action, 25, 28–35, 128–34,
204–5, 209–14, 227, 232, 243–46
  militant research in, 90–95
Trans Mountain pipeline, 87
Trans-Pacific Partnership, 58
trick, the (Benjamin), 191–94
Tronti, Mario, 89
Trotskyism, 109, 112
Trudeau, Justin, 98
Trump, Donald, 3, 92, 143, 187, 189, 196, 201–2, 234, 247
  populism, 50–53, 56–59, 63–64, 198–99, 225–26
  racism, 5, 9, 53–59, 186, 194, 205
Turkey, 4, 9, 62–64, 66–69, 79, 198, 202
  Justice and Development Party (AKP), 67–68, 70
  neo-Ottomanism, 68–70
  Republican People's Party (CHP), 68
Twitter, use of, 35, 54

unions, 87, 98, 135, 149–51
  Detroit workers', 21–23, 30
  industrial, 11, 111–13, 119–20
  movement, 55, 58, 159–61, 166, 246–47
  racism, 55–59
  trade, 29, 34–36, 50, 55–59, 82, 138–40
United Auto Workers (UAW), 21–22, 56
United States, 9, 18, 71, 135, 137, 198
  activism in, 20–24, 30, 50, 124–25, 139, 152, 162, 234
  civil liberties in, 135–43
  elections, 12, 50–57, 206n2, 219, 225–26
  nationalism, 2, 5
  poverty, 51–52, 56
  racism, 50, 52–55, 58–59, 67, 104, 201–2, 237
  Southern strategy, 142–43
  see also Trump, Donald
universal basic income, 8, 150, 226
universalism versus particularism, *see* particularism versus universalism

vanguard, leftist, 23–24, 31, 130
  role of, 19–21, 122
veganism, 100, 166
violence, 17, 77, 210, 241

non-, 139, 142, 239
state, 2, 29, 36, 113–16, 136–40, 179n3, 225, 231, 237
politics of 53–59, 70, 76, 81–83, 92, 185, 232, 236
voters, 5, 12, 225–26
disenfranchisement, 54–55, 206n2
racism and, 50–59
unionized, 55–58

wage, 19, 23, 29, 59, 89–91, 119–20, 151, 154, 227
living versus minimum, 18, 34, 39–40, 44–45, 139
psychological, *see* whiteness, psychological wage
Wainwright, Hilary, 203–4
Wall Street Journal, 51
war, 241n1
civil, 2
Cold, *see* Cold War
on Terror, 76
see also World War I; World War II
War Measures Act (Canada), 140
water,
rights, 165–66, 176
struggles for, 86–91
world forums, 166
wealth, 199, 233
concentration of, 1–2, 42, 44, 149, 197, 202, 226
redistribution, *see* redistribution, wealth
Weil, Simone, 130
West, the, 71
characterization of, 76, 81
values, 66, 78, 83
whiteness, 21–23, 88, 93, 103, 200, 227
dispossession, 9, 51–52, 63, 185, 234, 236–39
privilege, *see* privilege, white
psychological wage, 9, 50, 58, 63–64, 67
voting and, 53–59
working-class, 58–59, 88, 120, 142, 185, 247
see also race; racism
Williams, Alex, 150–51
Williams, Raymond, 18

wish images, 11, 189–92, 194n3, 236
"witch hunts," 231, 234–35
Wolin, Sheldon, 199–201, 203, 205
Women's March (US), 50, 92, 186–87, 192
working class, 20, 124–25, 129, 233, 235
capacity building, 28–32, 36, 89–90, 103–5, 133, 245
capital versus, 89–91, 136, 139, 146, 197–200, 206n6
definition of, 17, 22, 29, 40–42, 82, 88–91, 109
engagement, 3, 8, 10, 28–31, 38–48, 108–16, 246
environmental concerns, 154, 159, 162
focus on, 28, 119–21
global movements, 64, 75, 78, 80–83, 197
migrant, 77, 80–88, 247
organizing, 28–31, 34–36, 87–88, 92–95, 101, 200–2
power of, 28–29, 36–37, 42–44, 89–90, 102
racism, 50–56, 59, 64, 67–69, 88, 120–21, 142
self-valorization, 91
socialism in, 25, 29, 32, 103, 110–16, 120, 161–67, 246
unionized, 56–58, 112, 120, 247
Workers' Communist Party, 109
Workers' Party (Brazil), 158–61
Workman, Thom, 32
World War I, 137–40, 217n1, 236
World War II, 26n1, 117, 151, 199–200, 217n1, 236

xenophobia, 5, 63, 77, 83, 98, 127

Yemen, 2

Zapatistas, 88
Žižek, Slavoj, 55, 59, 78